Frank Furedi
100 Years of Identity Crisis

Frank Furedi

100 Years of Identity Crisis

Culture War Over Socialisation

DE GRUYTER

ISBN (Paperback) 978-3-11-070512-6
ISBN (Hardcover) 978-3-11-070557-7
e-ISBN (PDF) 978-3-11-070889-9
e-ISBN (EPUB) 978-3-11-070893-6

Library of Congress Control Number: 2021940628

Bibliographic information published by the Deutsche Nationalbibliothek
The Deutsche Nationalbibliothek lists this publication in the Deutsche Nationalbibliografie; detailed bibliographic data are available on the Internet at http://dnb.dnb.de.

Cover image: elebeZoom / iStock / Getty Images Plus
Printing and binding: CPI books GmbH, Leck

www.degruyter.com

Acknowledgements

The author is indebted to Jennie Bristow, Ann Furedi, Stewart Justman, Ellie Lee, Jan MacVarish, Nancy McDermott, and the Centre for Parenting Studies at the University of Kent. I would like to thank my colleagues at the XXIst Century Foundation in Budapest for their encouragement and insights.

I am grateful to the Leverhulme Trust for the receipt of an Emeritus Fellowship, which provided support for this project.

Contents

Introduction

Through the attempt to understand the historical origins of a phenomenon that today we call 'identity crisis', this author came to the conclusion that the condition can best be understood as a symptom of the unravelling of moral authority. Stable identities are not only psychological but also moral accomplishments. They are supported by clarity about *meaning*, which in turn draws on authoritative moral guidance. Without such guidance, people's identities often become decentred and find it difficult to endow their lives with meaning.

The main argument outlined in this book is that identity and the crisis that often surrounds it, as well as its politicisation, are inextricably linked to the confusion that frequently envelops conflicts of values and moral norms. This development is particularly evident in the domain of socialisation and, as we argue, it is the way that socialisation has been historically managed that creates the conditions for the crystallisation of the contemporary form of identity crisis and the potential for its politicisation.

This book argues that 21st century cultural conflicts and related disputes over identity are the outcome of forces unleashed by the politicisation of the socialisation of young people in the late 19th century. Interest in the politicisation of socialisation was motivated by the belief that the demands of economic efficiency and social and political reform required the mobilisation of the idealism and energy of the young. It was claimed that a rapidly changing world required the re-engineering of the way young people were educated and socialised. To become truly modern and flexible they had to be distanced from the traditions and values of the past. To achieve this objective, old-fashioned moral norms had to be displaced by scientifically authorised values.[1] Challenging and de-legitimating prevailing cultural norms was seen as the precondition for producing enlightened and healthy personalities.

Once socialisation was diverted from its traditional goal of transmitting moral norms, its capacity to provide a bond that bound together the different generations was undermined. Yet, these bonds serve to underpin the common world inhabited by members of a community. Once this bond begins to unravel, what is left is a sense of self in search of a home. This sense of homelessness

1 We use 'moral' and 'moral norms' to refer to the foundational principles that provide society's standards of what is right and wrong. Values can be, but are not necessarily, derived from moral principle. They refer to the domain of worth and, as we suggest, they can be administratively or technically produced.

https://doi.org/10.1515/9783110708899-001

created a need for the science of psychology, which, as we explain, diagnosed this predicament as an identity crisis.

The ethos of contesting and changing culture underpinned the worldview of modernising groups of social engineers devoted to detaching their society from the past. This impulse was most systematically expressed by American progressivism. However, virtually every modernist movement – New Liberals in Britain, Social Democrats in Sweden, European socialists and eugenicists, communists, fascists – endorsed and embraced aspects of this outlook. Though they often advanced a utopian vision of a world fundamentally re-engineered in accordance with scientific principles, in practice they were often drawn towards the more modest goal of rationalising the process of socialisation. They adopted this as their main objective because they drew the conclusion that the most reliable way of changing culture and replacing traditional with modern values was through influencing the attitudes of young people.

Political movements, therapeutic professionals, pedagogues and modernising capitalists regarded the re-engineering of socialisation as the main site for social/cultural/economic reform and renewal. Their ambition and project transcended the conventional ideological divide as movements of different shades of opinion increasingly looked to technical and scientific solutions to the problems facing society. Invariably, they relied on psychology to assist the re-engineering of socialisation. This dimension of social engineering has been characterised as mental modernisation by a recently published study on this subject.[2] In the 1920s, a leading American sociologist described it as 'mental conditioning'.[3] I prefer to use the term *moral engineering* to highlight its twin objective of modernising morality through replacing prevailing norms with psychological values with a view to changing culture. Moral engineering is a moralising project that seeks to render moral newly invented values.

At times, John Dewey, the leading intellectual of the progressive movement, referred to the educational techniques used to re-engineer education as a form of 'moral engineering'.[4] Almost seven decades later, in 1988, an American philosopher calling for moral engineering described it as an 'intelligent effort to design

---

2 See chapter 1 in A. Jewett (2020) *Science under Fire: Challenges to Scientific Authority in Modern America*, Cambridge, Mass.: Harvard University Press.

3 F.H. Giddings (1924) 'Social work and societal engineering', *Journal of Social Forces*, 3(1), 7–15, at 10.

4 See the discussion in his chapter titled 'Reconstruction in moral conceptions', in J. Dewey (1920) *Reconstruction in Philosophy*, New York: H. Holt, p.160); see https://archive.org/details/reconstructionin00deweuoft/page/160.

institutions that will foster moral practices, perhaps moral horticulture'.[5] The displacement of moral norms by psychological and other types of administratively produced values has been integral to the project of moral engineering for over a century. As in the 20th, so too in the 21st century, moral engineering is devoted to the reconfiguration of moral norms. In the current era campaigns for 'raising awareness' convey the ambition of moral engineering. Typically, their objective is to convert people from values that are deemed outdated and pernicious to ones that are consistent with 'awareness'.

It turned out that the moral engineering of socialisation exacerbated a pre-existing problem, which was the question of what moral virtues a community should transmit to its young in the context of a rapidly changing world. The impulse to detach people from their community's norms helped weaken the already weak influence of moral authority. As one study observed, 'the inability of liberal societies to develop any institutional means of transmitting its own virtues' has 'precipitated a cultural crisis'.[6] The current expression of this crisis is an unprecedented level of concern with identity and the cultural conflicts that surround it.

Despite the significance of the question of inter-generational transmission of values, it has rarely gained the attention it deserves. Even when this problem exploded in the 1960s and unleashed a chain of events leading to the culture wars of the 21st century, the depth of the crisis of socialisation and its implication for society was underestimated. Socialisation has tended to be discussed as a technical matter, and it seemed as if the confusions surrounding its content were self-consciously ignored. That studied disinterest was in part due to the lack of clarity that adults possess about how to exercise their authority to the benefit of young people. It was also – as the following chapters indicate – due to the influence of an outlook that questions the very desirability of transmitting a community's long-held virtues to the young.

Advocates of the re-engineering of socialisation came to the view that if they were to reshape people then prevailing cultural norms also had to be altered. Consequently, the re-engineering of socialisation required the de-legitimation of the values of the past and the customs and practices associated with it. In its place professions involved with the management of socialisation opted for using techniques of psychological validation to replace the previous regime of education and childrearing. The experience of the past 100 years indicates that these techniques are insufficient for providing young people with the guid-

---

5 J. Kultgen (1988) *Ethics and Professionalism*, Philadelphia: University of Pennsylvania Press, p.181.

6 D. Walsh (1997) *The Growth of the Liberal Soul*, Columbia: University of Missouri Press, p.89.

ance they require to make their way in the world. The most important legacy of the regime of socialisation through psychological validation is the emergence of the permanent condition of an identity crisis. The origins of the politicisation of identity and the conflicts surrounding it can best be understood through exploring the emergence and gradual expansion of a technocratic impulse oriented towards the management of socialisation and of human behaviour.

Traces of the contemporary conflicts of culture can be found at the turn of the 20th century, when advocates of the engineering of socialisation concluded that if they were to reshape people then existing cultural norms had to give way to new, scientifically validated ones. The re-engineering of socialisation required the de-legitimation of the values of the past and many of the moral norms and practices associated with it. At a time when traditional sources of legitimation appeared exhausted, science seemed to possess a singular capacity to provide society with an authoritative guide to the future. It turned out that the application of science into the domain of values could not provide communities with the coherent sense of normativity required to guide the transition from adolescence to adulthood.

Socialisation was and is still, often interpreted as a discrete and stand-alone phenomenon to do with education and parenting. But it is much more than that because its practice raises questions about society's attitude towards its past and to its future. The displacement in recent decades of ideological conflicts by cultural ones indicates that, for decades, behind-the-scenes tensions within culture were becoming increasingly difficult to resolve.

Unlike the well-known ideologies, the different strands of counter-cultural forces did not and still do not have a recognisable name. Indeed, moral engineering, the instrumental application of science to problems of morality, politics and culture, played a subservient role to political movements that adopted its practices. The ideological outlook of social and moral engineering expressed the sentiments associated with *scientism*. Scientism purports to apply scientific principles to the domain of human behaviour, value and morality. Its advocates believe that they possess the insight necessary for curing the diseases of culture and for producing a new, enlightened, aware citizen. The main instrument for the 'engineering of the mind' is the science of psychology and this discipline has played a central role in the practice of scientism. Scientism has proved to be a protean ideology that has successfully penetrated political movements and most professions. Its use 'can assume very different functions in intellectual and ideological confrontations, according to changing contexts'.[7]

7 I. Mészáros (1989) *The Power of Ideology*, New York: Harvester Wheatsheaf, p.180.

The recurring theme promoted through scientism – an ideology without a name – is the necessity for cultural change. The achievement of this goal relied on re-educating society and the displacement of moral by health and psychological values. Promoting mental health as a foundational value, Lawrence K. Frank stated:

> Thus we may begin to see mental health as a long-term goal that can be progressively approached as we reorient all our ways of living, working, and playing, and, above all, as we modify and sometimes completely change many of our customary beliefs, assumptions, and patterns of action and feeling regarding human nature and human relations.[8]

Although relatively unknown today, Frank was a key player in the network of American Research Foundations involved in the business of modernising socialisation. His call for a cultural revolution to change human nature and rid society of 'customary beliefs' and 'assumption' echoed the sentiment held by professionals involved in the sphere of education, social work and mental health.

In recent decades the practice of moral engineering has extended from the domain of socialising of youth to the re-socialising of adults. This reorientation is sometimes promoted through what is referred to by its advocates as 'liberal paternalism'. The most prominent advocate of this project, Cass Sunstein, coined the term 'nudge' to describe the policy of using paternalistic psychologically informed measures to protect people from themselves. His objective is to replace with what he perceives as unreliably formed moral judgments with the wisdom of behavioural science.[9] With nudging, the ideologically informed paternalism implicit in the practice of scientism becomes far more explicit than in previous times.

In the chapters to follow, we examine the evolution of this *ideology without a name*. Unlike in the past, when science and scientism played a subservient role in authorising the policies and behaviour of political institutions and idealogues, in recent times it often presents itself as an authority in its own right. For many politicians and policy makers their ideology is secondary to what 'The Science Says'. When pushed to account for their decision, they are likely to say 'we are following the science'. Instead of justifying their choice through the language of right and wrong, politicians insist that it is 'evidence based'. When proposing

8 L.K. Frank (1953), 'The promotion of mental health', *Annals of the American Academy of Political and Social Science*, 286, 167–174, at 167–168.

9 See C.R. Sunstein (2014) *Why Nudge? The Politics of Libertarian Paternalism*, New Haven: Yale University Press.

a new initiative, government statements begin with the mantra of 'Research Shows ...'.

One of the most curious features of 21st century political culture is that politics has become both intensely personalised but also deeply impersonal. In identity politics, the personal is political, the politicisation of emotion coexists with a form of technocratic governance where The Science claims final authority. How this has come about and how this development is linked to the cultural conflicts surrounding socialisation are the subject of this study.

The chapters to follow rely on a historical reconstruction of the trends driving the cultural conflicts surrounding socialisation. One reason why this subject matter requires a logical reworking of these trends is because the contemporary world suffers from a self-inflicted form of historical amnesia to the point that it struggles to retain a sense of the past. There is a tendency towards eternalising the problems confronting society and to read history backwards. This has led many to misunderstand the issues surrounding identity, and its problematisation and weaponisation.

Cultural change and the transformation of values and attitudes do not occur overnight, and they certainly do not affect different generations and sections of society in the same way. The conflicts over values discussed in this book took several generations to acquire a significant impact over the conduct of everyday life. Typically, most of the key trends discussed in this book – the discovery of adolescence, the unravelling of moral and adult authority, the politicisation of socialisation, the promotion of scientism, the displacement of the moral by the psychological – first gained momentum in the United States before spreading to other parts of the world. It was here that Identity Crisis was discovered and also where the legacy of the conflicts it unleashed is most visible. However, these trends have become global and it is evident that the conflicts described as the Culture War are not going away any time soon.

Throughout this book we refer to the unhappy term of 'social engineering'. It is a term that is used in a variety of different ways in the literature. Our usage of this term refers to the project of transforming moral questions into technical ones. In some instances, as with the current cohort of 'moral scientists', the project of reducing morality to objective truths is an explicit objective.[10] In most instances supporters of social engineering wish to 'unmask' the moral as a form of archaic dogma and replace it with 'evidence based' truths. The communication of a moral discourse through a technical language is one of the ways that scien-

10 See the discussion on 'moral science' in D.J. Hunter and P. Nedelisky (2018) *Science and the Good: The Tragic Quest for the Foundations of Morality*, New Haven: Yale University Press.

tism uses the authority of science to influence matters pertaining to public life. In this respect scientism has proved to be remarkably successful. Numerous studies demonstrate that technical and expert forms of decision making have displaced moral authority in many spheres of life.[11]

The principal medium through which scientism has displaced the moral is that of psychology, and more specifically the medicalisation of everyday life. Although at times social engineering expresses itself as an ambitious utopian project oriented towards transforming the world, in the end its focus is almost always on the question of how to take hold of and manage childrearing and education. The pursuit of this project has led to the intensification of generational conflict, the devaluation of adult authority, the distancing of communities from their past and an explosion of identity-related issues.

Throughout the chapters to follow we discuss the views of influential commentators, academics and experts whose views played a decisive role in the ascendancy of the cultural attitudes that challenged the prevailing norms. The views of prominent moral engineers did not always resonate with public opinion. Throughout the 20th century there was always a normative lag between expert opinion and ideals and the common-sense sentiments that prevailed in society. Nevertheless, decade by decade the gap between the two tended to narrow as expert opinion began to resonate first with the elites and then the middle class and gradually sprang roots in popular culture. However, the normative gap between expert opinion and common sense is never fully resolved. The never-ending campaigns to raise awareness that proliferate in the current cultural landscape show the durability of this normative gap.

Most criticisms of scientism emphasise its amoral and dehumanising technical ambition to control human behaviour. Such criticisms are often directed at the Enlightenment, and its secularising and Promethean ambitions. Our aim is not to question the appropriate exercise of the authority of science.[12] Our focus is on scientism: an ideology that inappropriately politicises science. It opportunistically uses the authority of science to transform culture and the conduct of human behaviour. Under the guise of value neutrality, scientism instrumentalises and professionalises human relations. Its project of de-legitimating traditional moral norms often results in the ascendancy of values that masquerade as scientific facts. The chapters to follow explore the connection between the impact of this ideology and the emergence of the cultural politics of identity.

---

11 See R. Wuthnow (1989), *Meaning and Moral Order: Explorations in Cultural Analysis*, Berkeley: University of California Press, p.68.

12 For a discussion of the challenges to the authority of science, see Jewett (2020).

Chapter 1: The Identity Labyrinth

'Identity' is more than a household term. Judging by the ceaseless stream of references to this word, transmitted through the mainstream and social media, identity has become the dominant cultural marker of our times. Yet, despite its constant usage, identity is not an attribute that anyone can take for granted. Individuals and groups self-consciously lecture people about how they want to be identified. Among the younger generations it has become fashionable to preface a statement with the words, 'I identify as ...'. That individuals feel obliged to broadcast their identity and to wear it on their sleeves is symptomatic of its tentative and ambiguous qualities. The statement 'I identify as ...' invites validation but it also hints at the possibility of being misunderstood, misrecognised and even overlooked and rejected.

The statement 'I identify as ...' conveys the impression that individuals get to decide their identity. And certainly, there is a veritable industry devoted to helping people customise their very own individual identity. Businesses promise to help find the 'real you' and provide you with an identity that will allow you to be different and stand out from the rest. Indeed, the imperative of differentiating individuals and groups is one of the main cultural drivers of the never-ending demand for identities. As one media company – appropriately named Identity – explains its mission: 'In a world where sameness is on the rise, *Identity* wins by imprinting every project with a visual sophistication and refreshing individuality'.[1]

Given the importance which individuals and society attach to identity, it is unsurprising that it has become a focus of anxiety and conflict. Indeed, the great emphasis that individuals confer on their identity intimates a sense of insecurity towards it. People who are confident about who they are and understand their place in the world do not feel the need to introduce themselves with the phrase 'I identify as ...'. Nor would they need to precede their comments on the media with phrases like 'as a working-class woman', or 'as a man of colour', or as a 'gay author', or as a 'Cis white woman'.

Most people have not yet adopted the usage of the cliché, 'I identify as ...'. Nevertheless, disquiet and defensiveness pervade deliberations on this subject. People intuit that identities can be lost and, in the age of digital technology, easily stolen. Businesses have responded to this concern by marketing what they

1 See https://identityid.com/ (accessed 22 February 2019).

https://doi.org/10.1515/9783110708899-002

brand as 'trusted identity'. One company sells a product called Augmented Identity, which it claims is an identity 'that ensures privacy and trust and guarantees secure, authenticated and verifiable transactions'. The company claims that its product 'allows us to truly enjoy life – because securing our **identity** is key to making our world a safer place'.[2]

Unfortunately, the experience of recent decades indicates that the goal of 'securing our identity' tends to elude most of us, most of the time. The problems associated with the project of 'securing our identity' are eloquently captured by the idiom of 'identity crisis'. The term originates from the 1940s and is associated with the work of the psychologist Erik Erikson. Erikson observed that many American soldiers returning from the Second World War found that 'their lives no longer hung together' and they struggled to find their place in the world.[3]

Erikson's concept of identity crisis drew attention to the challenge faced by young people as they attempted to cultivate a stable identity in order to develop 'the capacity of the ego to sustain sameness and continuity'.[4] His attempt to understand and explain what he saw as a difficult but normal developmental phase faced by young people provided important insights into some of the tensions faced by adolescents as they made their transition to adulthood. At the time 'identity crisis' was a rarely used clinical term that referred to a phase in the psychological development of adolescents.

In the 21st century, usage of the term 'the crisis of identity' transcends the world of adolescents and has insinuated itself into everyday life. Erikson himself was surprised at the ease and the speed with which the concept of identity crisis was reconfigured to apply to a bewildering variety of situations.[5] The phrase 'identity crisis' ceased to be focused on adolescents struggling to break free from their dependence on their parents and develop the psychological resources necessary for attaining adulthood. In 1965, the Canadian psychoanalyst Elliot Jaques invented the concept of the mid-life crisis. He noted that the crisis occurred around the age of 35 and in some cases lasted until a person reached 65 years of age.[6] The last decade of the 20th century saw the invention of a new age-related

---

2 See www.idemia.com/we-stand-augmented-identity (accessed 19 February 2019).

3 E.H. Erikson (1968) *Identity: Youth and Crisis*, New York: W.W. Norton & Company, p.42.

4 E.H. Erikson (1964) 'Identity and uprootedness in our time', in Erikson, E.H. *Insight and Responsibility: Lectures on the Ethical Implications of Psychoanalytic Insight*, London: Faber & Faber, p.95.

5 Erikson (1968).

6 E. Jaques (1965) 'Death and the mid-life crisis', *International Journal of Psychoanalysis*, 46(4), 502–514.

crisis, the 'quarter-life crisis': a condition of anxiety about the future, which afflicts people in their 20s.[7]

In 1968, Erikson reflected that during the previous 20 years, identity's 'popular usage has become so varied and its conceptual context so expanded that the time may seem to have come for a better and final delimitation of what identity is and what it is not'.[8] However, instead of the meaning of this word being clarified and its usage confined to a limited range of circumstances, its application has continued to expand and expand.

When Erikson cautioned his public about the promiscuous use of identity in the 1960s, he pointed to what now seems like a relatively few examples. A few years later the term 'identity crisis' was used to describe the predicament faced by individuals of all ages, minorities, ethnic groups, women, and public and private institutions. Even America was said to face a crisis of identity. By the late 1970s, the very term 'identity' was almost always associated with a problem if not a crisis. The coupling of identity with crisis has continued to expand and is used to highlight the challenges faced by just about any institution, person, group or idea. To take some random examples featured on *Google:* 'The Identity Crisis of Sustainable Development',[9] 'The Identity Crisis of Feminist Theory',[10] 'The Identity Crisis of the Ultra Rich',[11] 'The Online Identity Crisis'.[12]

Back in 1968, Erikson also drew attention to the emergence of a phenomenon that would become far more prominent in the decades to follow. He pointed to an unprecedented explosion of identity-talk by the 1960s counter-cultural movement as well as by other sections of society. 'We are witnessing an exacerbated "identity-consciousness"', he stated. He added:

> For whereas twenty years ago we gingerly suggested that some young people might be suffering from a more or less unconscious identity conflict, a certain type tells us in no uncertain terms, and with the dramatic outer display of what we once considered to be inner secrets, that yes, indeed, they have an identity conflict – and they wear it on their sleeves.[13]

---

7 See A. Robbins and A. Wilner (2001) *Quarterlife Crisis: The Unique Challenges of Life in Your Twenties*, New York: Tarcher.

8 Erikson (1968) p.17.

9 www.emeraldinsight.com/doi/abs/10.1108/WJSTSD-08-2013-0033 (accessed 12 June 2019).

10 www.oxfordscholarship.com/view/10.1093/0195137345.001.0001/acprof-9780195137347-chapter-5 (accessed 12 June 2019).

11 www.bloomberg.com/news/articles/2019-02-08/the-identity-crisis-of-the-ultra-rich (accessed 12 June 2019).

12 www.bbc.co.uk/programmes/b07tqvvp (accessed 12 June 2019).

13 Erikson (1968) p.26.

Erikson's claim that the inner secrets surrounding people's internal identity conflicts were transformed into public statements anticipated the emergence of a culture where many people do wear their identity on their sleeves. Suddenly people's personal troubles were hurled into the public domain. The sociologist Erving Goffman, in his influential study, *Stigma* (1963), invented the phrase 'politics of identity'. Goffman portrayed identity as a 'public performance'.

But not even Erikson could have imagined the phenomenal ascendancy of what he characterised as identity consciousness. His reference to the wearing of identity on your sleeves was a metaphorical one. Today, people literally wear their identity on their sleeves. With so much at stake, many regard the identity they wear on their sleeves as a precious, private possession. The imperative of protecting the ownership of one's identity has in recent years led to an explosion of outrage directed at people who supposedly appropriate the hairstyles, clothes, the food recipes or the tattoos associated with other people's identity. These disputes about cultural appropriation often touch on petty details of what people look like.

With so much emotional, financial and political investment in identity it has inevitably become a site of conflict. Media commentators often draw attention to the heated rows that surround the politicisation of identity. However, disputes over identity are not confined to the political sphere; they play a prominent role in many spheres of public and private life. Take the case of Martina Navratilova, one of the greatest tennis players of recent times. She was vilified for arguing that it was not fair for trans-women to compete in women's sports. In response to her comment, Navratilova was dropped as ambassador by the LGBT sports body, Athlete Ally for her views.

Navratilova had stated in a tweet that 'You can't just proclaim yourself a female and be able to compete against women'. This statement was condemned by Rachel MacKinnon, a trans cyclist, who denounced Navratilova for trading 'on age-old stereotypes and stigma against trans-women'.[14] Sections of the media were at a loss to know who to support in this conflict: Navratilova, a well-known advocate of lesbian and gay rights, or MacKinnon, a vociferous proponent of trans rights. The question of who is and who is not a woman has turned into a highly polarised dispute between some feminists and lesbians on one side and trans activists on the other. Evidently the statement, 'I identify as …' does not always resolve the matter of how we want to be seen.

---

14 www.theguardian.com/sport/2019/feb/17/martina-navratilova-criticised-over-cheating-trans-women-comments.

With so much attention focused on identity, it is easy to overlook the fact that it is rarely clear what is meant by this term. During the past 50 years numerous commentaries have underlined the elusive and imprecise usage of the word 'identity'. A review of the concept in 1972 complained that Erikson's use of identity 'means something quite definite' but it was 'terribly elusive'. The reviewer wrote that the 'subtlety of Eriksonian identity helps account for the vagueness that soon enveloped the term, for his ideas are of the sort that cannot bear being popularized without at the same time being blunted and muddied'.[15] The psychiatrist Robert Coles noted in the 1970s that the terms identity and identity crisis had become 'the purest of clichés'.[16] 'Identity is a rather bewildering concept, not least because it is associated with an incredible range of behaviour and human faculties', wrote the sociologist Sarah Moore.[17]

The social psychologist, Roy Baumeister contends that despite the ceaseless references to identity, 'we lack a clear idea of what identity actually is'.[18] Numerous explorations of the meaning of identity allude to its multiple and often nebulous usage. One study of the concept of identity suggests that it is the very ambiguity of its meaning that permits its usage in a wide variety of situations.[19] It seems evident that lack of precision about its use has not inhibited the growing importance of the term because it offers a cultural idiom or metaphor through which individuals and groups believe they can gain meaning about the human condition.

The ease with which the concepts of identity crisis and identity have been detached from their clinical settings points to a wider demand for a concept that can be used to illuminate the human predicament. Originally definitions of identity emphasised the sense of sameness and continuity felt by individuals towards themselves and their place in the world. Since the 1960s the term has been used as a synonym for 'who you are', 'how you see yourself' and 'how others see you'. At the same time identity is frequently portrayed as something external to a person that must be found. The search for an identity often conveys a consumerist impulse of finding the right fit for yourself. So, too, does the idea of

---

15 R. Coles (1974) 'Review of Dimensions of a New Identity by Erik H. Erikson', *The New Republic*, 8 June, p.23.

16 See Coles (1974) p.23.

17 S. Moore (2010) *Ribbon Culture: Charity, Compassion, and Public Awareness*, Houndmills: Palgrave, p.21.

18 R.F. Baumeister (1986) *Identity: Cultural Change and the Struggle for Self*, Oxford: Oxford University Press, p.3.

19 L. Giorgi (2017) 'Travelling concepts and crossing paths: a conceptual history of identity', *European Journal of Social Science Research*, 30(1), 47–60.

experimenting with identities. The concept of identity experimentation communicates the idea of choice. Identities that are the product of experimentation often refer to relatively superficial aspects of life such as hair colour, style of clothes, genre of music, or the ribbon or wristband you wear.[20]

Since the 1970s numerous experts have drawn attention to the increasing demand for the concept of identity. John Marx, a sociologist, noted that in the mid-1970s there was a 'precipitous upsurge in both public and scientific preoccupation with questions of identity'. He added that '"Identity crises" are held responsible for almost every conceivable kind of dissatisfaction and disagreement – ranging from generational and marital discord to foreign policy and international relations'.[21] A decade later, in the mid-1980s, a group of sociologists pointed to the rapid growth in the everyday usage of the term 'identity crisis'. They concluded that 'we know of no other concept that emerged so rapidly and visibly both as a technical term and stock cultural coin'.[22]

Since the 1980s interest in identity has exploded. Time and again scholars and commentators point to an increase in demand for identity. Towards the end of the 1990s, the renowned sociologist Stuart Hall observed that 'there has been a veritable discursive explosion in recent years around the concept of "identity"'.[23] At the beginning of the 21st century, the political scientist Leonie Huddy echoed the same refrain: 'interest in the concept of identity has grown exponentially during the last decade or so within both the humanities and social sciences'.[24] A few years later Zygmunt Bauman, one of the leading sociological voices of the post-war era, reflected on what appeared to him to be the sudden prominence of identity in public discussions. He commented:

> It is a puzzle and challenge to sociology – if you recall that only a few decades ago 'identity' was nowhere near the centre of our thoughts, remaining but an object of philosophical meditation. Today, though, 'identity' is the 'loudest talk in town', the burning issue on everybody's mind and tongue.[25]

---

20 See Moore (2010).

21 J.H. Marx (1980) 'The ideological construction of post-modern identity models in contemporary cultural movements', in Robertson, R. and Holzner, B. (eds) *Identity and Authority: Explorations in the Theory of Society*, Oxford: Basil Blackwell, p.146.

22 A.J. Weigert, J.S. Teitge and D.W. Teitge (1986) *Society and Identity: Towards a Sociological Psychology*, Cambridge: Cambridge University Press, p.116.

23 S. Hall (1998) 'Introduction: who needs "identity"?', in Hall, S. and du Gay, P. (eds) *Questions of Cultural Identity*, London: Sage, p.1.

24 L. Huddy (2001) 'From social to political identity: a critical examination of social identity theory', *Political Psychology*, 22(1), 127–156, at 127.

25 Z. Bauman (2004) *Identity: Conversations with Benedetto Vecchi*, Cambridge: Polity Press, pp.17–18.

In his discussion of the 'puzzle' of identity, Bauman made a crucial point that is often overlooked by commentators. He wrote that if the 19th century 'classics of sociology' had 'lived long enough to confront it', they would be interested in 'this sudden fascination with identity, rather than identity itself'.

Identity has become a central theme in western societies because it provides a cultural framework through which people can define themselves as individuals and also as part of wider social constituencies. Gerald Izenberg contends that, between 1940 and 1950, the problem of the self was 'fundamentally redefined as that of personal identity'.[26] In a similar vein, the sociologist Ralph Turner wrote that identity provided a psychological narrative for the age-old problem of human alienation.[27]

Other features of human existence, such as the meaning of belonging to a community, an ethnic group or a nation, have also been redefined as an identity issue. The widespread usage of phrases like 'parenting identity' or 'professional identity' indicates that what is at stake is not just the redefinition of the self, but also the impulse to give meaning to it in a wide variety of institutional settings. The historian Peter Mandler has drawn attention to the 'linguistic drift' of the use of this term as the meanings attached to identity slipped away from its original meaning. He uses the term 'vernacularisation' to highlight the way social science concepts like identity become integral to everyday language and lose touch with their original meaning.[28]

Identity is best grasped as a cultural frame through which a variety of different concerns can be interpreted and communicated throughout society. In everyday language and communication, it works as a *rhetorical idiom* that captures the mood of uncertainty and insecurity that many of us experience in our everyday life. For many, identity is not merely a problem – it also constitutes a promise of validation and self-realisation. Those who seek salvation in the affirmation of their identities are supported by an impressive body of academic literature that provides a positive spin on what Erikson described as the problem of 'exacerbated identity consciousness'.[29] Individuals are encouraged to construct or invent their identity and to experiment with it.

---

26 G. Izenberg (2016) *Identity: The Necessity of a Modern Idea*, Philadelphia: University of Pennsylvania Press, pp.17–18.

27 R. Turner (1969) 'The theme of contemporary social movements', *British Journal of Sociology*, 20(4), 390–405, at 396.

28 P. Mandler (2019) 'The language of social science in everyday life', *History of the Human Sciences*, 32(1), 62–82, at 67.

29 Erikson (1968) p.26.

A surprisingly new phenomenon

People living in the 21st century can easily imagine that concern with identity has been a constant dimension of the human experience. In numerous instances, commentaries portray society's preoccupation with identity as the contemporary version of an age-old problem. Such observations are based on the premise that the search for identity or the impulse to gain validation for it are inherent to the human condition. From this standpoint, the problem of identity transcends different historical epochs and different cultures.

Most accounts treat identity as an eternal feature of human history. The distinguished social scientist Shmuel Eisenstadt asserted that constructions of collective identities 'have been going on in all human societies throughout history'.[30] A *Handbook of Identity Development* stated that 'identity has become an anchoring concept for the understanding of sameness and differences across human communities'.[31] Others qualify their representation of the problem of identity as integral to the human condition with the proviso that the intensity with which the issue preoccupies people varies in different historical circumstances. One study stated that 'in every age men ask in some form the question: Who am I? Where do I belong?' It added that 'the degree of awareness and the kind of emphasis with which these questions are asked vary at different periods'.[32]

This tendency to presume that in every age identity preoccupies human society also extends to reflections on identity politics. Both supporters and opponents assume that identity politics has an age-old history. One critic claimed that 'before the identity politics of the 1980s and 1990s, there was the identity politics of the 1930s and 1940s'.[33] A fervent advocate of identity politics dismisses the belief that it is a relatively recent phenomenon. He exhorted his opponents to 'pick up a history book' and added, 'identity politics is as old as America itself'.[34]

---

30 S.N. Eisenstadt (1998) 'The construction of collective identities: some analytical and comparative indications', *European Journal of Social Theory*, 1(2), 229–254, at 229.

31 K. McLean and M. Syed (2015) *The Oxford Handbook of Identity Development*, Oxford: Oxford Library of Psychology, p.22.

32 F.M. Lynd (1958) *On Shame and the Search for Identity*, London: Routledge & Kegan Paul, p.13.

33 L. Wieseltier (1994) 'Against identity', *The New Republic*, 27 November.

34 See Ruben Navarrette Jr in *USA Today*, 4 February, https://eu.usatoday.com/story/opinion/2019/02/04/identity-politics-trump-julian-castro-stacey-abrams-beto-orourke-column/2733935002/.

In recent times, the American political scientist Frank Fukuyama has claimed that 'human societies cannot get away from identity or identity politics'.[35] Fukuyama contends that identity grows out of the 'distinction between one's true inner self and the outer world of social rule'. He asserts that people's inner self constitutes the foundation for human dignity, which in turn is always in search of a positive recognition from others. He believes that the tension and disjunction 'between one's inside and one's outside' provides the basis for the formation of concern identity. The author contends that the idea of identity was born during the Reformation, when Martin Luther valorised the inner self over external institutions.[36]

Undoubtedly, Luther's affirmation of people's conscience and inner life played an important role in freeing individual from external constraint. But Luther's focus on people's inner life did not lead directly to a demand for recognition from other people or institutions. His exploration of his inner self, like those of others who followed him, may have led individuals to raise questions about their selves, but that had little in common with the way that identity has been conceptualised during the past 50 or 60 years. In contrast to the current era, where identity is often coupled with the consciousness of difference and uniqueness, in Luther's time identity referred to sameness.

Martin Luther would have found the contemporary conceptualisation of identity incomprehensible. Luther's predicament was framed and interpreted by him and his followers as a 'crisis of faith' and not a crisis of identity. As Izenberg points out, 'faith was a matter of divine truth and theological, not psychological need'.[37] The tension between inner self and external conditions was dealt with through a moral orientation that could be answered through existing universal terms. Luther was not interested in finding his 'true self' or acquire a unique identity but to find a way of living up to the expectations of universally valid moral commitments. Indeed – as we argue later in this book – it was the unravelling of moral authority, which was most dramatically expressed through a crisis of socialisation, that has led to the rise and rise of identity consciousness and the tendency to perceive the problem of the self through the optics of an identity crisis.

It is important to realise that concern with the self – which is a recurrent theme in history – was not until the post-Second World War era framed through

35 See F. Fukuyama (2019) *Identity: Contemporary Identity Politics and the Struggle for Recognition*, London: Profile Books, p.13.

36 Fukuyama (2019) p.27.

37 Izenberg (2016) p.433.

the medium of identity. Erich Fromm, in his *Escape From Freedom* (1941), used the concept of identity in relation to his concern with what he saw as the loss of the individual self in totalitarian societies. However, identity as '*substantive self-definition*, self-definition as *something*, which purportedly determines what I believe and do', came into 'common usage with work of Erikson'.[38]

Erikson wrote that the concept of identity emerged in response to the problems faced by individuals in the interwar era and the early 1940s. 'And so it comes about that we begin to conceptualize matters of identity at the very time in history when they become a problem', he stated.[39] He added, 'for we do so in a country which attempts to make a super identity out of all the identities imported by constituent immigrants'.[40] The problems to which he alluded were particularly noteworthy in the United States, and the social and cultural concerns of this society significantly influenced the way that the crisis of identity was portrayed and perceived throughout the world. This point is confirmed by a rigorous study of the semantic history of identity, which concludes that the formal conceptualisation of identity emerged first in the United States in response to a growing concern about what it meant to be an American.[41]

Far from there being a universal concern to 'possess an identity', this issue was absent in public deliberations throughout most of human history. Sigmund Freud famously talked of his Jewish identity in a speech in 1926 to refer to his inner self. His passing reference to identity can be construed as an acknowledgement of his ambivalence about his place in the world and anticipates the subsequent usage of the term. Arguably, it was the ambiguous position of Jews within European societies that led Freud to attempt to find a way of accounting for the Jewish dimension of his personality. Up to this point the very rare references to Jewish identity in published accounts referred to the need to preserve continuity with a Judaic distinct tradition.[42]

Izenberg points out that the first exploration of identity in the contemporary meaning of the term is to be found in Virginia Woolf's interwar novel, *Orlando*. He argues that it was the disruption to people's sense of who they were caused by the First World War that led to questions being raised about the meaning of

---

38 Izenberg (2016) p.24.

39 E.H. Erikson (1963) *Youth: Change and Challenge*, New York: Basic Books, p.78.

40 Erikson (1963) p.256.

41 See P. Gleason (1983) 'Identifying identity: a semantic history', *Journal of American History*, 69(4), 910–931, at 910.

42 See for example, 'Our duty to-day is to maintain our Jewish identity, and to preserve our Jewish institutions without faltering, without yielding. We must, with united forces, rally around our sacred Sabbath', in *The Menorah*, B'nai Brith, vol.11, p.158.

identity.[43] However, it would take until the 1940s and 1950s for the idea that identity was in crisis to crystallise and gain widespread public recognition.

The most authoritative account of the historical specificity of identity is provided by Marie Moran's *Identity and Capitalism* (2015). Moran offers a compelling case for her argument, that identity is a very new idea and it 'never "mattered" prior to the 1960s because it did not in fact *exist* or operate as a shared political and cultural idea *until* the 1960s'.[44] She points out that 'until the 1950s, or even the 1960s and 1970s, there was no discussion of sexual identity, ethnic identity, political identity, national identity, corporate identity, brand identity, identity crisis or "losing" or "finding" one's identity'. My own research into identity-related concepts indicates that, insofar as writers referred to national identity in the 19th century, their aim was to underline the sense of moral continuity of a community. As one Scottish clergyman stated in 1844; 'Upon what principle then, can the moral feeling of nations be explained, if not that of national identity which we are attempting to establish?'[45]

In the 19th century identity was essentially a moral construct and possessed a meaning that is very different from that of today. Our examination of the database of *Google N Gram Reader* indicates that in the 19th century concern with the stability and continuity of identity was often captured by the concept of *moral identity.* In its 19th century usage, this concept linked moral authority to an idea of identity that conveyed a sense of stability and immutability. Moral identity referred to its quality of sameness and continuity. Theologians and conservative commentators used this phrase to underline the importance of historical continuity. As a tract issued in 1827 by the American Unitarian Association indicated, 'the moral identity once broken, all other continuity goes for nothing, all other sameness is illusory'.[46]

It is only since the 1960s that identity has become a central category of the social sciences and is widely cited in both academic and popular monographs. Matters were different before the Second World War. For example, the *Encyclopaedia of the Social Sciences*, published in the early 1930s, 'carried no entry at all for identity'. It did have an entry titled 'Identification', which dealt with fin-

---

43 Izenberg (2016) pp.25–26.

44 M. Moran (2015) *Identity and Capitalism*, London: Sage, p.3.

45 See W. White (1844) *Christ's Covenant the Best Defence of Christ's Crown, etc: Our National Covenant, Scriptural, Catholic,* and *of Permanent Obligations*, Edinburgh: Kennedy, p.64.

46 Tracts of the American Unitarian Association, issues 71–125, 1827, p.75, https://books.google.co.uk/books?id=NtRMAQAAMAAJ&q=%22moral+identity%22&dq=%22moral+identity%22&hl=en&sa=X&ved=0ahUKEwiuh6TOjIzgAhUxpnEKHYCdD_4Q6AEIRjAG.

gerprinting and other techniques of criminal investigation.[47] Whatever the significance of the demand for recognition, it was not perceived or represented through the medium of identity at this point in time. In contrast to 1930, the 1968 edition of the *International Encyclopedia of the Social Sciences* carried a substantial article on 'Identity, psychosocial', and another on 'Identification, political'.

Although it is not possible to fix a date when identity emerged as an influential concept, all the evidence indicates that it was during the 1950s that identity became a rhetorical idiom through which people came to know and understand themselves and construct an understanding of what it means to be a human. The subsequent expansion of identity-talk was paralleled by the growing authority of psychology. It was the authority of psychology that provided the symbolic and intellectual resources necessary for propelling identity consciousness forward and providing an answer to the question of what it means to be a human.

> Thinkers try to answer the question from the symbols historically available to them. Traditionally, answers came from mythical, religious, theological, humanistic, philosophical, and everyday world views. In the past century, the rise of psychological and social sciences provided yet other symbols and models for addressing this question... 'Identity' became the translation of this era's answer to the seminal question.[48]

Although in recent times identity has mutated into a cultural attribute, in its early phase it worked as a moral and later as a psychological concept.

Even in the field of psychology, it took some time for identity to become an important focus of interest. There is no diagnostic category for identity in the 1953 edition of the *Diagnostic and Statistical Manual of Mental Disorder* (DSM) published by the American Psychiatric Association. The 1980 edition introduced the category of 'Gender Identity Disorder', and in 1994 'Personality Identity Disorder' replaced 'Multiple Personality Disorder'.[49] In the 1994 DSM, 'Identity Disorder' was downgraded to 'Identity Problem' on the grounds that apprehension over one's identity was so widespread that it could be considered as part of the new normal. In 2003, 'Identity Problem' was removed altogether, presumably because it was so widespread and normal that what clinicians had to worry about were those people who did not have such problems.

---

47 Gleason (1983) p.910.
48 Weigert, Teitge and Teitge (1986) p.30.
49 Izenberg (2016) p.3.

A 2010 review of the *PsychoInfo* noted that 54 per cent of all published material on this database that contained 'identity' as a keyword had been published in the previous decade, that is, after 1999. It indicated that 80 per cent of all identity-related articles were published between 1989 and 2010. Less than 4 per cent of articles with keyword 'identity' were published before 1970. The author of this study concluded that between 1970 and 2010 the previous interest of psychology in personality and character had been steadily displaced by identity.[50]

The relatively recent interest of psychology in the topic of identity indicates that reflections on the internal life of an individual or with the self have only been interpreted through the concept of identity since the late 1960s.[51] More fundamentally, even people's reflections on their selves need not be conducted through psychological concepts. The self has not always been a psychologically informed phenomenon. 'The mistake commonly made in histories of psychology is the assumption that all self-objectification must necessarily be psychological in character', writes Kurt Danziger in his study of how psychology developed its language.[52]

It is not possible to grasp the true significance of western society's adoption of the rhetoric of identity without situating it within a wider historical context. The current tendency to eternalise this development coincides with a propensity to overlook the specific features of the predicament facing individuals in 21st century society. A sensibility of historical amnesia dominates contemporary intellectual culture, which encourages a tendency to read history backwards.

Without attending to the historical dimension of the ascendancy of identity rhetoric, its analysis will tend to fail to capture the underlying cultural, social and political trends that have sustained its growing influence. To capture the distinct features of the cultural conflicts surrounding identity and its politicisation it is essential to logically reconstruct the historical influences that have led to their crystallisation.

The importance of a historical dimension for the topic of this study is also essential since what people think about identity and how it is conceptualised are themselves historically contingent. In its earliest formulation in the 1940s, the search for identity was often depicted in negative terms. Erich Fromm, who played a pioneering role in the development of the identity concept and was the first to use the term in relation to a crisis, argued that it was the loss

50 See S. Brinkmann (2010) *Psychology as a Moral Science: Perspectives on Normativity*, Berlin: Springer Science & Business Media, p.68.

51 Brinkmann suggests 1968 as a key moment when identity begins to take off as a central concept in psychology.

52 K. Danziger (1997) *Naming the Mind*, London: Sage Publications, p.24.

or the weakening of the self that created the need to 'feel a sense of identity'. He feared that the need for identity tended to encourage conformism. In his *The Sane Society* (1955), Fromm expressed his concern about people's need for a sense of identity in the following negative terms:

> What could be more obvious than the fact that people are willing to risk their lives to give up their love, to surrender their freedom, to sacrifice their own thoughts, for the sake of being one of the herd, of conforming, and thus acquiring a sense of identity, even though it is an illusory one.[53]

Fromm's statement reflected a widely shared consensus that feared that the need for a sense of identity might become a driver of the kind of destructive passions that led to fascism in the interwar era. William Whyte's bestseller, *The Organization Man* (1956), drew a direct link between the conformist ethos prevailing in American society and its growing preoccupation with individual identity. Whyte's views were characteristic of the attitude of critical commentators in the 1950s. Such sentiments stand in direct contrast to the more celebratory tone of post-1960s identity politics.

Taking a long view of developments, the historian Eric Hobsbawm explained that 'until the 1960s', the 'problems of uncertain identity were confined to special border zones of politics'.[54] Although the politicisation of identity has its origins in the 1960s, the term itself only acquired usage in the 1970s. To understand the genealogy of the usage of the term 'identity politics' we consulted the *Nexis* database of newspaper and periodical sources. The first reference to this term in a news story was in *The New York Times* on 24 June 1990.[55] By this time the term was widely used on campuses and by political activists but it had not yet acquired a noticeable presence in mainstream public life. There were 8 references to it in 1992 and 25 the year after. In 1995, it rose to 143. In 2000 there were 331 hits for 'identity politics', rising to 1140 in 2010. From this point onwards there was a steady year-on-year increase to 8923 in 2017, after which the number exploded further.[56]

53 E. Fromm (1955) *The Sane Society*, Greenwich: Fawcett Publications, p.64.

54 https://newleftreview.org/issues/i217/articles/eric-hobsbawm-identity-politics-and-the-left.

55 'A civil rights theme for a writing course campus life: Texas', *The New York Times*, 24 June 1990.

56 See *Nexis* database.

The changing perceptions of identity

Most commentaries of the ascendancy of identity tend to attribute its pervasive influence to the rapid pace of social and cultural change in what is often characterised as the post-modern era. This theme had already been emphasised by a member of Erikson's intellectual circle, the psychologist Kenneth Keniston, in the early 1960s. Keniston believed that in the rapidly changing world experienced in the United States it was difficult, if not impossible, to socialise young people to the point that they could gain stable identities. 'If growing up were merely a matter of becoming "socialized": that is of learning how to "fit into" society, it is hard to see how anyone could grow up at all in modern America, for the society into which young people will someday "fit" remains to be developed or even imagined', asserted Keniston.[57]

Keniston concluded that in a rapidly changing world the previous patterns of socialisation need to give way to a more explicit and conscious emphasis on identity formation. 'Oversimplifying', he stated, 'we might say that socialization is the main problem in a society where there are known and stable roles for children to fit into; *but in a rapidly changing society like ours, identity formation increasingly replaces socialization in importance*' (my emp.).[58] Keniston noted that even the 'achievement of identity' becomes 'more difficult in a time of rapid change'.[59] The main problem to which Keniston alluded was the absence of a stable system of values and ideals through which young people's identity could gain definition and acquire stability. He wrote that 'one of the chief tasks of identity formation is the creation of a sense of self that will link the past, the present and the future'. But what happens when 'the generational past becomes ever more distant, and when the future is more and more unpredictable'? Keniston's response to this question was that in such circumstances 'continuity requires more work, more creative effort'.[60]

During the past 60 years different versions of the thesis linking a supposedly rapidly changing world to the crisis of identity have been constantly reiterated by academics and media commentators. It is as if every generation of commentators feels compelled to attribute the status of omnipotence to the autonomous power of change. Change itself is depicted as an all-powerful force that destabilises or decentres people's identities. It is often represented through a language that

---

57 K. Keniston (1963) 'Social change and youth in America', in Erikson, E.H. (ed.) *Youth: Change and Challenge*, New York: Basic Books, p.178.
58 Keniston (1963) p.178.
59 Keniston (1963) p.178.
60 Keniston (1963) p.178.

hints at a fundamental rupture with the past. Terms like Globalisation, Risk Society, New Modernity, Late Modernity, Post-Modernity and Liquid Society draw attention to a runaway world of ceaseless change and fluidity that continually unravel individual and social arrangements.[61]

Arguments about the impact of rapid change often focus on its disorienting impact and influence on identity formation. They frequently refer to the impossibility of stable identity formation. The following statement clearly illustrates this approach:

> Perhaps stability and continuity in personal identity was true in the past – although that seems unlikely – but it is increasingly difficult, if not possible to achieve in the rapidly changing contemporary world. A stable, continuous personal identity over the entire life-cycle seems not merely atypical, but socially pathological and retarded in a post-industrial, post-modern world.[62]

From this perspective a stable identity is not merely impossible to achieve but it is also undesirable to possess in the so-called post-modern world.

Previously the loss of stable identity had been presented as a problem. In more recent times the difficulty of adopting a stable identity is frequently portrayed as a positive development by commentators whose preference is for identities that are constructed or invented. Post-modernist writers dismiss what they depict as traditional ideals of the self and of identity. They assert that 'the fixed subject of liberal humanistic thinking is an anachronism that should be replaced by a more flexible individual whose identity is fluid, contingent, and socially constructed'.[63] Within the academic world – where these sentiments exercise considerable influence – such writers make a virtue out of the destabilisation of identity.

The claim that the post-modern condition undermines a 'unitary conception of identity' is often justified by pointing to a variety of social and cultural developments that have altered the structuring of society. Robert Dunn points to the disruption of traditional hierarchies, the influence of media consumption and the proliferation of lifestyles. He contends that 'a series of changes involving migration, transnational capital, communication technologies, and cultural expor-

---

61 See for example Z. Bauman (1991) *Modernity and Ambivalence*, Cambridge: Polity; A. Giddens (1991) *Modernity and Self-Identity: Self and Society in the Late Modern Age*, Cambridge: Polity; and U. Beck (1992) *Risk Society: Towards a New Modernity*, London: Sage.

62 Marx (1980) p.184.

63 See the discussion in C. Lemert (2011) 'A history of identity: the riddle at the heart of the mystery of life', in Elliott, A. (ed.) *Routledge Handbook of Identity Studies*, London: Routledge, p.18.

tation ... have been destabilizing identity in the West and throughout the world'.[64]

Explanations that dwell on the fluidity and instability of identity frequently imply that it is something that is chosen or invented. From this standpoint, identity is a pre-existing entity waiting to be constructed. This argument was forcefully advocated by Bauman, who contends that identity is 'revealed to us as something to be invented rather than discovered'.[65]

Not everyone agrees that the project of inventing identity is on balance a positive development. Critics have drawn attention to the compulsive imperative of identity construction that leads individuals down a neurotic consumerist path. The sociologist Charles Lemert has pointed to the pathologies of inventing yourself through body surgery, therapies and sexual experimentation. He raised concerns about Internet lives 'who essentially lose themselves in the self-transformation they undertake trying to catch up with the world'. He described this as a 'disturbing trend of early twenty-first century life'.[66] This sentiment is echoed by Anthony Elliott, who writes of a 'reinvention craze' driving people to undertake painful and expensive procedures to alter the way they look and 're-create their identities'. Examples of these 'reinvented identity practices' are cosmetic surgery, superfast weight loss diets and body augmentation.[67]

Cultural narratives of identity that emphasise its fluid and decentred character are implicitly and sometimes explicitly challenged by representatives of groups founded on an essentialist claim to identity. So, paradoxically the declaration of individual construction and choice best expressed through the rhetoric of 'I identify as ...' coexists with an outlook that perceives identity as destiny. It seems that many individuals and groups simply cannot let go of the conviction, that though sometimes elusive, they are born with or into a pre-given identity. Paradoxically, the fantasy of invention and reinvention of identity runs in parallel with the belief that we 'are born this way'. Lady Gaga's 2011 hit, 'Born This Way' captures the fatalistic sensibility that people are born to identify as gay or lesbian. From this perspective sexual orientation is biological destiny and not a matter of choice. As she puts it in her song; 'there ain't no other way':

> Oh there ain't no other way
> Baby I was born this way

64 R.G. Dunn (1998) *Identity Crises: A Social Critique of Postmodernity*, Minneapolis: University of Minnesota Press, p.12.

65 Bauman (2004) p.15.

66 Lemert (2011) p.18.

67 See A. Elliott (2013) *Reinvention*, London: Routledge, pp.11, 94–95.

Baby I was born this way
Oh there ain't no other way
Baby I was born this way.[68]

Groups that are wedded to their collective identity often insist that there is something naturally or culturally pre-given in their identity. The trend towards this fossilisation of identity is most systematically expressed by those who draw on biology and genetics to legitimate their identity status. For some time now there have been attempts to discover a so-called 'gay gene' that would endow this form of sexual identity with the legitimacy of science.[69] While some have claimed that there are genetic markers that co-relate with homosexuality, others have suggested that the origin of sexual orientation is epigenetic in character. Epigenetics focuses on the way that environmental factors can modify people's genes and potentially influence human attitudes and behaviour.[70]

Many members of the gay, lesbian and trans communities embrace the genetically based version of sexual orientation because they believe that it normalises and validates their identities. Since the turn of the 21st century adherents of the claim that people are 'born this way', and their sexual orientation is genetically based, have often adopted a fiercely dogmatic orientation to those who question their view. Those who challenge the view that sexual orientation is innate have become targets of anger and abuse. In 2012, the actress Cynthia Nixon provoked a backlash from the gay community when she told *The New York Times* that homosexuality was a personal choice for her. One gay blogger, John Aravorsis, reacted to her supposedly anti-gay comment by asserting that 'every religious right hate monger is now going to quote this woman every single time they want to deny us our civil rights'.[71]

Identity has become a focus of heated controversy. Some perceive it as an outcome of choice; others as naturally endowed. Many groups and individuals regard their identity as the defining feature of their existence, while others attach little significance to it. Certainly, the view that identity is fluid and is an accomplishment to be realised or chosen exists in an uneasy relationship with an essentialist, fossilised account that emphasises its opposite. Since the 1970s sup-

68 www.youtube.com/watch?v=wV1FrqwZyKw.

69 See the discussion in K. O'Riordan (2012) 'The life of the gay gene: from hypothetical genetic marker to social reality', *Journal of Sex Research*, 49(4), 362–368.

70 See S. Reardon (2015), 'Epigenetic "tags" linked to homosexuality in men', *Nature*, 15 October, www.nature.com/news/epigenetic-tags-linked-to-homosexuality-in-men-1.18530.

71 Cited in www.dailymail.co.uk/tvshowbiz/article-2094099/Cynthia-Nixon-gay-choice-Actress-seeks-clarify-comments-causing-outrage.html.

porters of identity politics have played an important role in contributing to the ascendancy of an essentialist version of identity.

Identity: a problem of normativity

Explanations that associate identity-related problems with the consequences of the rapid pace of change have a point insofar as they draw attention to the challenge that people face when forced to adapt to new circumstances. However, rapid change has been a continuous feature of the modern era and was widely commented on a long time before the emergence of the idiom of identity. Explanations that attribute causal significance to change cannot account for the fluctuating perceptions of identity during the past century. Such theories cannot adequately explain why it shot into such prominence in the early 1970s, and why it has become so thoroughly politicised since the 1990s. Change itself is not simply an autonomous and objective phenomenon. It is perceived and interpreted through a system of meaning. How change is perceived is fundamentally a cultural accomplishment, as is the significance that communities and individuals attach to identity.

Stable identities are underpinned by clarity about *meaning*, which in turn draws on authoritative moral guidance. Without such guidance, people's identities become decentred. Identity, and the crisis that often surrounds it, is inextricably linked to the confusion that often envelops conflicts of moral norms.

Erikson wrote at length of a 'normative identity crisis' facing adolescents. The chapters that follow show that the crisis of norms is not merely confined to adolescents. The most useful way to understand the phenomenon encompassed by the term 'identity crisis' is as a sublimated expression of the unravelling of moral authority and the crisis of socialisation. Often, it is through the experience of an identity crisis that people and groups become aware of the absence of an authoritative moral authority that could give guidance and meaning to their lives. Erikson drew attention to this development when he noted that 'cultural identity' required that 'certain fundamentals of morality' be taken 'for granted'.[72]

Identity and the crisis that often surrounds it, as well as its politicisation, are inextricably linked to the confusion that frequently envelops conflicts over moral norms. This process is particularly evident in the domain of socialisation and, as we argue, it is the way that socialisation is managed that creates the conditions

72 E.H. Erikson [1950] (1995) *Childhood and Society*, London: Vintage, p.255.

for the crystallisation of the contemporary form of identity crisis and the potential for its politicisation.

Concern about identity, and the political controversies that surround it, constitutes one of the defining elements of the current zeitgeist. But a long time before identity became such a prominent public and political issue, the confusions surrounding it had become a matter of concern to those who feared that its loss could pose an insurmountable challenge to the healthy conduct of public and private life. Decades before the term 'identity crisis' was invented in the 1940s, psychologists, educators, political commentators and policy makers devoted their energy to tackle this, as yet unnamed, problem facing individuals in society.

Concern about character and personality, the mass man, the alienation of people from society, the apparent attractiveness of totalitarian ideology, the growing influence of a conformist culture, the difficulty that adolescents had in making the transition to adulthood were some of the themes that touched on issues which were eventually voiced through the term, the 'crisis of identity'.

The meaning of identity has fundamentally changed over the centuries. Historically, identity has been associated with the characteristics of sameness and continuity. This outlook was articulated by the philosopher William James in his *The Principle of Psychology* (1890). James stated that:

> The sense of our own personal identity, then, is exactly like any one of our other perceptions of sameness among phenomena. It is a conclusion grounded either on the resemblance in a fundamental respect, or on the continuity before the mind, of the phenomena compared.[73]

However, since it was first formulated by the ancient Greeks in this manner, identity's meaning has undergone important alterations. Whereas throughout most history, identity conveyed the connotation of sameness and continuity, in recent decades it has become associated with the *imperative of differentiation*. The contrast between continuity and constant construction, invention and reinvention of identity allows us to understand what is its most interesting and distinct feature in the 21st century. It has also become a prominent feature of identity politics, where the segmentation of identity groups into new ones has led to the proliferation of different groups.

Whereas for pre-modern and many modern societies the qualities of sameness and continuity were held in high regard, in our times the quest for flexibility, differentiation and difference has acquired positive connotations. As Bau-

73 W. James [1890] (1950) *The Principle of Psychology*, Mineola: Dover Publications, p.334.

meister noted, 'the increased desire for identity appears to be an increased desire for differentiation not continuity'.[74] The impulse towards differentiation is to a significant degree encouraged by the cultural valuation of individuality. The consciousness of the individual self was the precondition for the emergence of a sense of identity. However, the intensification of the consciousness of the individual self did not directly lead to the growing interest in identity. As we discuss in the chapters to follow, for a variety of reasons the meaning of the self altered, as it became bereft of moral clarity and began to understand itself through the medium of psychology. As the type of individuality valued and sought changed so did the way that people understood their self.

The American social critic Christopher Lasch noted in the 1970s that the kind of individuality with which people identified had altered. He commented that individuality which was realised through work and vocation had given way to one that sought fame and aspired to celebrityhood regardless of achievement.[75] Although some scholars trace the origins of this trend back into the 19th century, it was in the late 1960s and 1970s that the trends outlined by Lasch acquired systematic and culturally dominant form.[76]

The detachment of individuality from achievement encouraged the process of differentiation from others. Since the scope for the acquisition of genuine differentiation is relatively limited, the quest for it heightened concern with one's identity. 'The obstacles to the individuality created by living in a modern collective society make the appetite for differentiation difficult to satisfy', concluded Baumeister. He added that 'the quest for identity expresses that problem and that appetite'.[77]

The shift from gaining identity through work and achievement to an aspiration to be affirmed regardless of achievement has significantly contributed to the destabilisation of identity. In comparison to the early 20th century, it has also endowed the self with a relatively passive quality. It – far more than the impact of rapid change – has contributed to disorganisation of the individual sense of identity. A strong sense of self and a stable identity is accomplished through active work. 'Identity is safest of course, where it is grounded in activities', com-

---

74 Baumeister (1986) p.142.

75 C. Lasch (1979) *The Culture of Narcissism: American Life in an Age of Diminishing Expectations*, New York: Warner Books.

76 P. Cushman (1995) *Constructing the Self, Constructing America: A Cultural History of Psychotherapy*, New York: Da Cappo Press, p.63, argues that what he calls the 'therapeutic ethos' began to emerge in America in the 1830s.

77 Baumeister (1986) p.147.

mented Erikson. He believed that it was through the acquisition of vocation and work that young people resolved their identity crisis.[78]

The relationship between a sense of active agency and the development of a stable identity is well explained by the philosopher Hannah Arendt. Arendt stated that people's identity is realised through action. She believed that it is action that discloses our unique identities. She wrote that 'in acting and speaking, men show who they really are, reveal actively their unique personal identities and thus make their appearance in the human world'.[79]

The contemporary world has become estranged from Erikson's and Arendt's version of an identity developed through the act of agency and work. Today identity is often perceived as bestowed by nature or by membership in a particular community. In contrast to its previous version, personhood has acquired a strikingly passive form. In western societies, identities are treated as sacred and ready-made objects that need to be validated and esteemed regardless of someone's accomplishment. The obligation to respect identity has acquired the character of an ideological dogma in relation to group identities. In such cases identities are conferred by either nature, institutions or cultural conventions, rather than earned.

The main driver of the problems under discussion is the detachment of identity from normativity. It is the detachment from moral norms that has lent identity an unstable, arbitrary and fluid form. Most accounts claim that the fluidity of identity is a consequence of the post-modern condition and the rapid acceleration of change. While these conditions influence the forms that identity assumes, I contend that the decisive influence on the problematisation of identity is a lack of clarity about the moral values that underpin the self. As the philosopher Christine Korsgaard pointed out, 'you can't maintain the integrity you need in order to be an agent with your own identity on any terms short of morality itself'.[80] According to Korsgaard, normative standards provide the principles through 'which we achieve the psychic unity that makes agency possible'. Psychic unity with society's moral norms provides the normative resources for what Korsgaard characterises as *self-constitution*, the possession of which is the precondition for a dynamic sense of identity.[81]

---

78 E.H. Erikson (1974) *Dimensions of a New Identity: The 1973 Jefferson Lectures in the Humanities*, New York: W.W. Norton & Company, pp.105–108.

79 H. Arendt (1998) *The Human Condition*, Chicago: University of Chicago Press, p.179.

80 C.M. Korsgaard (2009) *Self-Constitution: Agency and Integrity*, Oxford: Oxford University Press, p.xii.

81 Korsgaard (2009) pp.7, 19.

What is generally referred to as the crisis of identity should be interpreted as a response to the unravelling of moral authority. In turn, the weakening of moral authority has both undermined the status of adulthood and led to a crisis of socialisation. The significance of this development has acquired its most striking expression in society's struggle to endow meaning to people's identity. This development was eloquently explained by the sociologist Peter Berger and his collaborators in their classic study, *The Homeless Mind* (1974). The authors of this text drew attention to the weakening of what they characterised as the 'identity defining powers of institutions'. Their emphasis on the difficulty that society's institutions had in providing norms and values through which individuals could lend meaning to their values drew attention to what would – with the passing of time – turn into one of the greatest problems facing public life. At the time, they wrote:

> Stable identities (and this also means identities that will be subjectively plausible), can only emerge in reciprocity with stable social contexts. Therefore, there is a deep uncertainty about contemporary identity. Put differently, there is a built-in identity crisis in the contemporary situation.[82]

Almost half a century later the 'deep uncertainty' about identity to which they referred has become a far greater source of conflict and tension than the authors could have imagined in the 1970s. Erikson's crisis of identity has become a source of conflict and is one of the main drivers of a process that frequently goes under the name of a culture war. As we shall see, surprisingly this conflict begins around disputes about how children should be raised and socialised.

---

82 P. Berger, B. Berger and H. Kellner (1974) *The Homeless Mind*, Harmondsworth: Penguin, p.86.

Chapter 2: Before Identity Crisis Was Given a Name

On 4 August 2020, *The New York Times* reported on the case of BethAnn McLaughlin, who in a statement acknowledged that through her Twitter account, 'MeTooSTEM', she had invented the false persona of a female Native American anthropologist at Arizona State University. @Sciencing_Bi was portrayed as a Hopi anthropologist, who was allegedly the victim of sexual harassment by a Harvard professor. The announcement of the death of this non-existent person due to COVID-19 complications prompted widespread expressions of grief, including a memorial service organised on Zoom.[95] Numerous individuals who identified with the victim identity of the fictitious @Sciencing_Bi were no doubt pained by this act of deception. They were forced to confront the fact that in the 21st century, identity is not always what it seems.

In a world where identity has become so important, it often serves as a medium through which people make a statement about themselves.

Today we have become accustomed to the existence of 'pretendians', that is, people who pretend to be who they are not. Given the cultural valuation attached to the identity of a victim, it is not surprising that in the United States there have been numerous examples of white people embracing a black or a Native American identity. During her campaign for nomination to be the Democratic Party's presidential candidate in 2019, Senator Elizabeth Warren faced criticism for her assertion that her DNA allowed her to claim Native American heritage. As one member of the Cherokee Nation complained about '"pretendians," or people pretending or claiming to be Native':

> Pretendians perpetuate the myth that Native identity is determined by the individual, not the tribe or community, directly undermining tribal sovereignty and Native self-determination. To protect the rights of Indigenous people, pretendians … must be challenged and the retelling of their false narratives must be stopped.[96]

95 www.sciencemag.org/news/2020/08/twitter-account-embattled-metoostem-founder-suspended (accessed 20 October 2020).

96 www.hcn.org/articles/tribal-affairs-how-pretendians-undermine-the-rights-of-indigenous-people (accessed 12 October 2020).

https://doi.org/10.1515/9783110708899-003

Would-be pretendians are unequivocally warned to Keep Out! All access to Native American identity is denied. Evidently, identity has become a site of conflict and of competitive claims making.

Competing claims about identity and who has the right to identify themselves as members of a particular group suggest that these disputes are intertwined with a cultural and psychological condition that is frequently diagnosed as an identity crisis. This condition is frequently alluded to by pretendians, whose personal narratives have been exposed as false. Just listen to the words of Jessica Krug, a white history professor at George Washington University who admitted to claiming a black identity. In her confession to a blog post on the *Medium* website she acknowledges that she has been a serial pretendian. She wrote that

> To an escalating degree over my adult life, I have eschewed my lived experience as a white Jewish child in suburban Kansas City under various assumed identities within a Blackness that I had no right to claim: first North African Blackness, then US rooted Blackness, then Caribbean rooted Bronx Blackness.[97]

Jessica Krug, a serial consumer of different black identities, wrote that her actions were an outcome of her mental health issues.

In a world where psychological determinism is used to explain people's behaviour and action, it is not surprising that Krug blamed her embrace of a black identity on her childhood trauma. She wrote;

> Mental health issues likely explain why I assumed a false identity initially, as a youth, and why I continued and developed it for so long; the mental health professionals from whom I have been so belatedly seeking help assure me that this is a common response to some of the severe trauma that marked my early childhood and teen years.[98]

So long as people are estranged from who they are, it is unlikely that pretensions to an idealised identity will cease. At a time when it has become socially acceptable for a biologically born man to identify himself as a woman and a biologically born woman to adopt the identity of a man, dramatic shifts in the presentation of the self are the new normal.

The estrangement from one's self, which often leads to a quest for a (new) identity, is in historic terms a relatively recent development. It is in literature

---

97 https://medium.com/@jessakrug/the-truth-and-the-anti-black-violence-of-my-lies-9a9621401f85 (accessed 15 October 2020).

98 https://medium.com/@jessakrug/the-truth-and-the-anti-black-violence-of-my-lies-9a9621401f85 (accessed 15 October 2020).

that we first encounter people who seek to reinvent themselves through the adoption of a new persona. Miguel de Cervates' novel *Don Quixote* (1605) portrayed the first encounter with the dramatic act of reinvention. In this, the first modern novel, Alonso Quixana is disenchanted with his unremarkable role of a Spanish country gentleman. In his fantasy, he is someone else and he identifies with the role of an honourable and dignified knight and adopts the name of Don Quixote.

Not unlike a 21st century pretendian, Don Quixote self-consciously reinvents his identity, assumes the manner of a chivalrous knight and sets forth on a life of adventure. Today, we diagnose men like Don Quixote, who embark on a dramatic quest for meaning, as suffering from a mid-life identity crisis but back in the early 17th century, before the emergence of the discipline of psychology, there was no name for identity-related afflictions.

Finding one's place

The attempt to find one's place in the world, which drove Don Quixote to madness, was a challenge faced by a significant cohort of young people in the 18th century. A new modern world appeared to put into question many of the prevailing norms and conventions that gave meaning to human experience. This quest for meaning – particularly for young people – acquired its most vivid expression in the new genre of the romantic novel.

Anxieties about changing values and behaviour and finding one's place in the world were most clearly and imaginatively expressed through literature, particularly through the genre of the novel. During the 17th and 18th centuries the intensity with which these problems were brought to life by literature, itself became a matter of concern. Don Quixote himself served as an early illustration of the risks associated with reading. According to Cervantes, Don Quixote was an obsessive reader, who 'whenever he was at leisure (which was mostly all year round) gave himself up to reading books of chivalry' to the neglect of other activities. Consequently, his reading overwhelmed his imagination to the point that he lost the ability to distinguish between fiction and non-fiction.

With the development of a mass reading public in the 18th century, numerous readers found the reality portrayed in novels more directly relevant to their selves than that which they encountered in their normal everyday existence. It is in the 18th century that the troubles surrounding the realisation of the self came to be openly recognised and discussed. It was principally through the new genre of the novel that the theme of tension between the aspiration for self-realisation and the social and cultural obstacles to it became a focus for discussion. Reading allowed individuals to develop thoughts in accordance with their own personal circumstances and inclinations, which sometimes did not conform to official sentiment – creating tension between the authority of the self and the prevailing moral order.

Romantic novels in particular included frustrated characters who felt that their life was thwarted by onerous rules and conventions, which prevented them from being true to themselves. An awareness of the gap between their day-to-day existence and who they felt they were meant to be, pointed to the need for the attainment of an identity that seemed to elude many readers of fiction.

For many young people, the novel provided a medium through which for the first time they could find their self. The novel held up a mirror to what had previously only been intuited or hinted at, and it gave meaning to all those traces of one's self that one had struggled to express or understand. In this respect Jean-Jacques Rousseau's novel published in 1761, *Julie, or the New Heloise*, is particularly pertinent. In *Julie*, a triangular relationship of the main protagonists stands in stark contrast to prevailing forms of stolid, limited and limiting relations. On the publication of *La Nouvelle Heloise* Rousseau was inundated with letters – written mainly by women, but also by men – indicating that they felt he had written the novel just for them: that it was really about them in particular, that he had captured their self in the novel. They saw in *Julie* a story of yearning, transgression and redemption that resonated with their own imagination, desire and sensibility.

Rousseau's *Julie* played an important role in the development of 18th century romanticism and of romantic literature. His sensitivity to the predicament faced by alienated youth provided insights on which future writers would draw to develop the concept of adolescence and identity crisis. Other authors, too, were driven towards the depiction of characters at the threshold of adulthood. The association of emotional upheaval and preoccupation with the self and young adulthood acquired widespread public recognition in the aftermath of the publication of Johann Wolfgang von Goethe's *The Sorrows of Young Werther* in 1774.

Werther became the media sensation of the 18th century. It touched a raw nerve and led to widespread disquiet on both sides of the Atlantic. This was a story of unrequited love that led to the act of suicide by the main character of the novel. Goethe's sympathetic depiction of Werther and of his demise drew attention to the turbulent emotional upheavals experienced by young people attempting to endow their life with meaning. For many readers, Werther's attempt to gain moral freedom from existing stultifying conventions through ending his life symbolised the dramatic circumstances faced by young people who felt that they were thwarted from realising their destiny. For many young readers, Werther's *crie de coeur:* 'Ah, this emptiness! This terrible emptiness that I feel in my breast', expressed their own sense of loneliness and estrangement.

The publication of *Werther* turned into an almost instant media event, becoming the first documented literary sensation of modern Europe. The novel was translated into French (1775), English (1779), Italian (1781) and Russian (1788), and repeatedly republished in different editions. There were more than 20 pirated editions published within 12 years of the novel's appearance in Germany. *Werther* also enjoyed a remarkable success in the United States, becoming one of the bestselling novels before the War of 1812 and having a powerful influence on the early American literary public.[99]

Werther provided the focus for a very early example of a phenomenon that would be labelled in the 20th century as a youth subculture. At the time, a generation of idealistic and romantic youth adopted Werther as their hero, many memorising excerpts from his letters and imitating the affectations associated with the persona of their tragic idol. According to one account, the 'youth of Europe learned his speeches as they learned Hamlet's'.[100] To many of them, Werther personified an identity to which they were attracted and which they were ready to imitate. It was as if this fictitious character evoked by Goethe appeared as a vibrant living role model to many young readers.

It was widely reported that young men and women were weeping for days, even weeks, over his tragic demise. Groups of young men adopted the fashion of wearing yellow trousers in combination with blue tailcoat and high boots in imitation of Werther's appearance in the novel. This novel also exercised a powerful impact over young people in the United States. The fans of *Werther* were disproportionately composed of readers who at the turn of the 20th century would be called adolescents. As one study noted, 'many of them were boys on the cusp of manhood', like the one a British traveller came across in Georgetown in 1798, who 'delighted in the perusal of the Sorrows of Werther [and] perfumed his handkerchief with lavender'.[101]

With hindsight it is evident that the young men who imitated Werther's appearance and adopted his affectations were not only identifying with their hero but also adopting his identity. Like Don Quixote, who dressed up as a knight, devotees of Werther pursued their fantasy by dressing up in the style of their

99 For a discussion of the impact of Werther on 18th century society, see F. Furedi (2015) *The Power of Reading: From Socrates to Twitter*, London: Bloomsbury.

100 See G.C. Minois (1999) *The History of Suicide: Voluntary Death in Western Culture*, Baltimore: Johns Hopkins University Press, p.367.

101 Cited in R. Bell (2011) 'In Werther's thrall: suicide and the power of sentimental reading in early national America', *Early American Literature*, 46(1), 93–120, at 95.

hero. They were also the pioneers of performing distinction. Unlike the insensitive and pedestrian, fans of Werther were advertising their sensibility of awareness. Centuries later artefacts of awareness would be mass produced as literally millions of young people displayed their awareness through the ribbons and bracelets that they sported.

The Sorrows of Young Werther is considered to be a central accomplishment of Germany's *Sturm und Drang* literary movement. This movement's preoccupation with the realisation of the individual self and people's internal anguish and internal life resonated with the feelings and outlook of many young people in the late 18th and 19th centuries. *Werther* directly appealed to a sensibility that experienced the prevailing social and moral order as constituting a barrier to the cultivation and development of the individual self. It was the contradiction between the aspiration to the realisation of individual personality and the conventions of society that Werther struggled to transcend. The tragic consequences of his struggle served to highlight his supposed heroic quality and reinforced his appeal to the novel's readers. In this regard, readers' response was influenced by the emergence of a new individual-oriented romantic fashion that valorised the intense emotional experience and self-discovery.

In the case of Werther, an obsessive sensibility of the self coexisted with an immature rejection of the duties and responsibilities associated with prevailing conventions. That, nevertheless, his persona became a focus of celebrity adoration indicates that prevailing fashion resonated with his behaviour. In the decades that followed the publication of *Werther*, sections of middle-class society came to the conclusion that whimsical and self-obsessed behaviour was both a normal and an understandable feature of young adulthood. At the time, this turbulent phase in young people's lives was not yet called adolescence. It would take several decades before the emotional upheavals linked to this phase of development would gain the attention of psychologists, who would then go on to diagnose the anguish and self-obsession of Werther as a normal symptom of the phase of adolescence.

The belief that the turbulent phase of emotional upheaval was a normal feature of young people's lives gradually crystallised into the conviction that they were not yet ready for adulthood. Devotees of Werther and other young people were no longer children but neither were they in a position to assume the role associated with adulthood. One consequence of this way of perceiving human development was to imagine that young people inhabited a distinct stage in the life-cycle; one that distinguished them from both children and adults. The invention of this distinct stage of youth had the effect of creating and increasing the distance between childhood and adulthood. To bridge the distance between these two phases of development, a new stage – soon to be called adolescence – was constructed.

The formulation of the idea of adolescence is usually associated with the work of the French philosopher, Jean-Jacques Rousseau. In his discussion of the emotional upheavals brought on by puberty, he wrote of 'the child who is moody and erratic, and has a more or less strong aversion toward parental authority'. He observed that 'it does not want to be led anymore ... it does not want to have anything to do with the adult, it is unreasonable, and mutinous, in short, it is unmanageable'.[102] Rousseau's description of this rebellious phase of adolescent life highlighted an attitude and form of behaviour that was widely recognised by observers in the 18th and 19th centuries. Rousseau perceived adolescence as a tumultuous phase of transition to adulthood during which young people learn to adjust to the role expected of them by society. In his study *Émile*, he used the terms 'rebirth' and 'second birth' to capture the process through which an adolescent would be reborn as an adult.[103]

Rousseau also alluded to this turbulent phase as a period of crisis during which young people develop a sense of who they are and acquire the maturity necessary for assuming, and learning to adjust to, the responsibilities that are usually linked to adulthood. His discussion of this process of adjustment anticipated the 20th century characterisation of this process as that of an identity crisis.

Rousseau's three-stage model of development posited the bridging stage –adolescence – as far shorter than 21st century views on this subject. He referred to the emotional crisis associated with the transition to adulthood as very brief – 'ce moment de crise, bien qu'assez court'.[104] Since the 18th century, this bridging period between childhood and adulthood has steadily increased, and in the 21st century the crisis of adjustment is rarely perceived as very short. As Koops noted, 'since Rousseau, adolescence has not only increased in duration, but also in intensity'.[105] Koops used the term 'infantilisation' 'to describe a historical process that from the 17th century, led to childhood gradually lasting longer and the distance between children and adults steadily increasing'.[106]

---

102 Cited in W. Koops (2019) 'Does adolescence exist?', *Japanese Journal of Adolescent Psychology*, 30(2), 89–98, at 89.

103 See the discussion in W. Koops and M. Zuckerman (2003) 'Introduction: a historical developmental approach to adolescence', *History of the Family*, 8(3), 345–354.

104 Cited in Koops and Zuckerman (2003) p.89.

105 Koops (2019) p.90.

106 Koops (2019) p.89.

The discovery of adolescence

In the 21st century adolescence is perceived as a taken-for-granted stage in human development. Its attributes are a focus of discussion and debate among social scientists in general and psychologists in particular. Since adolescence has become intensely psychologised during the past century, it is easy to overlook the fact that its literary representation as a distinct stage preceded its formulation as a scientific concept. Society's preoccupation with the management of adolescence surfaced within the context of the powerful cultural upheavals surrounding values and norms that accompanied the rise of modernity in the 18th century.

The early psychological theories of adolescence tended to draw on the literary representations of the identity crisis of youth, which they rebranded in a scientific language. This approach characterises the work of the American psychologist Stanley Hall, whose two-volume study, *Adolescence: Its Psychology and Its Relation to Physiology, Anthropology, Sociology, Sex, Crime, Religion, and Education* (1904) served as the point of reference for this subject. In this study, which is said to be the beginning of scientific and scholarly research on adolescence, Hall drew on the romantic sensibility towards youth expressed by the *Sturm und Drang* movement and Rousseau to conceptualise the personality traits most associated with adolescence. His work and that of other psychologists ensured that the spirit of Romanticism, with its 'affirmation of a realisable, essential self, found scientific legitimation'.[107]

Following Rousseau, Hall asserted that 'adolescence is a new birth', during which 'the higher and more completely human traits are now born'.[108] Rousseau's idea of adolescence as second birth informed Hall's account. In this way, 'Rousseau's ideas became stable elements not only of western folk psychology but also of academic psychology'.[109] Rousseau's idealisation of second birth as the outcome of a developmental crisis also provided the cultural underpinning for 20th century theories of identity crisis.

Hall was strongly influenced by the insights and romantic sensibility of the *Sturm und Drang* movement and by its literary representations of the emotional upheavals represented by youth. He was fulsome in his praise for Goethe and

---

107 See E. Illouz (2008) *Saving the Modern Soul: Therapy, Emotions, and the Culture of Self-Help*, Los Angeles: University of California Press, pp.22–57.

108 S. Hall [1904] (1916a) *Adolescence: Its Psychology and Its Relation to Physiology, Anthropology, Sociology, Sex, Crime, Religion, and Education*, vol. 1, New York: D. Appleton & Company, p.xiii.

109 Koops and Zuckerman (2003) p.347.

observed that 'perhaps no one ever studied the nascent stages of his own life and elaborated every incident with such careful observation and analysis'.[110] He wrote that 'Romance, poetry, and biography furnish many admirable descriptions of the psychic states and changes characteristic of every stage of ephebic transformation'.[111] Hall's discussion of the psychological characteristics of adolescence bears all the hallmarks of the influence of romantic literature. He venerated adolescence, and described himself as one who was 'an almost passionate lover of childhood', who for long believed that this phase of youth was 'one of the most fascinating of all themes, more worthy, perhaps than anything else in the world of reverence, most inviting study, and in most crying need of a service we do not yet understand how to render aright'.[112]

Although Hall's *Adolescence* presents itself as a work of scientific psychology, it often reads as a compilation of the available folk knowledge on the meaning of youth derived from literature and non-literary sources. Hall, like many 19th century commentators, was fascinated with youth and it is difficult to avoid the impression that his interest in the subject matter was motivated by the feeling that something important was lost in the transition to adulthood. At times, he portrays adulthood as a stage that is inferior to what preceded it. There is a clear tone of regret in his statement that 'in one sense, youth loses very much in becoming adult'.[113] His yearning for youth exists in an uneasy relationship with the need to uphold adult authority. From this standpoint, Hall's contribution can be seen as an early example of the contemporary tendency to recycle the problems of adulthood as issues facing youth.

Adolescence often comes across as a homage to youth. In its Preface, Hall suggests that his study 'can appeal only to those still adolescent in the soul'.[114] He reminds his readers that 'the best definition of genius is intensified and prolonged adolescence', a phase that 'only poetry can ever describe'.[115] In many instances, this supposedly scientific text resembles an updated version of a Platonic dialogue, inspired by the 'charm' of the 'noble love of adolescent boys'.[116] Though framed in the language of modernist science, *Adolescence* com-

110 Hall [1904] (1916a) p.581.
111 Hall [1904] (1916a) p.513.
112 Hall [1904] (1916a) p.xviii.
113 S. Hall [1904] (1916b) *Adolescence: Its Psychology and Its Relation to Physiology, Anthropology, Sociology, Sex, Crime, Religion, and Education*, vol. 2, New York: D. Appleton & Company, p.90.
114 Hall [1904] (1916a) p.viii.
115 Hall [1904] (1916b) pp.90, 302.
116 Hall [1904] (1916a) p.513.

municates a sense of disillusionment with modernity. More widely, through the emerging narrative of adolescence numerous 19th century commentators expressed their ambiguous reaction to the dictates of modernity. The idealisation of youth and of its emotions offered a unique opportunity for freely voicing a romantic anti-rationalising sensibility.

In part the invention of the concept of adolescence and the growing interest in this phase of young people's lives were motivated by concern about the problems and behaviour of young people. Despite his romantic idealisation of youth, Hall, like most of his colleagues, was worried about what he perceived as the disorderly, unpredictable and delinquent behaviour of adolescents. Hall described this phase of life as 'the age of sentiment and of religion, of rapid fluctuation of mood' which intensified 'self-feeling' and which encouraged an 'exaggeration and excess' of ambition and sentiments. He believed that such sentiments could lead to the quest for noble deeds, but could also drive young people in self-destructive directions. 'Never has youth been exposed to such dangers of both perversion and arrest as in our own land and day', warned Hall.[117]

The literary evocation of adolescence and its subsequent representation through the language of psychology has their origins not so much in the empirical reality of young people as in the anxieties of adults about their own values. As the historian Joseph Kett contends, in the 19th century:

> Rather than describing the experience of teenagers, the discourse on adolescence in this and subsequent periods has primarily reflected the challenges that adults saw to their own values and the ways in which they adapted to change.[118]

In other words, it was through the narrative about youth that emerged in the 18th and 19th centuries that adults attempted to understand their own confusions and response to the cultural changes brought about through the rise of modernity. Adulthood and its meaning were rarely discussed in its own terms. Instead, the recycling of moral anxieties through the predicament faced by youth provided the narrative through which adults tried to interpret their own predicament in face of the changing conditions confronting them.

---

117 Hall [1904] (1916a) p.xv.

118 J.F. Kett (2003) 'Reflections on the history of adolescence in America', *History of the Family*, 8(3), 355–373, at 356.

Why was adolescence invented?

Accounts of the invention of adolescence rarely perceive this development as more to do with the challenges facing adults than with the discovery of biological or psychological characteristics of youth. Most studies of this discovery attribute it to the experience of broad structural and social changes – especially in American society. In particular the transformation of family life, the demands of a modern industrial economy and urbanisation are seen to provide the sociological underpinning for the construction of the bridging phase of adolescence. In effect, adolescence came to be represented as 'a form of psychology and behavior exhibited by pre-adults' that emerged in the 19th century as an outcome of the 'peculiar social conditions' that 'prevailed at the time'.[119] As one study explained, the '"discovery" of adolescence can be related to certain broad changes in American life – above all, to changes in the structure of the family as part of the new urban and industrial order'.[120]

According to the dominant narrative, the invention of adolescence in the 19th century was closely linked to the transformation of the family, particularly the reduction in the number of children. This decrease in family size allowed parents to make a greater emotional investment in their child than in previous times. Phillipe Aries, the influential historian of childhood, argued that unprecedented parental concentration on the child led to the loss of freedom of children.[121] This exercise of control coexisted with the expansion of the phase of children's dependence on their parents, which in turn created a cohort of pre-adults, who were 'not yet in control of their destiny':

> Confronted by this expanded period of control, whether at school or with parents, facing an increasingly industrial complex and changing world, youth became bewildered and confused about the process of becoming an adult and thereby spawned what historians identify as the unique psychological features of adolescence.[122]

In numerous studies these psychological features of adolescence are attributed to the specific socio-economic context of the 19th century. The tension between

---

119 See V.C. Fox (1977) 'Is adolescence a phenomenon of modern times?' *Journal of Psychohistory*, 5(2), 271–290, at 271–272.

120 J. Demos and V. Demos (1969) 'Adolescence in historical perspective', *Journal of Marriage and Family*, 31(4), 632–638, at 632.

121 P. Aries (1962) *Centuries of Childhood*, New York: Vintage, pp.413–415.

122 Fox (1977) p.273.

dependence on parents at a time when young people yearn for independence is said to create many of the psychological strains of adolescence.

According to this narrative, the socio-economic transformation of capitalist society led to the expansion of education, which in turn altered the status of youth and intensified generational segregation while increasing children's dependence on parents. These changes led to the emergence of an unprecedented degree of generational separation of children from adults. The unique adolescent experience of the 19th century emerged out of this separation.

Theories of adolescence focused on the loss of freedom of young people who were intensely aware of the fact that they were pre-adults who were not yet in control of their destiny. As Skolnick outlined this story;

> Thus, economic, familial, and cultural changes transformed the experience of growing up; adolescence became an important stage of the individual's biography. The opening of a gap between physical maturation and the attainment of social adulthood led to the psychological characteristics that have come to be known as the adolescent experience – the urge to be independent from the family; the discovery of the unique and private world of the self; the search for an identity; and the questioning of adult values and assumptions which may take the form of idealism, or cynicism, or both at the same time.[123]

Different versions of this account present adolescence and its problems as the outcome of a changing socio-economic landscape. From this perspective, these new problems invited the science of psychology to engage with what was in the 19th century supposedly a relatively new phenomenon.

Undoubtedly, the radical socio-economic changes of the 19th century had a major impact on people's lives. Industrialisation and urbanisation intensified the distinction between activities carried out at home and at work. The structure of the family underwent important modification, and most children and many young people were drawn into schools and ceased to participate in the world of work. Though these changes significantly altered the experience of growing up it does not necessarily follow that they led to the emergence of the emotional traits that Hall and other psychologists attributed to adolescence.

There is considerable evidence that the emotional and personality traits attributed to adolescence by psychologists were identified and discussed in detail centuries before the arrival of the science of psychology. Aristotle's description of the volatility and emotional turbulence of youth anticipated Hall's formulation of this adolescent trait. Indeed, Hall explicitly refers to Aristotle's description

---

123 A. Skolnick (1975) 'The limits of childhood: conceptions of child development and social context', *Law and Contemporary Problems*, 39(3), 38–77, at 63.

of adolescence and asserts that this Greek philosopher gave the 'best characterisation of youth'.[124] Aristotle regarded adolescence as the third stage of life that followed infancy and childhood. In his writing, he described the inner tension experienced by youth in a language that would later be captured through the rhetoric of storm and stress:

> The young are in character prone to desire and ready to carry any desire they may have formed into action. Of bodily desires it is the sexual to which they are most disposed to give way, and in regard to sexual desire they exercise no self-restraint. ... If the young commit a fault, it is always on the side of excess and exaggeration. ... They regard themselves as omniscient and are positive in their assertions.[125]

Aristotle both idealised youth – 'they are inclined to be valorous' while expressing concern about its lack of restraint – 'they are slaves, too, of their passions'.[126] Over 2000 years ago, Aristotle outlined in detail many of the adolescent traits that modern psychology supposedly discovered in the late 19th century.

The historian Vivian Fox provides numerous illustrations that indicate that 'adolescent personality traits were identified and described in a manner similar to the modern characterizations of adolescence well before the modern era'.[127] She claims that the years of adolescence were depicted as a transitional phase well before the 19th century. Inner turmoil, 'storm and stress and emotional tensions related to sexual desire were described in detail by numerous authors, the most famous of which is the *Confessions* of St Augustine'.[128]

With hindsight, it appears that what was significant about the 19th century psychology of adolescence was not that it discovered something new but that it attached an unprecedented degree of significance to a phenomenon that had been in existence for a long time. In this respect the work of Hall and other psychologists can be seen to reflect the concerns that were widely circulating in society. The frequently voiced assertion that Hall's concept of adolescence captured a 'real change in the human experience, a change intimately tied to the new kind of industrial society that was emerging in America and Europe', is only partially accurate.[129]

---

124 Hall [1904] (1916a) p.522.
125 Cited in Fox (1977) p.274.
126 Cited in Fox (1977) p.274.
127 Fox (1977) p.273.
128 Cited in Fox (1977) p.275.
129 This claim is advanced by K. Keniston (1970) 'Youth: a "new" stage of life', *American Scholar*, 39(4), 631–654., at 632.

The discovery of adolescence was stimulated by the difficulty that adult society experienced in relation to the challenge of socialising and influencing the behaviour of young people. As Baumeister commented, in the absence of clarity about moral authority, 'it was unclear as to what version of fundamental truth' adult society culture 'imparts to its adolescents'.[130]

The 18th and 19th centuries saw the steady erosion of the influence of traditional institutions and moral norms. Hitherto the tensions and conflict between generations coexisted with a system of more or less shared values. In contrast, from the 19th century onwards inter-generational conflict was often articulated through the competing values held by the old and the young. The emotional intensity with which young people rebelled against prevailing conventions was linked to the degree with which the traditions of the past retained their influence. This point was recognised by Hall, who wrote that emotional turbulence of adolescence was more likely to erupt in the United States of his time than 'in older lands with more conservative traditions'.[131]

In the 19th century the weakening of traditional conventions was a constant theme in American commentaries on childrearing. Concerns were regularly raised about the apparent loss of parental authority. Parenting books 'imparted the same message: the authority of parents must be established early in a child's life and firmly maintained throughout the years of growth'.[132] These calls for the restoration of parental authority often unwittingly conveyed a tone of defensiveness and confusion. This defensive tone reflected the realisation that parental authority had lost its previous unquestioned valuation. The traditions that had hitherto underpinned parental authority had lost much of their force.

Ambiguity towards the moral status of adulthood ran in parallel with the idealisation of youth. Among progressive circles the young were increasingly portrayed as the bearers of progressive change while the old were often depicted as the repositories of the archaic traditions of the past. This sentiment was shared by Hall, who believed that the 'future of our race' depended on the 'increased development of the adolescent stage', which he characterised as the 'bud of promise for the race'.[133]

Fascination with youth and the idealisation of the innocence of the child were paralleled by calls to restrain parental control. Competing claims about the best way of bringing up children reflected the erosion of consensus on the role of adult authority. Jacob Abbott, a well-known writer of children's books,

130 Baumeister (1986) p.112.
131 Hall [1904] (1916a) p. xvi.
132 See Demos and Demos (1969) p.632.
133 Hall [1904] (1916a) p.50.

was aware of the dilemma facing parents on this score. In his *Gentle Measures in the Management and Training of the Young* (1871), Abbott indicated that there were three modes of managing children. These were 'Government by manoeuvring and Artifice', 'By Reason and Affection' and 'By Authority'.[134] Abbott was in no doubt that the management of children demanded the exercise of 'that absolute and almost unlimited authority which all parents are commissioned by God and nature to exercise over their offspring during the period while the offspring remain dependent upon their care'. At the same time, Abbott advised parents to adopt 'gentle methods' and techniques in the management of their children. He noted that such gentle methods are not a substitute for authority, but they can 'aid in establishing and maintaining it'.

Despite Abbott's insistence that childrearing required the exercise of 'absolute and almost unlimited authority', the reader of his book was likely to gain the impression that successful parenting depended on 'gentle' pedagogic and psychological skills. The implication of his approach was that, at the very least, mothers and fathers had to adopt an approach to childrearing that was different from the way that parental authority had been exercised in the past. In a roundabout way Abbott called into question the status adult of authority. For once authority is conceptualised as a form of management that relies on the use of psychological technique, it becomes deprived of its moral content. In such circumstance, adulthood loses some of its moral status, and its capacity to influence the younger generation diminishes.

In the minds of many 19th century observers the challenge of influencing the younger generation was intertwined with a lack of clarity about what was expected of adults. Indirectly, the discovery of adolescence helped turn a troublesome value-related problem into a more manageable technical/psychological one. Through the attribution of unprecedented significance to the emotional traits of young people, confusions regarding moral norms were recast as psychological ones. Such confusions were naturalised as the emotional traits of adolescence.

The discovery and the conceptualisation of adolescence offered a provisional solution to the challenges faced by adult authority. This was the cultivation and institutionalisation of a moratorium on the assumption of adulthood and the responsibilities associated with it by young people. Following Hall, psychologists argued that young people required this 'gentle' phase where through limiting the intensity of adult control, adolescents could cultivate their identity freed from the burden of adult responsibilities. The normal and natural demands of

134 J. Abbott (1871), *Gentle Measures in the Management and Training of the Young*, www.gutenberg.org/cache/epub/11667/pg11667-images.html (accessed 3 May 2019).

this moratorium relieved some of the pressure on adults regarding the exercise of their authority.

Slowing down the transition to adulthood

The moratorium on the assumption of the responsibilities of adulthood created the conditions that permitted adolescence to acquire qualities that distinguished it from both childhood and adulthood. With the passing of time these qualities were perceived as the natural psychological or biological attributes of adolescents.

Unlike children, adolescents possessed a degree of freedom from parental control and in contrast to adults they were given latitude to experiment and adopt forms of spontaneous behaviour that would be frowned upon in later life. Hall noted 'youth must have its fling', which required 'the need of greatly and sometimes suddenly widened liberty'. He recognised that youth still needed 'careful supervision and wise direction' but this had to be exercised 'from afar and by indirect methods'.[135] It is likely that in giving youth permission to 'have its fling', Hall was not only acknowledging but also justifying a practice that had become a fact of life for at least a minority of young people. However, psychology's advocacy of a psychosocial moratorium during which young people could have their fling helped boost and legitimate the cultural narrative of adolescence.

Psychologists and educators idealised the transition period as one where people could enjoy the kind of freedom or lack of restraint that they were unlikely to experience either in childhood or in adulthood. One psychologist called on adults to create the condition of freedom for adolescents in the following terms:

> We can surround youth with encouragement. There need be no sneering superiority, no ridicule, no tyrannical authority, no dogmatic over ruling, nothing to undermine the confidence and assertion that are necessary to approach work and love on an adult basis. We can have young people as free as possible to develop their own interests, free to discover for themselves, to experiment, even to make mistakes. We can give them freedom to experiment in the ordering and control of their own group life as well as their individual interest.[136]

135 Hall [1904] (1916b) pp.90–91.

136 J. Taft (1921) 'Mental hygiene problems of normal adolescence', *Annals of the American Academy of Political and Social Science*, 98(1), 61–67, at 66.

This narrative of freedom was rarely realised in practice. Nevertheless, this commentary titled 'Mental hygiene problems of normal adolescence' echoed the approach adopted by the professional advocates of a moratorium.

The gradual acceptance of the moratorium – first in the US and later throughout much of the western world – was shaped by powerful cultural impulses reflecting confusions about the exercise of adult authority. As we discuss in the chapter to follow, these confusions centred on the capacity of adult society to socialise the new generation. In part young people were freed from direct adult control because their elders were far from certain about how to exercise their authority. As Kett argued, adults 'were uncertain where to draw the line with youth'.[137] Since the 1950s, lack of clarity about where to draw the line between adolescence and adulthood had become progressively a greater problem.

The advocacy of a moratorium was not the cause of the gradual removal of young people from work and economic life. Nor did it precede the expansion of education and enrolment of growing numbers of adolescents into high school. The conceptualisation of a moratorium served as a medium through which a new narrative of youth was reconciled with the new socio-economic circumstances. With hindsight, the really important 'discovery' was not so much that of adolescence but of the need for a moratorium – that is, the need to slow down the process of transition to adulthood. Therefore, the institutionalisation of a prolonged bridging period between childhood and adulthood should not be interpreted as a response to the biological or psychological difficulties that inhere in the adolescent condition. Rather, as Koops indicates, insofar as adolescents find it difficult to grow up, it is because 'they are not accepted by the grown-up world'.[138]

The difficulty that the grown-up world had in accepting young people into adulthood was often justified on the ground that in previous times society was too hasty in forcing its unprepared youth to grow up. Though these sentiments first gained influence in the US, they had spread to other parts of the world by the early 20th century. In England, the educator and social reformer Margaret McMillan criticised previous generations for hurrying children into premature adulthood. In her 1909 article 'Adolescence', she claimed that this stage of development was ignored until the arrival of 'Brain Specialists'. 'Our ancestors ignored it in their ignorance', she claimed. She observed that

> Adolescence is a period of growth through which some human beings pass on their way to Adult Life. Some are allowed to pass through and out of it happily, but for others this stage

137 Kett (2003) p.369.
138 Koops (2019) p.89.

> of becoming is ignored, or slurred over, so that the child is hurried into manhood or womanhood by a short cut as it were.[139]

McMillan and other British advocates of adolescence did not merely condemn the supposed ignorance of their ancestors. Their target was their contemporaries, who in their ignorance continued to 'hurry' children into adulthood. Towards the end of the First World War, a commentary in *The Athenaeum* warned that the 'age of adolescence demands a care which we have not yet accorded it'. The commentator asserted that

> Growing boys and girls live in a society which does not understand them, which presses them into adult organization and, instead of developing as Nature ordained they should, they are thwarted, repressed and distorted.[140]

In its appeal to the authority of Nature, this call to give children time to grow up reflected the romanticised narrative of youth that influenced the sensibility of many educators and reformers at the time. However, unlike 18th century Romanticism, its early 20th century version relied on the authority of science such as McMillan's 'Brain Specialists' or psychologists to legitimate their views on adolescence.

The elaboration of a moratorium – the relaxation of pressures for adult activity during adolescence – was the work of psychologists, educators and social workers like McMillan. Many commentators on this subject were critical of prevailing childrearing and pedagogic practices and regarded themselves as the defenders of the interest of the young against a failing moral order. As Kett commented; 'the psychologists, social workers, and educators who fashioned an institutionalized moratorium for adolescents held highly negative perceptions of the work ethic and success myth that had permeated earlier conceptions of youth's role'.[141] Their narrative of adolescence was influenced by anti-modernist impulses that surfaced in the late 19th century.

Hall, too, was worried about the negative effect of 'overcivilization' on the development of young people. Hall's fear that overcivilization led to the loss of masculinity and undermined young people's mental health influenced his view of adolescence. His support for a moratorium was in part expressed in a language with clear anti-modernist overtones:

---

139 M. McMillan (1909) 'Adolescence', *The Highway*, 2(15).

140 'The nation's youth', *The Athenaeum*, 1917, pp. 119–120.

141 Kett (2003) p.371.

> [The adolescent] must have much freedom to be lazy, make his own minor morals, vent his disrespect for what he can see no use in, be among strangers to act himself out and form a personality of his own, be baptized with the revolutionary and skeptical spirit, and go to extremes at the age when excesses teach wisdom with amazing rapidity, if he is to become a true knight of the spirit and his own master.[142]

Centuries previously, the aspiration to become a true knight inspired Don Quixote to embark on his futile quest. At the turn of the 20th century, psychology offered youth permission to embark on a voyage free from restraint and the burden of adult responsibility. Later, in the post-Second World War era, this moratorium was represented as a phase during which young people could experiment with cultivating their identity and overcome their crisis of identity. At least that was the theory. It is unlikely that Hall would have anticipated that six decades after the publication of *Adolescence*, the moratorium would be celebrated as an end-in-itself, with millions reluctant to complete their journey to the land of adulthood.

The institutionalisation of adolescence

During the decades following the discovery of adolescence, its advocacy led to its gradual institutionalisation through the steady expansion of education. In the UK, supporters of expanding compulsory education used the discovery of adolescence as a key argument for promoting their cause. Some went so far as to claim that the post-First World War reconstruction of the nation depended on providing new opportunities for the education of adolescents:

> We are beginning now to discover adolescence and the most important test of sincerity and determination in the cause of Educational reconstruction will be found in the boldness with which we approach the problem of adolescent education.[143]

During the interwar era calls for education reform focused on the necessity for schooling adolescents. It is worthy of note that at the time, the most important official report on the reform of schooling in the UK, *The Hadow Report* (1926), was titled *The Education of the Adolescent*.[144]

---

142 S. Hall (1971) 'Adolescence and the growth of social ideals', in Rapson, R. (ed.) *The Cult of Youth in Middle-Class America*, Lexington: D.C. Heath and Co., pp.35–41.

143 'The nation's youth', *The Athenaeum*, 1917, p.120.

144 See www.educationengland.org.uk/documents/hadow1926/ (accessed 8 January 2016).

As in the UK, so, too, in the US, advocates of social reform took up the cause of adolescents to support their claim for the extension of compulsory education. As the historian Paula Fass remarked, 'taking up the banner of adolescence, educators reimagined the US public high school as an institution that could address the needs of immigrants and other Americans, while maintaining a democratic idiom in a transforming world'.[145] In part because of the unique prosperity of the US, advocates of the cause of adolescence were more successful than their counterparts in the UK. As Fass noted, by the end of the interwar era they had succeeded in transforming the 'US high school into a socialising institution for adolescents'.[146]

The expansion of schooling was not simply motivated by pedagogic imperatives. Around the turn of the 20th century many educators came to the conclusion that retaining students in schools as long as possible was an end-in-itself. Kett observed that 'the preponderance of opinion among public educators began to shift away from this meritocratic, survival-of-the-fittest pedagogy to a greater emphasis on the value of retaining students in school as long as possible'.[147] This point was echoed by Fass, who wrote that 'educators opened wide the doors of high school because they were intent on keeping students there for as long as possible'.[148]This emphasis on retention was in part motivated by the impulse of shielding adolescents from the supposed outdated influence of their families.

The objective of retention was realised through the expansion of education. The steady growth of the public high school provided the cultural infrastructure for the flourishing of adolescent consciousness. Through the retention of young people in schooling until the age of 16–18, it also contributed to the slowing down of the process of transition to adulthood. As Fass explained:

> The comprehensive public high school transformed the aims of education from being a limited period directed toward making the young literate and reliable citizens into a training institution for variously defined social and economic purposes. Rather than a short transi-

145 https://aeon.co/essays/adolescence-is-no-longer-a-bridge-between-childhood-and-adult-life (accessed 9 December 2020).
146 https://aeon.co/essays/adolescence-is-no-longer-a-bridge-between-childhood-and-adult-life (accessed 9 December 2020).
147 Kett (2003) p.384.
148 https://aeon.co/essays/adolescence-is-no-longer-a-bridge-between-childhood-and-adult-life (accessed 9 December 2020).

> tion period of personal uncertainty and discovery, adolescence became a prolonged sojourn of development spent among other youth.[149]

The high school gave 'American adolescents an institutional platform and visibility', notes Fass.[150] It gave prominence to adolescence and provided the institutional foundation and resources for what would eventually be characterised as 'teen age' or youth culture. Consequently, until the 1950s adolescents were far more visible in the US than in any other part of the world.

However one conceptualises the forces driving the discovery of adolescence, it is evident that by the 1920s and the 1930s concerns about the moral order and about society's capacity to adjust to a changing world were often interpreted through the prism of adolescence. A heightened awareness of the challenge of maintaining stability in the face of change was gained through focusing on the problems of adolescence. Social scientists coined the term 'adjustment' to capture the process through which adolescents learned to come to terms with their place in the world. It was through the narrative of adolescent adjustment that society often sought to explain the cultural tensions thrown up by change. Although the term was often used with reference to the psychology of personal adjustment, it also referred to society's capacity to come to terms with changing reality.

Social scientists often portrayed adjustment as the essence of the condition of adolescence. According to the authors of 'Adolescence: psychosis or social adjustment?' (1935):

> Adolescence is a crisis in social adjustment. In our Western civilization many of the major demands of life are made upon the adolescent within a few years. He must achieve self-direction. He must make a vocational choice. He must adjust to our pattern of sex behavior. He must achieve, from our welter of conflicting values, a satisfying philosophy of life.[151]

Yet, in a world of conflicting values, where a 'satisfying philosophy of life' was by all accounts difficult to attain by adults and adolescents alike, it is evident that the problem of adjustment transcended the predicament facing young people.

That adjustment to prevailing social norms was mainly discussed through the problematisation of adolescence is understandable since it is through the at-

---

149 S.P. Fass (2016) *The End of American Childhood: A History of Parenting from Life on the Frontier to the Manged Child*, Princeton: Princeton University Press, p.135.

150 Fass (2016) p.141.

151 H.W. Zorbaugh and L.V. Payne (1935) 'Adolescence: psychosis or social adjustment?', *Journal of Educational Sociology*, 8(6), 371–377, at 374.

tempt to socialise the younger generation that the confidence of adults in their cultural outlook is tested. In her discussion on 'Mental hygiene problems of normal adolescence' (1921), the American psychologist Jessie Taft raised uncomfortable questions about whether adults possessed the wisdom and confidence required to help adolescents adjust to the world they faced. She asked if adults are 'wise enough and grown up enough' so that 'we can give the adolescent an interpretation of sex and human behavior which will enable him to face frankly his own cravings and inferiorities real and imagined and adjust to them in a constructive spirit'.[152] Reading between her lines, one gains the impression that she had doubts as to whether 'parents and teachers' were 'wise' and grown up and 'well adjusted'.

By the 1940s adolescent adjustment was represented as the pathway through which young people resolved their crisis of identity and developed the maturity required to play the role of confident adults. However, as we shall see, the problem of adjustment raised the question of 'adjustment to what'? Could adult society provide the cultural resources through which most young people could acquire an identity so that they could make their way in the world?

The moratorium described by Hall and other psychologists provided adolescents with an opportunity to define who they were and what they believed in. Western culture tended to support the quest for identity and idealised its youth. As Aries concluded, 'our society has passed from a period that was ignorant of adolescence to a period in which adolescence is the favorite age'. He added that 'we now want to come to it early and linger in it as long as possible'.[153] Erikson, too, was attracted to this age, and following Hall he underlined its importance for personal development. To the tensions that inhered in the course of the moratorium he gave the name 'identity crisis', and argued that society must do what it can to give adolescents the freedom and space they need to resolve this crisis in a satisfactory manner.

One development that Erikson did not count on was that in the post-Second World War era, circumstances conspired to make 'adolescents of us all' and, as is now widely recognised, 'identity crisis becomes the typical biographical crisis of the modern person'.[154] But even he would have been surprised by the frenetic borrowing and consuming of identities that characterise the Jessica Krugs of this world.

152 Taft (1921) p.67.

153 Aries (1962) p.30.

154 Weigert, Teitge and Teitge (1986) p.8.

In this chapter, we have argued that the invention of adolescence had little to do with the discovery of the psychological traits associated with youth. Nor was it a direct outcome of socio-economic changes to the structure of society and family life. The expansion of education did not create the adolescent but constituted a response to the prevailing consensus that insisted that young people were not ready for adulthood. Our conclusion from the available evidence is that in response to the difficulty that adult society had in accepting young people into its ranks, it opted to postpone the point at which the transition to adulthood was to be completed.[155]

155 A similar conclusion is advanced by R. Epstein (2010) *Saving Our Children and Families from the Torment of Adolescence*, Fresno: Quill Driver Books.

Chapter 3: The Cultural Contradictions of Adulthood

The sentimentalisation of adolescence discussed in the previous chapter ran in parallel with the modern society's unease with the process of ageing. This sensibility was fuelled by the consciousness of a world that was rapidly changing. In the 19th century, perceptions of rapid change were often optimistically interpreted as a marker of progress. The young were frequently portrayed as the bearers of change while the old were represented as obstacles to progress. Though the old were still formally venerated as the personification of maturity and wisdom, their authority was in practice often contradicted by the sentiment that they represented a bygone age. Perceptions of a rapidly changing world reinforced this trend and adulthood became increasingly associated with the past.

Inter-generational relations were frequently represented as coextensive with the interaction between the present and the past. As the sociologist Jennie Bristow noted in the literary representation of these trends, 'intense generational conflict' served as an 'allegorical representation of progress and social change'.[1]

During the 19th century, political movements communicated their commitment to change through designating themselves as parties of the young. The Young Italy movement founded by Giuseppe Mazzini was paradigmatic in this respect. It self-consciously endowed the young with the responsibility of creating a unified Italian nation. Similar sentiments motivated the Young Turks in northern Greece, who played a leading role in the overthrow of the Ottoman Empire. Throughout Europe, nationalist movements portrayed youth as the symbol of liberation and progress. On the other side of the Atlantic, the 'Young America' movement, with its quest for the new, often presented itself as the instrument for the realisation of the nation's destiny.[2]

The cult of the young was regularly counterposed to the archaic ways of the elder generation. In the 19th century, literature often touched on the conflict between the cultural attitudes of different generations. Ivan Turganev's powerful novel, *Fathers and Sons* (1862) offers a powerful dramatisation of a growing generational divide. Despite resistance from traditionalist quarters, the idealisation of the young swiftly gained momentum and became ascendant by the turn of the 20th century. Idealisation of the young coexisted with anxiety about their capaci-

1 J. Bristow (2015) *Baby Boomers and Generational Conflict*, New York: Palgrave Macmillan, p.27.

2 G. Wallach (1997) *Obedient Sons: The Discourse of Youth and Generations in American Culture, 1630–1860*, Amherst: University of Massachusetts Press, ch. 5.

https://doi.org/10.1515/9783110708899-004

ty to play a constructive role – the appellation of the 'Lost Generation' for those who came of age at the end of the First World War reflected this concern. Despite such anxieties, the idolisation of the young became steadily more pronounced from the 1920s. Fascist movements in particular lionised the young and praised them for their physical strength, idealism and self-sacrifice. Joseph Goebbels – soon to be Hitler's Propaganda Minister – remarked that 'The old ones don't even want to understand that we young people even exist. They defend their power to the last. But one day they will be defeated after all. Youth finally must be victorious.'[3] The glorification of youth coupled with the devaluation of the elderly was a theme that resonated with totalitarian ideologies – left and right – during the interwar era.

Writing in 1942, one of America's leading social scientists, Talcott Parsons, indicated that 'a tendency to the romantic idealization of youth patterns seems in different ways to be characteristic of modern Western society as a whole'.[4] His point was echoed in the early 1960s, when a social scientist remarked; 'Yet we still share with the ancient Greeks the wish that "youth should not be spoiled by old age." We try to stay young.'[5] In the 21st century the romantic idealisation of youth has acquired unprecedented momentum. The media's sanctification of Greta Thunberg is underwritten by the claim that the young are putting right the problems created by their parents' generation.

The sentimentalisation of youth developed in parallel with growing scepticism directed at the ways of the older generations. At the turn of the 20th century it appeared to many that the ways of the old were fast being displaced by rapid social, technological and cultural change. Commentators on both sides of the Atlantic insisted that the world was now subjected to constant change, which demanded that society adapt to new circumstances. This prognosis of ceaseless change was coupled with the conclusion that the young were likely to be far more effective in adjusting to new realities than their elders. As Eisenstadt, one of the leading sociologists of generations, explained, 'the necessity of a continuous adjustment to new changing conditions has emphasised the potential value of youth as the bearers of continuous innovation, of noncommitment to any specific conditions and values'.[6]

---

3 Cited in www.britannica.com/topic/fascism/Volksgemeinschaft (accessed 6 July 2018).

4 T. Parsons (1942), 'Age and sex in the social structure of the United States', *American Sociological Review*, 7(5), 604–616, at 607.

5 K. Naegele (1962) 'Youth and society: some observations', *Daedalus*, 91(1), 47–67, at 52.

6 S.N. Eisenstadt (1963), 'Archetypal patterns of youth', in Erikson, E.H. (ed.) *Youth: Change and Challenge*, New York: Basic Books, p.41.

Eisenstadt also noted that the focus on 'instrumental adaptability' to new circumstances turned ageing into an empty 'meaningless passage of time'.[7] The meaninglessness accorded to the 'passage of time' and to ageing stood in contrast to the adulation of youth. The flip side of the celebration of youth was the devaluation of ageing. In particular, this attitude influenced the outlook of many thinkers and commentators associated with the progressive movement at the turn of the 20th century. A leading radical progressive intellectual, Ralph Bourne, wrote a veritable manifesto – *Youth And Life* (1913) – which portrayed the young as the saviours of civilisation. Adults were viewed by him as obstacles to progress:

> There is no scorn so fierce as that of youth for the inertia of older men. Adults are little more than grown-up children. This is what makes their arrogance so insulting. ... Youth has no right to be humble. The ideals it forms will be the highest it will ever have, the insight the clearest, the ideas the most stimulating. The best that it can hope to do is to conserve those resources, and keep its flame of imagination and daring bright.[8]

In the eyes of Bourne, there was little to be valued in adulthood. He explained that it is the young 'who have all the really valuable experience'.[9]

At the turn of the 20th century, Bourne and many leading American liberals invested their hopes in the youth because it appeared to them that, unlike their elders, they were not weighed down by the traditions of the past. Bourne portrayed the young as the saviours of civilisation. He called on intelligent youth to be 'the incarnation of reason pitted against the rigidity of tradition'.[10]

Bourne believed that the experience of the elderly counted for little since it was based on a bygone age that was made irrelevant by the impact of rapid change. Not only were the older generations irrelevant, but their behaviour and attitude also held back young people from realising their destiny. In an accusatory tone, Bourne complained that 'an unpleasantly large proportion of our energy is now drained off in fighting the fetishes which you of the elder generation have passed along to us'.[11]

Sentiments similar to those of Bourne were voiced throughout Europe. The Italian Futurist movement worshipped novelty and youth and communicated

---

7 Eisenstadt (1963) p.41.

8 R.S. Bourne (1913) *Youth And Life*, New York: Houghton Mifflin, p.13.

9 Cited in S. Burt (2007), *The Forms of Youth: Twentieth-Century Poetry and Adolescence*, New York: Columbia University Press, p.21.

10 Cited in S. Kaplan (1956), 'Social engineers as saviors: effects of World War I on some American liberals', *Journal of the History of Ideas*, 17(3), 347–369, at 351.

11 Cited in Wallach (1997) p.154.

an unrestrained sense of contempt for the old. *The Futurist Manifesto*, published in 1909, warned young people that

> To admire an old picture is to pour our sensibility into a funeral urn instead of casting it forward with violent spurts of creation and action. Do you want to waste the best part of your strength in a useless admiration of the past, from which you will emerge exhausted, diminished, trampled on?[12]

The *Manifesto* depicted ageing as a form of social death that possessed no redeeming features. It observed:

> The oldest among us are not yet thirty years old: we have therefore at least ten years to accomplish our task. When we are forty let younger and stronger men than we throw us in the waste paper basket like useless manuscripts![13]

The sentiments articulated by the Futurists were more extreme than most commentaries devoted to the glorification of youth. Nevertheless, this movement exercised an important influence on the aesthetic sensibility of several generations of young Europeans, particularly in the domain of art, design and architecture.

The association of youth with progressive change and reform became widespread in the aftermath of the First World War. Responsibility for this catastrophic global conflict was assigned to a short-sighted and irrational older generation. Numerous commentaries – fiction and non-fiction – portrayed the older generations as incompetent, irresponsible and self-deluded. The stupidity and callousness of adult authority were frequently denounced for causing the pointless death of millions of young men who perished on the battlefields of Europe. This act of generational betrayal was eloquently dramatised by Erich Maria Remarque in his influential novel *All Quiet on the Western Front* (1929). In this angry novel, the young people who come of age during the Great War perceive themselves as the casualties of their incompetent elders. That this novel became an instant international bestseller showed that the resentment of the betrayal of the older generation resonated with the interwar cultural imagination.

An essay titled 'Youth at the Helm', published in the British literary magazine *The Athenaeum* (1918), highlighted the growing sense of estrangement from the traditional attitudes towards respecting one's elders. It asserted that 'one of the most irritating experiences – and one, moreover, which all young

---

12 www.societyforasianart.org/sites/default/files/manifesto_futurista.pdf (accessed 2 February 2020).

13 www.societyforasianart.org/sites/default/files/manifesto_futurista.pdf (accessed 2 February 2020).

men must suffer – is to be told with all the emphasis which portly men of 50 and upwards are able to command that "You'll grow wiser as you grow older" or "I used to think like that, but I've learnt better since"'. The anonymous author of this essay repudiated the coupling of wisdom with old age. He insisted that experience was overrated. 'The value of experience to civilisation, however, is not primarily positive and constructive. Experience is the nitrogen which dilutes the oxygen of Youth', he observed. This author had no doubt that 'progress means the victory of Youth over Experience'. He suggested that whatever reservation one had about youth in previous times, the First World War revealed that the elderly could not be trusted. He predicted that the future 'will be a world of Youth for Experience will be even more at a loss and more discredited'.[14] This author's derision of experience anticipates the ascendancy of the values of flexibility, nimbleness, agility and adaptability in the late 20th century.

The conviction that experience no longer counted for very much was widely held among intellectuals and cultural influencers during the early 1900s. The English writer, and social commentator H.G. Wells, regarded by many as a prophetic critic of society, dismissed the experience of the past as irrelevant to the conditions of the early 20th century. In his novel *The New Machiavelli* (1911), Wells' progressive liberal protagonist observed that the world had changed so much that 'suddenly, almost inadvertently, people found themselves doing things that would have amazed their ancestors'.[15] This sensibility of ceaseless change was often drawn towards the conclusion that the new ways of 'doing things' relied on harnessing the energy, idealism and capacity for risk taking of the youth.

The identification of youth with the future and the older generations with the past implicitly – and gradually explicitly – called into question the moral status and authority of adults. The prevailing consciousness of temporality associated ageing with inflexibility and a dogmatic commitment to an increasingly irrelevant past. In contrast, youth was deemed to possess the potential to adjust to a constantly changing world and forge a path towards the future.

This sensibility gained greater and greater influence during the course of the 20th century. Writing in the aftermath of the so-called 'youth revolt' of the 1960s, Erikson surmised that 'even in a period of rapid change, adolescence seems to serve the function of committing the growing person to the possible achieve-

14 *The Athenaeum*, issue 4626, February 1918, p.73.
15 Wells [1911] (2005) *The New Machiavelli*, London: Penguin Books, p.35.

ments and the comprehensible ideals of an existing or developing civilization'.[16] Erikson believed that adult society was likely to have difficulty in sharing authority with the young because they mistrusted themselves and were defensive and uncertain about their role in society. He concluded that, having discovered the adolescent, 'we must dare to ask: *What, really, is an adult?*'[17] Another way of posing Erikson's question is that 'With devaluation of experience, what is the point of adulthood?'

Why was adulthood not discovered?

As it happens Erikson's query about the status of adulthood was not a rhetorical one. Throughout most of the 20th century, the psychologists, social scientists, commentators and policy makers who had a lot to say about children and adolescents were conspicuously disinterested in adulthood. Until the 1970s, the concept of adulthood waited to be discovered. Anyone attempting to ascertain what commentators and experts had to say about adulthood would be hard put to come across any serious study of this subject. This absence has been noted by a number of sources. As early as 1933, one study stated that 'in the ordinary discussion of adult education the meaning of *adulthood* has been taken for granted. Everybody knows – until he attempts to tell it – what it means to be grown up.'[18]

In an important monograph, 'Searching for adulthood in America' (1976), the historian Winthrop Jordan wrote that 'it is an interesting commentary on our culture that we find ourselves asking: What does adulthood mean?'[19] Jordan noted that whereas growing interest in the different stages of the life-cycle around the turn of the 20th century led to the 'discovery of adolescence', no such discovery occurred in relation to adulthood. Jordan pointed to the late development of academic interest in the idea of adulthood – for example, as late as 1968 the *International Encyclopaedia of the Social Sciences* had articles on 'Aging' and 'Adolescence' but none on adulthood.[20] He expressed his surprise that 'it took until 1975 for a symposium on adulthood to materialize'.[21]

---

16 E.H. Erikson (1970) 'Reflections on the dissent of contemporary youth', *International Journal of Psychoanalysis*, 51, 154–176, at 156.
17 Erikson (1970) p.175.
18 R. Kotinsky (1933) *Adult Education and the Social Scene*, New York: D. Appleton-Century Company, p.3.
19 W.D. Jordan (1976) Searching for adulthood in America', *Daedalus*, 105(4), 1–11, at 1.
20 Jordan (1976) p.8.
21 Jordan (1976) p.8.

The Preface to a collection of papers given at the 1975 symposium echoed Jordan, and stated that the 'archives for the study of adulthood still wait to be created'.[22] Stephen Graubard, the author of the Preface, wrote that 'adulthood figures rarely in the scientific literature of our time: it has none of the concreteness that attaches to terms such as "childhood" or "adolescence"' and encompasses as a 'catch-all category everything after 18 or 21'.[23] Thirty-five years after this symposium, an essay on the 'changing semantics of youth and adulthood' reiterated Graubard's point and stated that 'adulthood is under-theorized in sociology'. It added that this was truly 'remarkable'.[24] Five years later, in 2015, a book devoted to the very study of adulthood repeated the same point: 'Adulthood is the one stage in life that lacks a history'.[25]

Although there is general agreement that the study and elaboration of the concept of adulthood is a relatively undeveloped subject, there has been little attempt to explain why this should be so. Jordan merely suggests that adulthood was a condition that used to be simply assumed as a process but 'it now seems to demand explanation'.[26] While Jordan is right to suggest that the ideal of adulthood can no longer be taken for granted, he has not explained why it was and still remains a relatively neglected subject.

Looking back over the available evidence, the absence of a serious intellectual engagement with adulthood is striking. As late as the 1970s, most discussions of adulthood took the form of an afterthought to the problem of adolescence. Adulthood was discussed in the context of adolescents transitioning towards it.[27] However, what young people were transitioning to was often dealt with perfunctorily and in passing.

Our examination of literary sources and several on-line databases suggests that the term 'adulthood' was rarely used until the 20th century. The first reference to adulthood in the *Oxford English Dictionary* is to an item in a veterinary

---

22 See S.R. Graubard (1978) 'Preface' to Erikson, E. (ed.) *Adulthood*, New York: W.W. Norton, p.vii.

23 Graubard (1978) p.vii.

24 H. Blatterer (2010) 'The changing semantics of youth and adulthood', *Cultural Sociology*, 4(1), 63–79, at 78.

25 S. Mintz (2015) *The Prime of Life: A History of Modern Adulthood*, Cambridge, Mass: Harvard University Press, p.x.

26 Jordan (1976) p.10.

27 See for example, 'Adolescence to young adulthood', 1952), *The Coordinator*, 1(5), 14–17, www.jstor.org.chain.kent.ac.uk/stable/581270 (accessed 25 September 2020).

journal in 1850. It relates not to humans but to horses, and states that 'at five years old the horse arrives at adult-hood'.[28]

During the last two decades of the 19th century, there are a handful of references to adulthood, particularly in Christian publications, where it is used as an expression of maturity. The first use of the word 'adulthood' to convey positive connotations that I came across was in an 1893 edition of *Zion's Herald*, where it is said that a perfect man for Christ is an adult man and that 'perfect implies adulthood'.[29] Another issue of this publication notes that 'a state of adulthood in contrast with infancy' is 'a state involving the power of skilful discrimination in matters whose good or evil nature is doubtful'.[30]

Most references to adulthood in the late 19th and early 20th centuries contrast it unfavourably with that of childhood. In 1882, a commentator remarked that the Saviour makes provision for childhood, but the problem is 'irresponsible adulthood'.[31] Another religious commentator asserted that the purity of a child is 'more important than the maturity of adulthood'.[32] The tendency to portray adulthood as a stage that is morally inferior to childhood is clearly voiced in a poem, *A Child's Mind*, in May 1914, published in a London-based tabloid weekly, *Answers:*

> And wandering thus and talking on,
>   My spirit purged and chastened grows
> For in the innocence of youth
> I find more simple love and truth
>   Than e'er adulthood knows.[33]

The poem concludes by indicating that those who seek wisdom can do no better than 'with a simple spirit heed, a thoughtful child's mind'.[34]

In some instances, the influence and role of adulthood towards children were depicted as far from benign and were portrayed as potentially damaging to children. At the 1897 meeting of the National Education Association of the United States, one of the speakers declared that the 'child can never become its real self so long as *adulthood* blights it and dwarfs it by daring to stand be-

28 'Adulthood, n.'. *OED Online*, Oxford University Press, www-oed-com.chain.kent.ac.uk/view/Entry/2846?redirectedFrom=adulthood (accessed 21 September2020).
29 'Another misused word',1893, *Zion's Herald*, 71(7), p.52.
30 J. Mudgs (1893), 'Our monthly sermon: Christian perfection', *Zion's Herald*, 71(37), p.290.
31 'The earthly probation the best', 1882, *Zion's Herald*, 59(45), p.356.
32 J.A. Wood (1884) 'Purity and maturity', *Zion's Herald*, 61(3), p.18.
33 'A child's mind', 1914, *Answers* 52(23), 9 May.
34 'A child's mind', 1914, *Answers* 52(23), 9 May.

tween it and God'. The speaker added that 'adulthood must not interfere so much with childhood'.[35] At this point in time many educators assumed that adulthood needed to be restrained to give children more space to develop. An article in the *Methodist Magazine* in 1898 observed that 'the greatest improvement yet wrought by the new education is the altered attitude of *adulthood* toward childhood in disciplining it'. It warned that 'the reformation of the coercive ideals of *adulthood* has only well begun'. It concluded by stating that 'adulthood must not interfere so much with childhood'.[36]

Dickens As An Educator (1900), authored by the Canadian educator James Laughlin Hughes, presented a series of unattractive traits of adulthood that leads it to disrespect childhood. He wrote that, by 'false ideals of coercive law adulthood has been made repressive instead of suggestive, depressive instead of helpful, dogmatic instead of reasonable, tyrannical instead of free, "child quellers" instead of sympathetic friends of childhood'. He directed his fire at 'kind but thoughtless adulthood', which is 'most grievously unjust to childhood, because it fails to consider how things appear to the child'.[37]

In some instances, adults were not only accused of being far too controlling but also of refusing to assume their responsibility towards the younger generations. These sentiments were directed at parents who resisted adopting modes of behaviour associated with maturity. An article titled 'Parents who haven't grown up' in a 1925 edition of *Harper's Monthly Magazine* indicts mothers and fathers who do not want to grow up, since adulthood means 'discipline, self-control, judgment, responsibility, and justice'. Ernest Grove, the author of this article, who was a Professor of Social Science at Boston University, had no doubt that 'one of the perils of young life' is the 'emotional immaturity of the parent'.[38] Whereas many commentators wanted to restrain the exercise of too much adulthood on the ground that it served as an obstacle to child development, Grove identified parental rejection of adulthood as the problem. Both versions offered an unattractive version of adulthood.

Although by no means a dominant theme, the condemnation of immature adults who are morally inferior to the younger generation recurred fairly regular-

---

35 See https://books.google.co.uk/books?id=UW8kAQAAMAAJ&q=%22adulthood%22&dq=%22adulthood%22&hl=en&sa=X&ved=2ahUKEwjAsI-trPPrAhUHV8AKHUsjBpUQ6wEwBHoECAUQAQ (accessed 23 April 2019).

36 https://books.google.co.uk/books?id=YMIQAAAAIAAJ&q=%22adulthood%22&dq=%22adulthood%22&hl=en&sa=X&ved=2ahUKEwjAsI-trPPrAhUHV8AKHUsjBpUQ6AEwDXoECA4QAg (accessed 15 June 2019).

37 J.L. Hughes (1900) *Dickens As An Educator*, New York: D. Appleton & Co., pp. 66, 75.

38 E.R. Groves (1925) 'Parents who haven't grown up', *Harper's Monthly Magazine*, 151, p.571.

ly in the 20th century. Writing in the late 1960s, Erikson suggested that parents appear to their children as 'overgrown boys and girls'.[39] In recent decades the theme of immature adults who wish to be 'forever young' has been a frequent topic of discussion in the media.

Classical views about the wisdom and maturity of adulthood continued to be communicated in everyday settings by traditionalist commentators. In contrast, scepticisms directed towards adulthood – particularly the role of parents – dominated the thinking of cultural influencers, educators and psychologists throughout much of the 20th century. Educationalists and psychologists often perceived adults as out of touch and diagnosed adulthood as a rigid and backward-oriented condition.

The cultural anthropologist Margaret Mead, who played a central role in promoting the idealisation of adolescence, communicated a distinctly downbeat account of adulthood. 'All adults are to some extent out of touch with the newest patterns of behavior as they most particularly affect the behavior of adolescents', she wrote in 1940.[40] Other experts were far less charitable and acted as if it were their job to insulate young people from the toxic influence of adults. L.K. Frank, who played a central role in the promotion and institutionalisation of the new science of childhood in the US, continually called into question the view that adults possessed the wisdom and maturity required to guide the development of the young.

Frank held parents responsible 'for so many of the tragedies among adolescents'. He observed that 'we are beginning to realize that the very family life that enjoys the highest social approval for its conformity' to 'traditional practices and beliefs, may, ironically enough, be responsible for the misconduct and disastrous lives of the children and youth who have been subject to that kind of child rearing'.[41] Frank was no cultural outlier. He was Foundation Officer with the Laura Spelman Rockefeller Memorial and the General Education Board during the 1920s and the 1930s. Later, he became Director of the Caroline Zachry Institute for Human Development, 1945–1950, and Chairman of the International Preparatory Commission for the International Congress on Mental Hygiene, London, 1948. According to one account, Frank was 'the architect and administrator of several major foundation-sponsored programs in child development and parent education and in culture and personality'. He formulated and advanced a socio-political project for the development and dissemination of new, '"enlightened"

39 Erikson (1968) p.30.

40 M. Mead (1940) 'Social change and cultural surrogates', *Journal of Educational Sociology*, 14(2), 92–109, at 104.

41 L. Frank (1940) 'The family as cultural agent', *Living*, 2(1), 16–19, at 18.

methods for socializing children and adolescents'.[42] He was in regular contact and collaborated with the leading authorities on adolescence, and his negative appraisal of the role of adults in children's development was more or less shared by them.

There was of course a normative lag between the negative attitude towards adulthood expressed by Frank and other clinical and academic experts and the general public. Within communities, everyday discussions on generational tensions and about the challenge of bringing up children were rarely accompanied by a negative framing of adulthood. It would take time before the moral devaluation of adulthood would gain a wider hearing and become a recurrent theme in popular culture. Mintz pointed out that 'the emergence of a more sceptical and even cynical attitude towards adulthood did not occur overnight'.[43] There were traces of this attitude in the late 19th century but it wasn't until the 1940s that it gained significant institutional support, and it would take another couple of decades before the devaluation of adulthood came to be reflected in popular culture.

Mintz's study represents one of the very few attempts to account for the shifting of attitudes towards adulthood. In his discussion of American coming-of-age novels that deal with the trials of making the adjustment to adulthood, he noted that

> Over time, we can detect within these American coming-of-age tales a striking shift in attitude. Whereas the earlier works viewed the achievement of mature adulthood positively, during the twentieth century growing numbers expressed disdain and alienation from the attributes of conventional adulthood. Some books like Anzia Yezierska's *Bread Givers* (1925), and especially those that followed *Catcher in the Rye*, are more cynical, critical, or ironic tales of alienation, disaffection, and angst.[44]

Mintz added that 'if literary depictions of coming of age have grown more ambivalent or even hostile toward conventional adulthood, the same is true in real life'.[45]

Adulthood is not only seen as morally inferior to youth but is also frequently depicted as an undesirable and unattractive phase of life. In 1963, Keniston pointed out that young people 'frequently view the more public aspects of adult life as empty, meaningless, a rat race, a futile treadmill'. He asserted

---

42 D. Bryson (1998) 'Lawrence K. Frank, knowledge, and the production of the "social"', *Poetics Today*, 1, 401–421, at 403.

43 Mintz (2015) p.46.

44 Mintz (2015) p.45.

45 Mintz (2015) p.45.

that 'adulthood suffers by comparison with childhood' with its imaginative life of 'spontaneity, freedom, and warmth'.[46] Writing more than half a century later, Mintz echoed the same theme; 'today, many young adults view the traditional markers of adulthood with suspicion and contempt, associating adulthood with weighty, unwelcome responsibilities, closed-off options, and stultifying, button-down conformity'.[47]

In the 21st century it is difficult to come across any positive accounts of adulthood in popular culture. While the current mood of disenchantment with adulthood is unparalleled, it is essential to note that its devaluation is not a novel phenomenon. One reason why adulthood was not discovered at the same time as adolescence was because the attention of psychologists and social investigators was almost entirely focused on young people. Unlike adults, the youth were seen as susceptible to expert guidance. The young were seen to possess potential; many psychologists and educators regarded them as a pliable material that could be moulded and influenced to become the bearers for progress. In contrast, bereft of potential and energy, adulthood was depicted as lacking in vigour, as exhausted and an obstacle to change. No wonder that many of the early explorers of adolescence soon declared that the 20th century would be the 'century of the child'.[48]

The psychologist and educator William Kessen described the attitudes that characterised 'century of the child' advocates as a 'salvationist view of children'.[49] According to this view, children were by nature innately good, with impulses that needed to be allowed to flourish and develop. Proponents of the salvationist view of children believed that, through social engineering, the reform of education would lead to the reform of society. This sentiment, which was particularly influential among child psychologists, endures to this day. Kessen wrote that child psychologists, 'whatever their theoretical stripe, have taken the Romantic notion of childish innocence and openness a long way towards the several forms of "if only we could make matters right with the child, the world would be a better place"'. He added that the 'child became the carrier, of political progressivism and the optimism of reformers'.[50] This point is emphasised in

46 Keniston (1963) p.177.
47 Mintz (2015) p.69.
48 See T.R. Richardson (1989) *The Century of the Child: The Mental Hygiene Movement and Social Policy in the United States and Canada*, New York: State University of New York Press.
49 W. Kessen (1979) 'The American child and other cultural inventions', *American Psychologist*, 34(10), 815–820, at 818.
50 Kessen (1979) p.818.

Jane Golden's *Babies Made Us Modern*, where she argues that it was through the care of babies that psychology created a new modern understanding of the self.[51]

In the 1920s, American and English progressive educators believed that children could play a vital role in the moral regeneration of the nation. 'This regeneration was to be achieved through developing the spiritual life of the child, primarily by means of promoting individual creativity', noted one study of this movement.[52] From this perspective, the exercise of adult authority at home and in schools tended to be seen as an obstacle to the spontaneous development of a child.

Psychologists, along with the influential Mental Hygiene movement, were drawn towards the salvationist ethos and argued that the 'scientific promotion of well-being in childhood could prevent adult dysfunctions'.[53] This belief was linked to the conviction that the road to progress was founded on the influence that psychologists and educators could exert on children. According to a study of this movement, the 'mental hygiene paradigm originated with the premise that society could be perfected through the socialization of children'.[54] An alliance of psychologically informed 'child savers' believed that adults, and particularly parents, stood in the way between it and children.

Unlike adults, who were stuck in their ways, children were malleable and open to the guidance provided by enlightened expertise. This point was strongly underlined by a group of psychologists at the end of the Second World War in their *Peace Manifesto*. In this *Manifesto*, its main author Gordon Allport elaborated the premise on which psychology based its differential attitude towards adults and children.

> In planning for permanent peace, the coming generation should be the primary focus of attention. Children are plastic; they will readily accept symbols of unity and an international way of thinking in which imperialism, prejudice, insecurity, and ignorance are minimized.[55]

The belief that children were plastic and could be influenced to adopt the kind of progressive sentiments that could prevent wars and conflicts inspired many psy-

---

51 J. Golden (2018) *Babies Made Us Modern: How Infants Brought America into the Twentieth Century*, Cambridge: Cambridge University Press.

52 W.E. Marsden (1997) 'Contradictions in progressive primary school ideologies and curricula in England: some historical perspectives', *Historical Studies in Education*, 9(2), 224–236, at 228.

53 Richardson (1989) p.2.

54 Richardson (1989) p.2.

55 G.W. Allport (1945) 'Human nature and the peace', *Psychological Bulletin*, 42(6), 376–378, at 376.

chologists and child professionals with hope. As we shall see, this sentiment also encouraged them to adopt policies of social engineering that were designed to harness the malleability of children to the realisation of political objectives.

The devaluation of adulthood

It is frequently argued that the devaluation of adulthood, and particularly the authority of parents, was the outcome of profound socio-economic changes. In his study of adulthood, Mintz contends that the loss of respect for the status of the elderly in the US was due to the fact that in the late 19th century 'old age was increasingly associated with dependency, physical disability, mental debility, and a host of character problems including depression, bitterness, hypochondria, and an inability to absorb new ideas'. He added that other factors that contributed to the negative perception of old age were 'mounting economic dependency of the elderly, in an increasingly urban and industrial society'. He also cites 'an increasing incidence of chronic degenerative conditions amongst the elderly as medical advances reduced the number of deaths caused by infections and epidemic disease and extended life expectancy'. Finally, Mintz attributes changing attitudes towards adulthood to 'a cult of youth, which regarded the elderly as inflexible, unadaptable, and out of step with the times, and as inefficient and unproductive workers'.[56]

It is likely that some of the developments cited by Mintz contributed to the unravelling of adult authority. However, it should be noted that rapid economic change, urbanisation and increased life expectancy did not lead to a loss of respect for the elderly in many cultures such as in Japan or China. Nor should youth culture be perceived as one of the causes of the decline of adult authority. On the contrary, the rise of youth culture should be understood as a symptom of the decline of the cultural and moral status of adulthood. As early as 1938, the philosopher George Boas drew attention to the estrangement of adults from adulthood:

> We who have grown up so hanker after childhood that we openly deny our years. Has there ever been a period when adults so brazenly have pretended to be young? No matter what their age, our women dress and act like girls, our men like undergraduates. The greatest compliment you can pay a person is to remark upon his youthful appearance. Everything is done to conceal the fact that human life lasts longer than 25 years.[57]

---

56 See Mintz (2015) p.10.

57 G. Boas (1938) 'The century of the child', *American Scholar*, 7(3), 268–276, at 274.

In 1942, Parsons related the rise of youth culture to the decline of the appeal of adulthood. He remarked that youth respond to adulthood 'negatively' and noted that 'there is a strong tendency to repudiate interest in adult things and to feel at least a certain recalcitrance to the pressure of adult expectations and discipline'.[58]

Mintz is right to draw attention to a narrative that portrayed adults, and particularly older adults, as inflexible and out of step with a rapidly changing world. However, this narrative was not simply a direct response to social change. The cultural script of adult irrelevance expressed the point of view of a coalition of anti-traditionalist, progressive, technocratic professionals, whose project of moral engineering directly targeted beliefs and practices that were rooted in the old ways. Their social scientific knowledge often served to validate the promotion of subordinating the status of adulthood to the authority of the expert. Their outlook towards the old was justified on the ground that in a rapidly changing world adults struggled to keep up with their children. From this perspective, not only were adults out of touch with a constantly changing world but their archaic ideas could only confuse and misguide the younger generation. They were portrayed as both irrelevant and a negative influence on young people. The conclusion drawn by the experts was that the socialisation of young people required the intervention of professional social engineers, who, unlike most parents, possessed the most up to date, modern ideas. *The devaluation of adulthood was not so much the direct outcome of socio-economic changes but of the professionalisation of the management of inter-generational relations.*

Throughout the 20th century there persisted a '*normative lag* between common sense and social science discourse' on adulthood.[59] The diagnosis of the inflexible and out of touch adult was developed and promoted by experts such as psychologists, child professionals and educationalists. Through the decades their discourse gained a wider influence through its promotion by the media, commentators and cultural influencers. However, throughout the 20th century the normative lag between expert knowledge and common-sense views ensured that this negative diagnosis of adulthood had less influence over folk knowledge and communities than on circles of professionals. Nevertheless, with the passing of time this negative diagnosis gained greater and greater authority, which eventually led to the wider cultural devaluation of adulthood and of the attributes associated with it, such as maturity, experience and responsibility.

---

58 Parsons (1942) p.607.

59 H. Blatterer (2007) *Coming of Age in Times of Uncertainty*, New York: Berghahn Books, p.10.

The line of attack against the authority of adulthood developed along three different fields. First, adulthood was indicted on account of its inflexibility, its inability to move with the times and its adherence to out of date archaic values. Secondly, adulthood was attacked for its supposed negative influence on the development of young people. Thirdly, the values associated with adulthood came under fire – particularly those of maturity and responsibility – on the grounds that they constrained spontaneity and freedom enjoyed by youth.

From its conceptualisation as a distinct stage, adulthood was often unfavourably contrasted with youth on the ground of its inflexibility. The inability of adults to adapt to changing circumstances was and remains a constant theme in the literature on inter-generational relations. In his analysis of the situation in interwar Germany, Fromm painted a picture of desperate, disoriented adults faced with being left behind by the younger generations. He asserted that during the upheavals in post-First World War Germany, 'the older generation was bewildered and puzzled and much less adapted to the new conditions than the smarter younger generation'. Fromm added that 'the younger generation acted as they pleased and cared no longer whether their actions were approved by their parents or not'.[60] Fromm's description of the repudiation of the moral status of adulthood by the 'smarter younger generation' implied that in the context of the new conditions adult authority rightly lost its legitimacy.

Typically, attacks on adult authority were also linked to its alleged failure to rise to the challenge of guiding and socialising young people. The ineptitude of adults in the domain of childrearing was often attributed to differences in generational experiences and values. 'Not only are parent and child, at any given moment, in different stages of development, but the content which the parent acquired at the stage where the child now is, was a different content from that which the child is now acquiring', argued Kingsley Davis in 1940. Davis, who was a demographer with a keen interest in generational interaction, concluded that when parents attempt to socialise their children, they 'apply the erstwhile but now inappropriate content'.[61]

Davis was sympathetic to the predicament faced by adults whose outlook based on the experience of the past lagged behind that of the adolescents they attempted to influence. He believed that this situation could not be remedied because parents could not 'modernize' their point of view, because they were the product of their own childhood experiences:

60 E. Fromm [1941] (1969) *Escape From Freedom*, New York: Holt, p.83.

61 K. Davis (1940b) 'The sociology of parent–youth conflict', *American Sociological Review*, 5(4), 523–535, at 524.

> He can change in superficial ways, such as learning a new tune, but he cannot change (or want to change) the initial modes of thinking upon which his subsequent social experience has been built. To change the basic conceptions by which he has learned to judge the rightness and reality of all specific situations would be to render subsequent experience meaningless, to make an empty caricature of what had been his life.[62]

Davis' argument about the time and cultural lag between the experience and outlook of generations was widely shared by experts by the early 1940s. Inter-generational conflict was often interpreted and explained through the model of differential generational experience.[63]

In contrast to Davis' sympathetic depiction of an adulthood steeped in the experiences of the past, politically motivated commentators accused the older generations of wilfully misleading the young by subjecting them to their archaic prejudices. Their narrative of condemnation focused on the damage that adults, particularly in their role as parents, allegedly inflicted on their children. The psychiatrist Brock Chisholm, who was the first Director of the World Health Organisation (WHO), adopted a strident tone in his denunciation of old taboos that the old impose on the young. He argued that

> Old ideas and customs are generally called 'good' or 'sound,' and new ideas, or experimental thinking or behavior, are usually labeled 'bad,' 'unsound,' 'communist,' 'heretical,' or any of many other words. The power these words have obtained over much of the race is astonishing. They are the symbols of the control that older people and the past have, and cling to, over young people and the future.[64]

Chisholm blamed the outbreak of world wars and conflicts on the imposition of the old ways on young people. 'We have swallowed all manner of poisonous certainties fed us by our parents, our Sunday and day school-teachers, our politicians, our priests', argued Chisholm.[65]

Chisholm's attack on the 'old ways' was linked to his romanticised idealisation of children. He called for the protection of 'that freedom present in all children', which has been 'destroyed or crippled' in the past through the imposition of adult control. His call for liberating children from the clutches of their elders

---

62 Davis (1940b) p.525.

63 C. Kluckhohn and H.A. Murray (1953) 'Outline of a conception of personality', in Kluckhohn, C. and Murray, H.A. (eds) *Personality: In Nature, Society, and Culture*, London: Jonathan Cape, p.28.

64 G. Chisholm (1947) 'Can man survive?', *A Review of General Semantics*, 4(2), 106–111, at 107.

65 G. Chisholm (1946) *The William Alanson White Memorial Lectures*, Baltimore: W.A. White Psychiatric Foundation, pp. 7, 9.

was conveyed in a radical and provocative tone. But similar sentiments were widely circulated by child professionals, though expressed in a far more restrained manner. As Director of the WHO and a leading figure in the international mental health establishment, Chisholm enjoyed significant global authority. In a 'Foreword' to Chisholm's published lecture on this subject, Abe Fortas, who was the American Under Secretary of the Interior, praised his call to put aside the 'mistaken old ways of our elders'.[66]

Adults were not simply condemned for imposing the old ways on the younger generations – they were also blamed for inflicting a variety of mental health problems on their children. During the 1940s and 1950s, the behaviour of authoritarian-inclined adults was diagnosed by psychologists as the outcome of repressive forms of childrearing. Writing in the midst of the war against Nazi Germany, Frank warned that 'it begins to appear that those who threaten or defeat social order are the individuals who have been warped and distorted by their nurture and rearing'.[67] By the mid-20th century similar sentiments were frequently conveyed by psychologists, parenting experts and child professionals. As the historian Joanne Meyerowitz outlined:

> In one widespread formulation (simplified here), parents – with the blessings of their culture – repressed their children, which caused frustration in early childhood, which in turn caused aggression and neurosis in adult citizens. This formula could be used to explain social ills in various cultures. In one common variation, authoritarian German fathers repressed their children who then grew up to be fascists and racists; in another, smothering American mothers reared delinquent or homosexual sons. As one commentator noted, 'The clinging mother is the great emotional menace in American psychological life, the counterpart to the domineering father in England and on the Continent'.[68]

The cumulative effect of the representation of parents as the cause of children's mental health problems drew attention to yet one more unattractive feature of adulthood.

The claim that adults were unwittingly messing up young people was routinely promoted by experts whose unflattering representation of parenthood served as an invitation for their professional services. This attitude was regularly

66 Chisholm (1946) p.1.

67 L.K. Frank (1941) 'What can psychiatry contribute to the alleviation of national and international difficulties? A symposium: social order and psychiatry', *American Journal of Orthopsychiatry*, 11(4), 620–627, at 620.

68 J. Meyerowitz (2010) 'How common culture shapes the separate lives: sexuality, race, and mid-twentieth-century social constructionist thought', *Journal of American History*, 96(4), 1057–1084, at 1073.

advocated from the interwar era onwards. Writing in 1930, the British parenting expert Jean Ayling warned that 'most of the children of my acquaintance are already badly damaged at an early age'. Her solution was to limit the role of parents, since they have a 'strictly bounded domain of usefulness', and to assign the wider task of child socialisation to the helping professions.[69]

The authority of adulthood acquired its most corrosive dimension in relation to the ambiguity surrounding the value of maturity. '"Maturity" acts as a central metaphor encompassing normative achievements and attributes of adulthood', noted Harry Blatterer.[70] Yet, although maturity is a frequent object of praise and seen as essential for the exercise of authority and leadership in a variety of institutional settings, it also conveys undesirable and negative connotations in popular culture. The most extreme version of the narrative of anti-maturity can be found in the writings of the German psychoanalyst Wilhem Reich, who, according to one account, 'expressed his hatred of all doctrines of maturity'.[71]

The normative status of maturity was contested by the very construction of adolescence. The frequent description of adolescence as the 'best days of your life' conveys the implication that something precious is lost in the transition to adulthood. Bryan Adams' hit song, the 'Summer of '69', described a moment when he and 'some guys from school' set up a band and, looking back at that summer, he recalled wistfully:

> Oh, when I look back now
> That summer seemed to last forever
> And if I had the choice
> Yeah, I'd always wanna be there
> Those were the best days of my life.[72]

The phrase 'I'd always wanna be there' does not simply convey the sentiment of wishing to be forever young but also the implicit disavowal of the normative status of maturity and responsibility.

---

69 J. Ayling (1930) *The Retreat From Parenthood*, London: Kegan Paul, Trench, Trubner & Co., pp.204, 213.

70 Blatterer (2007) p.12.

71 See P. Rieff (2006) *The Triumph of the Therapeutic: Uses of Faith After Freud*, Wilmington: ISI Books, p.137.

72 See www.youtube.com/watch?v=9f06QZCVUHg&ab_channel=BryanAdams (accessed 4 July 2020).

Back in 1942, Parsons portrayed the values motivating the then emerging youth culture as one that directly contradicted the normative attributes of adulthood. He outlined his thesis in the following terms:

> Perhaps the best single point of reference for characterizing the youth culture lies in its contrast with the dominant pattern of the adult male role. By contrast with the emphasis on responsibility in this role, the orientation of the youth culture is more or less specifically irresponsible. One of its dominant features themes is 'having a good time' in relation to which there is a particularly strong emphasis on social activities in company with the opposite sex. A second predominant characteristic on the male side lies in the prominence of athletics, which is an avenue of achievement and competition which stands in sharp contrast to the primary standards of adult achievement in professional and executive capacities.[73]

During the 1940s adulthood and youth culture existed in an uneasy relationship with one another. Formally, the authority of adulthood still enjoyed significant cultural and institutional validation and youth culture tended to be dismissed as a phase rather than a desirable end point in life. But even at this point in time, the common-sense view of adulthood was questioned by the emerging professional discourse on the subject.

Margaret Mead highlighted the fragility of the authority of adulthood. Like Fromm, she too believed that the young were the 'smarter' generation:

> By and large, the American father has an attitude towards his children which may be loosely classified as autumnal. They are his for a brief and passing season, and in a very short time they will be operating gadgets which he does not understand and jokingly talking a language to which he has no clue.[74]

There is an unmistakable tone of derision in her description of the rejection of adults by the young. The child soon learns that grandparents are 'not really necessary', she wrote, and suggested that in America young people trust themselves more than their parents and their leaders.[75]

The positive narrative regarding the maturity of adulthood still competes with those that promote the antithesis of the qualities attributed to maturity. However, in contrast to the 1940s the moral status of adulthood rests on far more fragile foundations. As one observer commented recently, 'our social institutions and technological devices seem to erode hallmarks of maturity: patience,

73 Parsons (1942) p.92.

74 M. Mead [1942] (2000) *And Keep Your Powder Dry: An Anthropologist Looks at America*, New York: Berghahn Books, p.28.

75 Mead [1942] (2000) pp. 53, 105.

empathy, solidarity, humility and commitment to a project greater than oneself'.[76] Whereas previously maturity was associated with positive qualities, in the contemporary era popular culture often portrays it as an undesirable state and stage of life, if not a form of social death. There are of course historical precedents for the phenomenon of infantilisation. But this trend, which existed on the margins of social life, has in recent times gone mainstream, especially in the Anglo-American world.

The social science literature on adulthood has tended to underestimate the fragile normative foundation for maturity. It frequently claims that the problem only kicked in during the 1960s or 1970s, or even later. Writing in this vein, the social analyst Reuel Denney wrote in 1963 that previously there had been a 'general acceptance of a clear-cut idea of adult identity and maturity', before concluding that 'today' 'this concept no longer exists so clearly'.[77] Blatterer suggests that 'adulthood's *normative* status as the ultimate benchmark of adult maturity', though based on the experience of the 1950s and 1960s, still 'remains robust'.[78] Our analysis suggests that while adulthood persists as a model of maturity, it has lost much of its moral status and struggles to retain its role as a desirable destination in the life course. While maturity is associated with psychological health, there is an evident cultural trend that encourages young people to regard maturity as a status to be avoided.[79]

The recently invented word *adulting* is the rhetorical achievement of a culture that increasingly portrays the identity of an adult as one that no sensible person would enthusiastically embrace. In the Anglo-American world, adulthood is constantly portrayed as disagreeable and the responsibilities attached to it as an impossible burden. The tendency to portray adulting as an unusually difficult and unpleasant accomplishment that has to be taught coexists with a palpable sense of disenchantment with the status of adulthood. In all but name adulthood has become destabilised to the point that it has become a target of scorn and for many an undesirable identity. No wonder that adulting is an activity that many biologically mature individuals are only prepared to do on a part-time basis.

---

76 See S. Gottschalken (2018) 'The infantilization of Western Culture', *The Conversation*, 1 August, https://theconversation.com/the-infantilization-of-western-culture-99556 (accessed 6 September 2020).

77 R. Denney (1963) 'American youth today: the problem of generations', in Erikson, E. (ed.) *Youth: Change and Challenge*, New York: Basic Books, p.141.

78 Blatterer (2007) p.15.

79 See S.J. Schwartz, J.E. Côté and J.J. Arnett (2005) 'Identity and agency in emerging adulthood: two developmental routes in the individualization process', *Youth & Society*, 37(2), 201–229.

In 1970 Keniston pointed out that from the point of view of youth, adulthood appears as a state of stasis. He underlined 'its unconscious equation with death or nonbeing'. Consequently, he concluded that 'the desire to prolong youth indefinitely springs not only from an accurate perception of the real disadvantages of adult status' but also 'from the less conscious and less accurate assumption that to "grow up" is in some ultimate sense to cease to be real'.[80] This statement, made over half a century ago, captures a trend that has acquired greater visibility and force in the current era.

Transition to what?

In its original conceptualisation, adolescence was presented as a transitional phase in a jowurney towards adulthood. By the 1960s, there were clear indications that many young people did not want to embark on this journey. At this point, Keniston represented youth culture as 'an expression of the reluctance of many young men and women to face the unknown perils of adulthood'.[81] At the end of the decade Erikson observed that young people, 'transient as they are, declare the world beyond youth to be totally void and faceless'.[82]

The devaluation of adult identity has important implications for the process of transition from adolescence to adulthood. In effect it means, as Mintz contends, that 'the normative scripts of adolescent-to-adult-transition has broken down'.[83] Once adulthood becomes disparaged by significant sections of society, it ceases to serve as a desirable goal for generational transition. As Eisenstadt remarked, 'the close linkage between the growth of personality, psychological maturation, and definite role models derived from the adult world has become greatly weakened'.[84] In these circumstances the question of 'transition to what?' becomes pertinent.

The successful resolution of identity crisis during the phase of adolescence depends on the availability of a clear model of adulthood. The gaining of identity depends on understanding who you are and how you fit into society. Gaining such an identity is 'easier if the society already has a clear role that you are ex-

80 Keniston (1970) p.640.
81 Keniston (1963) p.178.
82 Erikson (1970) p.1576.
83 Mintz (2015) p.19.
84 S.N. Eisenstadt (1995) *Power, Trust, and Meaning: Essays in Sociological Theory and Analysis*, Chicago: University of Chicago Press, p.79.

pected to fill and respects you for filling it, and you have good role models'.[85] Erikson claimed that clarity about the meaning of adulthood is critical for the resolution of young people's identity crisis and the acquisition of a robust identity. He commented that without a clear 'definition of adulthood' any 'question of identity is self-indulgent luxury'. According to him, the 'problem of adulthood is how to *take care* of those to whom one finds oneself committed as one emerges from the identity period, and to whom one now owes *their* identity'.[86]

Since adulthood is meant to provide the model that guides the formation of identity, the weakening of its status and appeal has important implications for the process of transition from adolescence. This issue was alluded to by Erikson when he raised concerns about the problem of giving meaning to adult authority. He was critical of the failure of adult society to provide the leadership that adolescents required to resolve their crisis of identity. What was at stake was not simply a question of adults not providing inspiring leadership but also their inability to uphold the ideals to which the young should aspire. Erikson warned that 'we must not overlook what appears to be a certain abrogation of responsibility on the part of the older generation in providing those forceful ideals which must antecede identity formation in the next generation – if only so that youth can rebel against a well-defined set of older values'.[87]

Erikson's concern with the failure of adult society to provide the forceful ideas that are necessary to identity formation is to the point. However, the absence of such forceful ideals is not due to a character defect of the older generations. By the time Erikson penned his thoughts on this issue not only was the normative foundation of adulthood seriously undermined but also adult society was struggling to articulate the ideals and philosophical outlook needed to share with the younger generation. Over the decades the norms and values that guided generations in the past were systematically called into question by experts who continually claimed that rapid change had made them irrelevant. This loss of continuity had important implications for the cultivation of adolescent identity. 'For, recall that one of the chief tasks of identity formation is the creation of a sense of self that will link the past, the present and the future', asserted Keniston.[88] Having invested so much emotion and energy in renouncing the influence of the past and its traditions, psychologists and related professionals have made

85 R. Martin and J. Barresi (2006) *The Rise and Fall of Soul and Self*, New York: Columbia University Press, p.275.

86 Erikson (1968) p.31.

87 Erikson (1968) p.30.

88 Keniston (1963) pp.178–179.

a significant contribution to the erosion of the sense of continuity required for the formation of stable identities.

Back in 1950, Benjamin Spock, arguably the most influential parenting expert of the Cold War era, expressed the hope that the crisis of identity among the young could be overcome with a 'fundamental reemphasis on all childhood education, in which human feelings and family relations will become the core'. He added that 'the result to be hoped for is that the idea of eventually being a father or being a mother will sound like an exciting aim throughout childhood'.[89] Spock hoped that stable and well-defined roles could offer adulthood the meaning that could inspire the young. As subsequent events indicate, that hope proved to be illusory.

The detachment of the present from the past meant that adulthood lacked a narrative with which it could confidently assist the project of identity formation.

As an implicit refusal of accepting adulthood gained cultural force, the process of identity acquisition appeared increasingly problematic. A group of sociologists echo this point: 'contemporary society makes adolescents of us all, and thus identity crisis becomes the typical biographical crisis of the modern person'.[90] While this problem afflicts all the generations, its impact is particularly confusing for the young. 'True identity', remarked Erikson, 'depends on the support which the young individual receives from the collective sense of identity characterising the social groups significant to him: his class, his nation, his culture.'[91] As the following chapter explains, the prevailing regime of socialisation failed to answer the question of how to provide young people with a collective sense of identity.

89 Spock is cited in W. Graebner (1980) 'The unstable world of Benjamin Spock: social engineering in a democratic culture, 1917–1950', *Journal of American History*, 67(3), 612–639, at 612.
90 Weigert, Teitge and Teitge (1986) p.8.
91 Erikson(1964) p.93.

Chapter 4: Identity, Socialisation and Its Tenuous Link with the Past

It is difficult to develop a sturdy sense of collective identity without a shared memory and a common attachment to conventions or customs that are rooted in the past. Collective identities are inter-generational accomplishments that are cultivated through the absorption of a common cultural inheritance. For socialisation to occur successfully, adults draw on the experience of previous generations to provide young people with a meaningful account of adulthood. Erikson remarked that the values with which children are trained 'persist because the cultural ethos continues to consider them "natural" and does not admit of alternatives'. He observed that:

> They persist because they have become an essential part of the individual's sense of identity, which he must preserve as a core of sanity and efficiency. But values do not persist unless they work, economically, psychologically, and spiritually; and I argue that to this end they must continue to be anchored, generation after generation, in early child training; while child training, to remain consistent, must be embedded in a system of continued economic and cultural synthesis.[1]

Through transmitting the legacy of the past, socialisation is integral to an inter-generational transaction whereby moral norms are communicated by authoritative adults to the young.

Although adulthood and childhood are often discussed as separate and stand-alone concepts, they exist and thrive as part of an inter-generational community where their relationship is mediated through a common web of meaning. Because they are heirs to a common past, adults are able to transfer to the young the cultural resources that they will need to make their way in this world. Through this generational continuity – which is not just biological but also cultural – the organic relationship between a community's present and past is reproduced and reinforced.

In this chapter we discuss the loss of the sense of the past and explain that this development has both undermined the status of adult authority and contributed to the emergence of the twin problems of socialisation and identity. Without a meaningful link to a past, conveyed through adults and institutions, the devel-

1 Erikson (1963) p.138.

https://doi.org/10.1515/9783110708899-005

opment of individual identity risks becoming destabilised and estranged from a common world.

The depreciation of the status of adulthood, discussed in the previous chapter, was closely linked to the devaluation of the normative legitimacy of the past. Once the past is regarded as irrelevant or, worse still, as the 'bad old days', the experiences of the older generations are also cast in a negative light. Adulthood becomes compromised by its association with the past, and instead of being able to serve as a model to the young it ceases to effectively serve that role. That is why the concurrent erosion of the status of adulthood and of the past was not a coincidence. Historically, the status of adulthood was linked to its capacity to transmit the wisdom and experience of the past to the younger generations. Erikson's reference to the 'collective sense of identity' which adults communicate to young people has as its premise the capacity of the older generation to communicate a model of identity to their offspring. However, with the loss of what the sociologist and critic Philip Rieff described as the 'sense of the past', cultural continuity became disrupted and the capacity of adults to serve as models to the young diminished.[2]

The term 'sense of the past' should not be confused with that of 'nostalgia for the past'. Nostalgia communicates a feeling of sentimentality towards a past that can never return. Its wistful affection for days gone by is often coupled with an impulse to avoid the challenges of the here and now by retreating into an imagined and idealised world of a previous era. The possession of a sense of the past is according to the literary critic Lionel Trilling, an 'actual faculty of the mind, "a sixth sense"', through which we become conscious of history and our place in it.[3] This sensibility does not mean obsessively looking back towards a distant land but a form of consciousness that regards cultural continuity as relevant for illuminating the human predicament.

Historically, generational relations were underpinned by an important element of cultural continuity. Throughout history the authority of the older generation over the young was taken for granted by all cultures. That did not mean that the young passively embraced the wisdom of the elders. What it meant was that even when they reacted against members of the older generations, young people still accepted the authoritative status of adulthood. Until modern times, the revolt of the youth was directed at the elders rather than cultural values that they personified. Often the elders were accused of not living up to the

---

2 Rieff (2006) p.4.

3 L. Trilling (1957) 'The sense of the past', in Trilling, L., *The Liberal Imagination: Essays on Literature and Society*, New York: Doubleday Anchor Books, p.189.

ideals of the past. With the rise of modernity in the 18th century, the young often expressed their ambition through a distinct form of generational consciousness that emphasised their rejection of the old. Their reaction to the old ways was integral to a wider mood of psychic distancing from the past.

During the 19th century, the past ceased to be seen by many as offering a pattern for the present and innovation was recognised as both 'inescapable and socially desirable'.[4] At some point in the 20th century, the western world became estranged from the authoritative status of the past and often adopted the attitude of rejecting it altogether. Its obituary was captured by the title of the historian J.H. Plumb's book, *The Death of the Past* (1969). Though Plumb was sympathetic to the loss of authority of the past, he was sensitive to the fact that something important had been lost. He observed that 'whenever we look, in all areas of social and personal life, the hold of the past is weakening'.[5]

Until the early 20th century the socialisation of young people was assisted by a sense of cultural continuity which still prevailed despite the emergence of the tendency to question the value of the past. It was widely recognised that the transformation of young people into adults required their introduction to the ways of their culture. By the late 1930s many observers commented that society could not take its capacity to socialise the younger generations for granted. However, the relationship between this problem and the loss of the sense of the past was not always explicitly acknowledged.

Writing in 1939, the psychologist John Dollard explained that 'socialization is the process of training a human animal from birth on for social participation in his group'. Dollard added that 'he is socialized when he is capable of playing the role destined for him as an adult'.[6] Dollard and other experts dealing with the transition from adolescence to adulthood assumed that socialisation could not be taken for granted. Dollard observed that it 'seems clear from present data that socialization is a process full of conflict between the child and its trainers' and indicated that 'growing up is not a smooth automatic process of assimilating the folkways and mores'.[7] The folkways and mores of the past were less and less observed and what was acceptable to previous generations had in many situations ceased to motivate many members of the younger generations.

---

4 E. Hobsbawm (1972) 'The social function of the past: some questions', *Past & Present*, 55, 3–17, at 10.

5 J.H. Plumb (1969) *The Death of the Past*, London: Macmillan, p.66.

6 J. Dollard (1939) 'Culture, society, impulse, and socialization', *American Journal of Sociology*, 45(1), 5–63, at 60.

7 Dollard (1939) p.61.

Kingsley Davis echoed Dollard's sentiments and asserted that 'too often the child-and-society problem has been visualized as simply that of transmitting the cultural heritage'. He warned that 'society does not depend solely on transmitting its heritage but also on absorbing each new generation into its structure'.[8] Nevertheless, Davis understood that the transmitting of a cultural heritage was an important challenge facing society that other commentators ignored.

Unlike many of his colleagues who dismissed the importance of transmitting the values of the past, Davis feared that in its absence it would be difficult to forge the collective sense of identity that young people needed to give meaning to their lives. He believed that 'the integrating principle would diminish', and as the traditions of the past became dismissed as irrelevant 'the central values and common ends' of society would 'tend to crumble'.[9] By 1940, and certainly by the end of the Second World War, the unstated consensus among social science experts dealing with socialisation appeared to be; 'let it crumble'. Only a minority of social scientists appreciated what the loss of cultural continuity would entail for inter-generational relations. In opposition to his anti-traditionalist colleagues, Davis wrote that if 'many fundamental customs', which are dismissed as 'anomalous and worthless customs', were 'eliminated', society would be left 'strangely incapable of maintaining itself'.[10]

The problem highlighted by Davis did not simply relate to the impact of a loss of cultural continuity on society. The transmission of cultural heritage is not an abstract process that only affects institutions or high culture. To a child, adults personify culture and a model of life. When adults become uncertain about who they are and what it is that they should transmit, children become confused about the values with which they should identify. The difficulty of resolving the crisis of identity is an indirect outcome of the disruption of cultural continuity.

Baumeister claimed that 'the identity crisis became a feature of adolescence sometime around the end of the 19th century'.[11] He pointed out that previously parents and adult society had 'defined adult identity for individual' – but 'rather abruptly, however, the adult identity was left mostly up to the adolescent to decide and define'.[12] It is unlikely that the reluctance of adults to define the meaning of their identity for adolescents happened as abruptly as Baumeister sug-

8 K. Davis (1940a) 'The child and the social structure', *Journal of Educational Sociology*, 14(4), 217–229, at 217.
9 Davis (1940a) p.227.
10 Davis (1940a) p.229.
11 Baumeister (1986) p.103.
12 Baumeister (1986) p.103.

gests. However, Baumeister is right to underline the significance of the erosion of adult confidence in its capacity to socialise young people. He also rightly claims that the lack of clarity about how adulthood should be defined will eventually compromise the ability of young people to resolve their crisis of identity. Once it becomes problematic for identity formation to draw on a pre-existing model, identity itself is likely to become more and more of an issue. That is why in the first instance a crisis of identity should be understood as a symptom of the adult society's confusions about how to socialise.

The difficulty that adult society had in setting ideals for the young tended to be resolved – particularly by middle-class parents – through adopting techniques of psychological validation. By the late 1950s even professional supporters of such techniques began to worry that avant-garde parents were going too far in their reliance on psychological validation. In 1958, at the annual conference of the Child Study Association of America, Dr Harold Taylor, President of Sarah Lawrence College, pointed out that the 'first generation of "understood children" is now of college age' and warned that 'they bring with them a pathology of their own'.[13] By 'understood children' Taylor referred to young people who were constantly validated through techniques designed to make them feel good about themselves. Since this discussion on the college age generation of 1958, the reluctance of adult society to set ideals for the young has become a far more pervasive fact of life.

The problematisation of socialisation

Socialisation only became an object of study in its own right a half a century after the 'discovery' of adolescence. In the modern and contemporary sense of this term, socialisation gained usage in the late 1930s and early 1940s. It was also during this period that Erikson's concern with identity gradually led to his coining of the term 'identity crisis'. Danziger has drawn attention to the suddenness with which the study of socialisation became embraced by three disciplines: sociology, anthropology and psychology. As illustration of the prominence acquired by this concept, he cited two different papers, one written by Robert Park and the other by John Dollard, published in 1939 by the *American Journal of Sociology*, which had the term 'socialization' in their titles.[14] Danziger

---

13 Cited in D. Barclay, 'Experts challenge adults to set ideals for young', *The New York Times*, 25 March 1958.

14 K. Danziger (1976) *Socialization*, Harmondsworth: Penguin.

also pointed to the growing interest of psychologists in the concept. In 1937, the publication of *Experimental Social Psychology: An Interpretation of Research Upon the Socialization of the Individual* marked an important milestone in a new phase of interest in this subject.[15]

Danziger remarked that in view of the 'rare occurrence of the term in earlier writings', its sudden 'prominence suggests the operation of a powerful undercurrent of ideas'.[16] Until the 1930s the concept 'socialisation' conveyed a very different meaning from its subsequent usage. The term originally referred to the wider process of rendering economic and institutional activities social.[17] Until the 1930s the term did not merely refer to individuals but mainly to wider social processes. Left-wing narratives often advocated the 'socialisation of production', according to which industries would be owned by society. Some conceptualised socialisation as the counterpoint to that of individuation.[18] In 1909, the German sociologist Georg Simmel referred to socialisation as 'the form, in which the content of social organization clothes itself'. Simmel used the term as a variant of society and as a general form of social influence.[19] During the interwar decades this meaning was gradually set aside as socialisation was 'reconceptualized as a process occurring within individuals', whereby they acquire the 'facility to function as competent and cooperative members of society'.[20] How to turn adolescents into adults was now frequently portrayed as a problem.

Until the 1930s, the socialisation of the individual was rarely a specific focus of psychological or sociological study. It was 'a relatively uncommon term in psychology before 1940' but became 'a social scientific hit after the war'.[21] From the 1950s, socialisation became more and more a psychological concept and less and less connected to the workings of wider social trends. As one study noted, 'although social scientists linked socialization to an array of institutions, they causally connected it, both directly and centrally, to then central psychological constructs of personality, adjustment, pathology, identity, and achieve-

15 G. Murphy, L. Murphy and T. Newcomb (1937) *Experimental Social Psychology: An Interpretation of Research Upon the Socialization of the Individual*, New York: Harper & Brothers.
16 Danziger (1976) p.14.
17 See J.G. Morawski and J. St Martin (2011) 'The evolving vocabulary of the social sciences: the case of "socialization"', *History of Psychology*, 14(1), 1–25.
18 See R.M. Binder (1903) *Feeling as the Principle of Individuation and Socialization*, New York: Columbia University Press.
19 See G. Simmel (1909) 'The problem of sociology', *American Journal of Sociology*, 15(3), 289–320, at 54–55.
20 Morawski and St Martin (2011) p.4.
21 Morawski and St Martin (2011) p.2.

ment'.[22] In many scholarly discussions of this subject, socialisation appeared disconnected from its relation to the norms and values of culture. The traditional association of socialisation with connecting young people to their past was considered less and less to be a subject worthy of investigation.

With the reconceptualisation of socialisation, the concept became increasingly individuated, internalised and psychologised. As principally a psychological phenomenon, the focus of interest turned towards its process rather than its social or moral content. Discussions of socialisation could not avoid referring to the transmission of norms and values altogether, but looking back on the evolution of the discussion one is struck by the relative absence of serious commentary on the content of socialisation. Yet, the issue at stake was not just the process of how adult society would socialise the young but also the norms and values to be transmitted to them. By the 1950s it appeared that many adults were not sure if they had any stories to transmit to the young. Writing in 1954, Arendt feared that many adults had given up their responsibility for socialising children.[23] With the disruption of cultural continuity and a loss of the sense of the past, both the process but importantly the *content* of socialisation became an issue.

Loss of the sense of the past

The loss of the sense of the past was interpreted by social scientists and educators through the magnification and the objectification of the psychic distance between the present and the past. As we noted previously, from the late 19th century onwards change was often experienced and presented in a dramatic and mechanistic manner that exaggerated breaks, ruptures and the decoupling of the present from the past. This response is entirely understandable at a time when the scale of social transformation made it difficult for many – including social scientists – to draw on the resources of the past to make sense of a new world. The author of a study of 'The sense of the past and the origins of sociology' argued:

> The generation that gave birth to sociology was probably the first generation of human beings ever to have experienced within the span of their own lifetime socially induced social change of a totally transformative nature – change which could not be identified, ex-

22 Morawski and St Martin (2011) p.2.

23 H. Arendt [1954] (2006) 'The crisis in education' in Arendt, H., *Between Past and Future*, New York: Penguin, pp.188–189.

plained and accommodated as a limited historical variation within the encompassing order of the past.[24]

The influence of this cultural conjuncture on the subsequent evolution of the social sciences is evident to this day. One manifestation of this trend is the 'academic and intellectual dissociation of history and sociology'.[25] Many social scientists concluded that if indeed the experience of the past could no longer illuminate the present, there was little point in studying it.

The estrangement of social scientists and educators from the past was not simply a direct reaction to the scale of social transformation but also an outcome of the technocratic vision of their project. As Dorothy Ross pointed out, by the turn of the 20th century social scientists felt 'deeply alienated from the past' and driven to an 'aggressive effort to control history through positivist science'.[26]

Progressive educators and commentators in particular insisted that in a constantly changing world, it was pointless to socialise children to embrace values that would very soon become outdated. They claimed that since children had to be adaptable and flexible, they should not be weighed down by the burden of old dogmas. The conviction that people inhabited a world that was qualitatively different from that of their parents served as the premise for the claim that the knowledge and insights acquired over previous centuries had lost their relevance. These views have endured to this day and continue to influence the work of experts charged with the task of engineering the curriculum.

In education it was and continues to be frequently asserted that old ways of teaching are outdated precisely because they are old. Knowledge itself was called into question because apparently in a world of constant flux it has a short shelf-life and is continually overtaken by events. Consequently, what's important is not what we know in the here and now but our preparedness to adapt to change. Dewey claimed that because of the rapid pace of change, when a child's 'school course is completed he will be just about a decade behind the march of progress'.[27] The implication of this statement was that no sooner did a child gain knowledge in the classroom then it reached its sell-by date.

---

24 P. Abrams (1972) 'The sense of the past and the origins of sociology', *Past & Present*, No. 55, 19–32, at 22.

25 Abrams (1972) p.32.

26 D. Ross (1991) *The Origins of American Social Science*, Cambridge: Cambridge University Press, p.253.

27 Cited in C. Keck (1908) 'The socialization of the child', *Journal of Education*, 67(4), 91–92, at 91.

Dewey, who was one of the leaders of the American progressive movement, self-consciously adopted a philosophical orientation that sought to challenge the influence of the traditions of the past in education. Dewey regarded change as a potential source of progress which also called into question the meaning of traditional and transcendental values.[28] His argument for educational reforms rested on his diagnosis of rapid change, which he believed demanded the 'relaxation of social discipline and control'.[29]

In the United States, education reformers directed their fire against the traditional curriculum on the grounds that it was dated and likely to be irrelevant to the needs of society. Journals that catered for a reform-conscious middle-class audience published articles with titles such as 'Our Medieval High Schools – Shall We Educate Children for the Twelfth or The Twentieth Century' and 'Medieval Methods for Modern Children'.[30] These sentiments pervaded one of the key statements of progressive educators, the *Cardinal Principles of Secondary Education* (1918). The statement warned that while 'society is always in the process of development' institutions of education are 'conservative and therefore ... [tend] ... to resist modification'.[31] The belief that education was far too medieval and resistant to change was not only held by progressive reformers but also by the modernist liberal technocrats committed to efficiency and the rationalisation of society. Writing in this vein, the steel baron Andrew Carnegie demanded educational reforms and warned those who send their sons to colleges, they 'waste energies upon obtaining a knowledge of such languages as Greek and Latin, which are of no more practical use to them than Choctaw'.[32] An informal alliance between technocrats devoted to the promotion of economic efficiency and of progressive reformers played an important role in displacing the traditional curriculum with a supposedly modern one, more attuned to a changing world.

In Britain, too, the fetishisation of change influenced attitudes towards education. The Fabian socialist and economist G.D.H. Cole was in no doubt that the traditional curriculum had to go. He wrote in 1931:

28 A. Zilversmit (1993) *Changing Schools: Progressive Education Theory and Practice, 1930–1960*, Chicago: Chicago University Press, pp.3–4.

29 J. Dewey (1902) 'The school as a social center', *Elementary School Teacher*, 3(2), 72–86, at 86.

30 R.E. Callahan (1962) *Education and the Cult of Efficiency*, Chicago: University of Chicago Press, p.50.

31 Cited in J.R. MacDonald (2017) *Reel Guidance: Midcentury Classroom Films and Adolescent Adjustment*, Thesis submitted to the faculty of the Virginia Polytechnic Institute and State University in partial fulfilment of the requirements for the degree of Master of Arts In History, p.34.

32 Cited in Callahan (1962) p.51.

> One thing is clear: the traditional approach will no longer do. Textbooks of political theory or science that were written only a few years ago – I am not forgetting that I wrote one myself – seem already quite out of date. For the issues in men's minds and the practical problems they are invoking political theory to help them solve, have undergone a rapid change.[33]

There is something performative about Cole's projection of a vision that called everything into question. His statement was not simply a reflection on the nature of rapid change and its impact on education but was also a declaration of passivity in the face of forces beyond human control. It also implicitly signalled an unwillingness to take responsibility for the ideas that he himself wrote 'a few years ago'.

Cole's dramatised account of the scale of change was echoed by numerous commentators. In his essay 'Education for change' (1938), the intercultural educator Stewart Cole left no one in doubt about the scale of change. Citing Dewey, he wrote:

> Great as have been the changes in our educational system in the last hundred years, and especially in the last thirty, they are nevertheless slight in comparison with those which must be undertaken in the next generation. How can education stand still when society itself is rapidly changing under our very eyes?[34]

It is important to note that the conviction that rapid change renders much of the knowledge of the past redundant has continued to influence educational policy to this day. This sentiment was widely promoted within pedagogic theory in the post-Second World War period. According to one account published in 1949, since the 'social order (including the form of government, the ways of life, the organization and management of business and industry) in the United States is in a constant state of change', it followed that schools 'should prepare young people to make adjustments to changes in life about them and to take part as leaders and bring about the desired change as rapidly as possible, but must [themselves] be in a constant state of readjustment to new and changing conditions in all areas of life'.[35] The argument that ceaseless change has rendered irrelevant the disciplinary knowledge of the past continues to influence policy makers to this day.

---

33 G.D.H. Cole (1931) 'The approach to politics', *The Highway*, 24, pp.7–8.

34 S. Cole (1938) 'Education for change', *Journal of Higher Education*, 9(1), 7–17, at 11.

35 H.R. Douglass (1949) 'Education of all youth for life adjustment', *Annals of the American Academy of Political and Social Science*, 265, 108–114, at 108.

In the interwar era, a new concept – the culture lag – was invented to capture the supposed tension between unchanging custom and attitudes and constantly changing reality. This concept, developed by the sociologist William Ogburn, was according to Dorothy Ross a 'refinement of the most pervasive historical idea of his era; namely, that American society was lagging in response to increasingly rapid economic change'.[36] According to this hypothesis, which was in vogue in the 1920s and 1930s, the 'material conditions of life changed more quickly than values and attitudes'.[37] The conclusion suggested by the notion of the culture lag was that what was needed was to leave behind outdated cultural attitudes and institutions and adjust to the demands of a new scientific and technological age.

The conservatism of educational institutions was often criticised as a prime example of the recently invented culture-lag hypothesis. The gap between the needs of a rapidly changing society and prevailing customs and values was frequently advanced as justification for insulating young people from the (often harmful) influence of the past. To close this gap, it was necessary to constantly update society's values and customs and ensure that young people were not burdened by archaic and useless knowledge. It often seemed as if advocates of the culture gap had become captives of a dogma that dictated that novelty was intrinsically superior to what preceded it. References to the cultural lag were frequently made in relation to the lag between material conditions and forms of family life and childrearing that were steeped in outdated customs. Supporters of the culture-lag concept seemed to believe that the need for reform was even more urgent in the sphere of socialisation than in the domain of formal education.

The assertion that rapid change rendered previous forms of socialisation obsolete was constantly repeated during the course of deliberation on this subject. Frequently problems associated with childrearing and inter-generational relations were attributed to the use of old – and therefore outdated – forms of socialisation. Lawrence Frank was critical of the 'family as a cultural agent' because 'most of the ideas and beliefs that are taught to the children with respect to these basic organizing concepts of life are obsolete and no longer credible except to those who have dedicated their lives to the perpetuation of the archaic and the anachronistic'.[38]

36 Ross (1991) p.444.
37 See P. Mandler (2013) *Return from the Natives: How Margaret Mead Won the Second World War and Lost the Cold War*, New Haven: Yale University Press, pp.3–4.
38 Frank (1940) p.16.

Most commentaries on socialisation were not as explicit and crude as Frank's in their condemnation of the old practices but they nevertheless shared the view that the rapid pace of change rendered these customs irrelevant. Kingsley Davis stated that 'extremely rapid change in modern civilization, in contrast to most societies, tends to increase parent–youth conflict, for within a fast-changing social order the time-interval between generations, ordinarily but a mere moment in the life of a social system, becomes historically significant, thereby creating a hiatus between one generation and the next'. He concluded that 'inevitably, under such a condition, youth is reared in a milieu different from that of the parents; hence the parents become old-fashioned'.[39]

Writing at the same time as Davis, Mead adopted the comparative approach of a cultural anthropologist to explain why traditional methods of socialisation were inappropriate to the needs of modern communities. She wrote that 'very few cultures have attempted the kind of explicit internalization of parental standards upon which ours depends'. By this she meant a system in which 'the child is expected to become like the parent' and is therefore 'expected to take the parent as a model for his own life style'. Mead claimed that the transmission of norms and values from one generation 'might work quite smoothly in a stable culture which was changing very slowly'. But in 'periods of rapid change, and especially when these are accompanied by migrations and political revolutions, this requirement of the system is unattainable'.[40]

In effect, Mead called into question the capacity of parents to socialise their children. In her writing the culture gap turned into an ever-widening chasm that left inter-generational relations problematic. Referring to American society, she wrote that 'all adults are to some extent out of touch with the newest patterns of behavior as they most particularly affect the behavior of adolescents'.[41] In Mead's account, the passing of cultural stability called into question the feasibility of a form of socialisation that relied on the older generation transmitting its values to the young. Mead eventually drew the conclusion that, rather than relying on the traditional approach to the transmission of values, it would be preferable to reverse this process so that the young (with the assistance of professional support) played an active role in their own socialisation and that of their elders.

---

39 Davis (1940a) p.523.
40 Mead (1940) pp.102–103.
41 Mead (1940) p.104.

The fetishisation of change

Looking back on the 20th century, it is difficult to avoid the conclusion that social scientists and educators often appeared to adopt an obsessive fascination with change. From the turn of the 20th century onwards and especially during the interwar era, change was portrayed as an omnipotent and autonomous force that rendered irrelevant the customs and cultural legacy of the past. Typically, change was presented in a dramatic and mechanistic manner that exaggerated breaks, ruptures and the decoupling of the present from the past. In this drama, the past appears as a passive victim of forces that continually highlight its irrelevance, ridicule its superstitious pretensions and expose its backward morality to a superior modern world. The assertion that we live in a qualitatively different world from that of our ancestors serves as a premise for the claim that the knowledge and insights acquired in the past have only a minor historical significance. From this standpoint, education is relieved of its responsibility to conserve the legacy of the past; on the contrary, children are encouraged to react against it.

Social scientists like Mead were prepared to acknowledge that in previous 'stable cultures' it was possible to transmit the legacy of the past. However, they insisted that was then and not in their new, fundamentally different world of unprecedented change. The futility of maintaining cultural continuity in the sphere of socialisation and education acquired the character of conventional wisdom in pedagogy and socialisation in the interwar period. When in 1932, the sociologist and social philosopher Helen Lynd rhetorically asked 'would a reorientation in terms of personality development be possible in a system so deeply committed to passing on a knowledge of the past as a basis for education', it was obvious that the answer would be a resounding, No![42]

Lynd reported that within the American college system 'there is a growing feeling that acquiring knowledge of the past experience of mankind is inadequate training for an unknown and largely unpredictable future'. Like Mead, she contrasted a stable past with an ever-changing present.

> In the past, education has laid its emphasis on things of permanence and stability; if not 'underneath are the everlasting arms,' at least 'until death do us part,' economic verities, and the laws of Euclid. But the one thing we can know about the institutional world in which the new generation will find itself is that it will wear a very different aspect from that of today.[43]

---

42 J. Lynd (1932) 'The modern American family', *Annals of the American Academy of Political and Social Science, 160, 197–204, at 197.*

43 Lynd (1932) p.194.

In effect Lynd dismissed the relevance of the collective inheritance of human culture. Even Euclid, whose insights continue to be relevant for educating children in mathematics, was dismissed as a has-been. And yet it can be argued that it is precisely in a changing world that young people require the sense of meaning that comes from an understanding of where they come from and where they stand in relation to their cultural legacy.

Pronouncements on the death of the past were often coupled with the dismissal of the intellectual capital derived from previous times. The philosopher Alfred North Whitehead's *Adventures of Ideas* (1933) was strident in its dismissal of what he characterised as the 'vicious assumption' that 'each generation will live substantially amid the conditions governing the lives of its fathers and will transmit those conditions to mould with equal force the lives of its children'.[44] He wrote that such conditions have irrevocably changed and 'we are living in the first period of human history for which this assumption is false'. Whitehead concluded that the relations between human life and the rate of change had fundamentally altered. 'In the past the time-span of important change was considerably longer than that of a single human life'; however, 'today this time-span is considerably shorter than that of human life, and accordingly our training must prepare individuals to face a novelty of condition'.[45]

From the 1930s onwards, the mantra that we live in a moment of unprecedented change that renders the ways of the past obsolete was repeated with ever greater intensity. During her long career, Mead herself regularly repeated this sentiment. Writing in the 1940s she highlighted this development. Two decades later she wrote that 'within two decades, 1940–60, events occurred that have irrevocably altered men's relationship to other men and to the natural world'. Consequently, 'the older generations will never see repeated in the lives of young people their own unprecedented experience of sequentially emerging change'.[46]

In the 1950s and 1960s it became difficult to encounter any serious attempts to defend traditional approaches to childrearing, education and socialisation. They bore the stigma of an association with the old. In his 1962 BBC Reith Lecture, the psychiatrist George Carstairs re-raised the problem posed by the cultural lag for childrearing practices. As usual he drew a mechanistic contrast between the stable ways of the past and the changing world of the 1960s.

44 A.N. Whitehead [1933] (1961) *Adventures of Ideas*, New York: Free Press, pp.92–93.
45 Whitehead [1933] (1961) p.93.
46 M. Mead [1970] (1972) *Culture and Commitment: A Study of the Generation Gap*, London: Panther Books, p.87.

> In primitive societies, patterns of child rearing are slow to change. Each aspect of tribal custom is regarded as the only proper way to behave; often the wrath of the gods is believed to be incurred if traditional habits are broken. To some extent, the same is true of childrearing in our own society. This has always been the domain of mothers and grandmothers, who have tended to cling to old familiar ways because until recent years they had relatively little education or experience of the wider world, certainly less than their daughters of the war and post-war years. It is, I believe, because of this time-lag in the modification of child-rearing practices that our emotional attitudes are sometimes anachronistic and ill-adapted to the changing realities of our society.[47]

Mothers and grandmothers clinging to 'old familiar ways' were cast into the role of villains, held responsible for the miseducation of young people. As it turned out, experts like Carstairs were far more articulate in their critique of supposed 'ill-adapted' childrearing practices than about outlining an effective way of socialising the younger generations.

Expert discourse advocating the necessity for abandoning the socialisation methods of the past did not directly influence the behaviour of the public. Attitudes towards culture do not get absorbed through reading experts' commentaries or attending academic lectures. Progressive educators continually felt frustrated about their inability to rid schools of practices that they deemed outdated and misleading.[48] Yet, with the passing of time the discrediting of the past and the call to abandon its values and customs had gained cultural hegemony. As one study published in 2010 noted, 'the notion that we are living in a permanently changing society has created a context in which parents feel that they no longer "know" what is good or bad for their children'.[49]

The elevation of change into an omnipotent power that demands that society breaks with its past is often interpreted as an illustration of the irrelevance of pre-existing knowledge and cultural practices. However, the way that change is perceived is not simply a physical or objective fact. Perceptions of change are mediated through cultural attitudes towards human experience. The degree of trust in the prevailing system of meaning plays an important role in influencing how society's relation to its past and future is perceived. So, if a community feels overwhelmed by change and distant from its past, its sensibility is not simply an expression of an acceleration of physical motion but a loss of cultural connection with the customs and values of the past.

---

47 George Carstairs 'The first years', Lecture 2, Reith Lectures, transmission 18 November 1962, Home Service, pp.5–6.

48 See Zilversmit (1993).

49 N. Vansieleghem (2010) 'The residual parent to come: on the need for parental expertise and advice', *Educational Theory*, 60(3), 341–355, at 341.

The dramatisation of change often conveyed a sense of fatalism towards forces that continually rendered everything that humanity achieved irrelevant. This sensibility did not merely highlight transience as the defining feature of the human condition. It also drew attention to the obsolescence of prevailing customs and institutions and, by implication, what humanity had achieved so far. In 1970, Keniston summarised what he perceived as the features of the unstable 'postindustrial society' of his time. He cited:

> a rate of social change so rapid that it threatens to make obsolete all institutions, values, methodologies and technologies within the lifetime of each generation; a technology that has created not only prosperity and longevity, but power to destroy the planet, whether through warfare or violation of nature's balance; a world of extraordinarily complex social organization, instantaneous communication and constant revolution.[50]

The dramatisation of change did not merely serve as an argument for fundamentally re-engineering education and socialisation. As we discuss in the chapters to follow, it was also used to legitimise the activity of social engineering by professionals who could help people to adjust to, and live with, a rapidly changing world.

A society's sense of temporality is an outcome of its relationship to its history and is particularly influenced by the way it regards its capacity to influence it. It is not the rapidity of change that has led to the loss of the sense of the past but the inability of significant sections of society to gain meaning from the values into which it was socialised. Although traces of this attitude are evident from the late 19th century onwards, it was the catastrophic experience of the First World War that served as a catalyst for what became in effect a dramatic cultural rupture with the previous era.

A consciousness of change and a sense of the transience of social arrangements need not encourage an attitude of hostility towards the past. It can coexist with a critical but still respectful sensibility towards custom and tradition. It is when the attitude of uncritical rejection of what precedes the present prevails that the fetishisation of change encourages the immature reaction of attempting to start the world anew.

The willingness to change, adapt and embrace uncertainty is one of the important and positive attributes of the modern era. However, these attributes become a caricature of themselves when they acquire the character of a dogmatic rejection of everything that precedes the present. Arendt warned against the tendency of modern man to rebel 'against human existence as it has been given, a

---

50 Keniston (1970) p.633.

free gift from nowhere' and 'which he wishes to exchange, as it were, for something he has made himself'.[51]

Discontinuity of culture

The loss of the sense of the past was not simply an outcome of society's perception of hyper-change. The sensibility of an ever-widening psychic distance between the present and the past was shaped by dramatic historical experiences – the most important of which was the First World War.[52] It is at this point that the phenomenon known today as the 'generation gap' acquired a powerful cultural significance. The cultural gap that opened up between the post-World War world and the pre-war era would in the decades to follow be experienced through generational tensions as the problem of identity.

The Great War fundamentally undermined the cultural continuity of the West. For many Europeans it appeared that their relationship with their past had become fatally undermined. Millions of people – especially the elderly – lamented the loss of the old order. It became apparent even to those who possessed a strong conservative impulse that there was no obvious road back to the past. Attempts to maintain a sense of the past were marginalised and overwhelmed by a zeitgeist that sought to create the world anew. The cultural influence of novelty captured the temper of the times. For many intellectuals and artists, the end of the war marked the beginning of a new cultural Year Zero. The sensibility of epochal rupture and disdain for the past dominated the modernist intellectual and artistic imagination. A more radical version of this sentiment was communicated by interwar radicalism, which fervently believed that a break with the past was both possible and necessary.

One of the most momentous and durable legacies of the Great War was that it disrupted and disorganised the prevailing web of meaning through which western societies made sense of their world. Suddenly the key values and ideals into which the early 20th century elites were socialised appeared to be denuded of meaning. In historical moments when people are confused about their beliefs, they also become disoriented about who they are and where they stand in relation to others. The psychiatrist Patrick Bracken writes about the 'dread brought on by a struggle with meaning'. In circumstances when the 'meaningfulness of our lives is called into question', people become painfully aware that they lack

51 Arendt (1998) pp.2–3.
52 See F. Furedi (2014) *First World War – Still No End In Sight*, London: Bloomsbury, chs 1 and 2.

the moral and intellectual resources to give direction to their lives.[53] 'Europe was exhausted, not just physically, but also morally', states a study of the 'crisis of confidence among European elites after the war'.[54]

The existential and moral crisis that unfolded in the aftermath of the First World War ruptured a sense of continuity with the past and disrupted people's sense of who they were. Consequently, it forced society and its individuals to ask the question of 'Who are we?' The sense of continuity across time is, as Baumeister stated, one of the defining criteria of identity. 'That criterion is hard to satisfy if the continuity is that of process of change rather than that of a stable component', he wrote.[55] As the sense of discontinuity prevailed over the sense of continuity, the conditions were created for the historical emergence of what would be referred to as a crisis of identity in the 1940s.

Suddenly, the taken-for-granted assumptions about civilisation, progress and the nature of change lost their capacity to illuminate human experience. As the prominent English historian H.A.L. Fisher acknowledged in 1934, he could no longer discern in history the 'plot', the 'rhythm' and 'predetermined pattern' that had appeared so obvious to observers in the past.[56] The cultural historian Paul Fussell claims that after the First World War it is difficult, if not impossible, to imagine the future as the continuation of the past; 'the Great War was perhaps the last to be conceived as taking place within a seamless, purposeful "history" involving a coherent stream of time running from past to future'.[57] A dramatic shift in the western world's sense of temporality had altered people's relationship to their past.

Although western society was already in the late 19th century predisposed towards detaching itself from its past, it was under the spell of the calamitous impact of the Great War that this sentiment came to capture the popular imagination. Cast adrift from the certainties provided by the taken-for-granted ways of doing things, a significant section of society found themselves asking the question of 'Who are we?' It was in this moment, when the unravelling of cultural continuity exposed the illusions of the past, that artists and intellectuals began to show an awareness of identity as a problem. In his study of the history

53 P. Bracken (2002) *Trauma: Culture, Meaning and Philosophy*, London: Whurr Publishers, pp.14, 207.

54 Muller, J.W. (2013) *Contesting Democracy: Political Ideas In Twentitieth Century Europe*, Yale University Press: New Haven, p.24.

55 Baumeister (1986) p.45.

56 Cited in M. Eksteins (1989) *Rites of Spring: The Great War and the Birth of the Modern Age*, Boston: Houghton Mifflin, p.291.

57 P. Fussell (1975) *The Great War and Modern Memory*, Oxford: Oxford University Press, p.21.

of the idea of identity, Izenberg observes that in all the literary works he examined, 'the turning point for the idea of identity is World War I'.[58]

In one of the earliest explorations of the subject of identity, the English philosopher John Locke claimed in the 16th century that identity reflected the continuity of memory through the changes undergone by the self. Since, as Locke explained, memory and individual identity are closely bound together, the loss of the sense of the past meant that many people found they could not take their personal identity for granted.[59]

Frequently the post-war years were labelled as an 'age of disillusionment'. Although rarely elaborated, the term 'disillusionment' referred to the loss of illusions in the norms and values of the pre-war order. The appellation 'illusion' served to communicate the sentiment that the values associated with the pre-war outlook were at best a product of self-deception and at worst of cynicism and dishonesty. In this way the past was not just condemned as irrelevant but also dispossessed of any redeeming qualities. Insulating the young generations from its malevolent influence became one of the goals of progressive educators. Many of them felt that they were in no position to provide moral guidance to the young. As a study of progressive educators in England pointed out, they regarded adults as 'unworthy models' who were likely to exercise a corrupting influence on children.[60]

What to transmit? The problem of normativity

For most historians the interwar era is best understood as an age of ideologies where new totalitarian regimes threatened to overturn the global order. However, while this hideous drama unfolded – leading to the Second World War and the Cold War – cultural authority became a constant focus of contestation. It was this veritable crisis of normativity that rendered problematic the transmission of values to young people.

In 1930, Winston Churchill drew attention to the crisis of normativity, which he experienced as the estrangement of his society from the values of the past. He observed:

58 Izenberg (2016) p.42.

59 P. Helm (1979) 'Locke's theory of personal identity', *Philosophy*, 54(208), 173–185.

60 R.J.W. Selleck (1972) *English Primary Education and the Progressives: 1914–1939*, London: Routledge & Kegan Paul, pp.94, 96.

> I wonder often whether any other generation has seen such astounding revolutions of data and values as those through which we have lived. Scarcely anything, material or established, which I was brought up to believe was permanent and vital, has lasted. Everything I was sure or was taught to be sure, was impossible has happened.[61]

Lord Eustace Perry echoed Churchill when he wrote in 1934 that there was 'no natural idea in which we any longer believe'. He added that 'we have lost the easy self-confidence which distinguished our Victorian grandfathers'.[62]

That the values into which Churchill was socialised in the late 19th century had lost much of their cultural influence was echoed by significant sections of the British Establishment. This sentiment was particularly influential among intellectuals and the teaching profession. Like many sections of the cultural Establishment, teachers felt reluctant and uncomfortable about educating young people to embrace the values of the pre-First World War era. Confusions about the normative foundation of authority were internalised by educators – many of whom believed that the traditional modes of classroom interaction needed to be radically revised.

The philosopher of education Geoffrey Bantock recalled the 'widespread revolt against authority' after the First World War and the 'waning confidence in adult values among the liberal "enlightened"'.[63] Many educators believed that their role was to protect children from being contaminated by unworthy adult values.[64] The clearest expression of the waning of confidence in adult values was a perceptible hesitancy and reluctance to take responsibility for the socialisation of the younger generations. This reluctance to transmit the experience and legacy of the past to the young was widespread among progressive educators in the interwar era. This group of educators were 'distressed and alienated' by the values that prevailed at the time and 'they shied away from imprinting the future generation with the marks of the present'.[65] This sentiment was forcefully articulated by J.H. Nicholson, a Professor of Education at Newcastle University. He lamented that 'we are an uneasy generation, most of us to some extent ill-ad-

---

61 W. Churchill (1930) *My Early Life*, London: Thornton Butterworth Limited.

62 Cited in P. Rich (1989) 'Imperial decline and the resurgence of British national identity', in Kushner, T. and Lunn, K. (eds) *Traditions of Intolerance*, Manchester: Manchester University Press, p.65.

63 G.H. Bantock (1952) *Freedom and Authority in Education: A Criticism of Modern Cultural and Educational Assumptions*, London: Faber & Faber Ltd, p.184.

64 Selleck (1972) pp.96–98.

65 Selleck (1972) pp.94 and 118–119.

justed to present conditions' and 'should therefore beware of passing on our own prejudices and maladjustments to those we educate'.[66]

Scepticism about the moral status of the prevailing values had important implications about the conduct of inter-generational relations. It had a particularly direct impact on education. Once adult society had lost the capacity to recognise itself through the values to which it was socialised, its capacity to educate children into a new system of meaning became compromised. Instead of confronting the question of how to conduct essential inter-generational transactions both within and outside education, the post-First World War decades saw a growing tendency to evade the problem. In many cases the erosion of the consensus about what kind of ideas to transmit to young people was and continues to be perceived as proof that adults do not have an authoritative role to play in this domain.

Sections of progressive educators attempted to make a virtue of the hands-off attitude towards socialising young people. Their advocacy of 'child-centred education' was to a significant extent motivated by their disenchantment with the exercise of adult authority. As one study of this form of pedagogy explained; 'Some adherents of the child-centred tradition believe that, in the interests of creativity and our needs for innovation in a rapidly changing world, the values of adults should not be imposed upon a child'.[67]

Writing in 1943 during the Second World War, Margaret Mead highlighted the reluctance of the interwar generation of parents to give clear moral guidance to their children. She noted that 'millions of young Americans were the first generation to be reared by parents who did not present themselves as moral role models'.[68] She added:

> [I]t is sufficient to point out that men who are twenty in 1942 were reared by members of a generation which betrayed a Cause which they had believed to be worth fighting for, a generation which spent twenty years heaping obloquy on those who had been fools enough to believe in it – especially on themselves. For the first time in American history, we have had a generation reared by parents who did not see themselves as knights of a shining cause.[69]

Although advocates of child-centred education and parenting did not go so far as to endorse the abdication of responsibility for socialising children, they continually called for the restraint of the exercise of adult authority.

---

66 See Selleck (1972) pp.118 – 119

67 H. Entwistle (1979) *Child-Centred Education*, London: Methuen & Co. Ltd, p.48.

68 Mead [1942] (2000) p.74.

69 Mead [1942] (2000) p.74.

Many social scientists and professionals dealing with family life saw little problem with the erosion of adult authority. When in 1950 the sociologist David Riesman drew attention to what he saw as the abdication of adult authority by parents and teachers, he was sharply criticised by Talcott Parsons. Parsons claimed that what Riesman characterised as the abdication of adult responsibility was actually a new and enlightened way of preparing the young for 'high levels of independence, competence and responsibility'. He rebutted Riesman by claiming that

> What Riesman interprets as the abdication of the parents from their socializing responsibility can therefore be interpreted in exactly the opposite way. If parents attempted to impose their role-patterns in a detailed way on their children, they would be failing in their responsibilities in the light of the American value system.[70]

Parsons, along with many of his colleagues, praised adults for not 'imposing' their views on the young. By the time he wrote his critique of Riesman, the view that adult values should not be imposed on children had migrated from a small circle of progressive educators to middle-class society.

Now and again questions were raised about the reluctance of adult society to transmit a normative outlook to the younger generations. Writing in 1952, the psychoanalyst Hilde Bruch questioned the wisdom of avoiding the exercise of adult authority:

> It has become fashionable in the world of psychiatry and psychology, not only in its immediate relation to child-rearing practices, to speak in sweeping, dramatic terms of the crushing effect of authority and tradition. The failure to recognise the essentially valid and sustaining aspects of traditional ways and of differentiating them from outmoded harmful and overrestrictive measures has resulted in a demoralized confusion of modern parents and this has had a disastrous effect on children.[71]

Though Bruch's criticism of her colleagues' normalisation of adult irresponsibility was well observed, it overlooked a more fundamental problem, which was that the older generations were far from clear about what values to transmit to the young. Since adults could no longer represent the past and its legacy to the young, there was little consensus about the stories they should transmit. In such circumstances they found it difficult to give meaning to their authority as adults.

---

70 T. Parsons, with White, W. [1961] (1970) 'The link between character and society', in Parsons, T., *Social Structure and Personality*, Chicago: Free Press, p.217.

71 H. Bruch (1952) *Don't Be Afraid of Your Child*, New York: Farrar, Straus and Young, p.54.

By the 1960s Erikson had become aware that the decline of adult responsibility posed a problem for young people attempting to resolve their crisis of identity.[72] He was in no doubt that young people relied on the normative outlook passed on to them by their elders to make their way in the world. Those adults who opted out of their generational responsibility were in effect choosing to 'remain juvenile'. Those who shirked responsibility 'for the generational process' had in effect become 'advocates' of 'an abortive human identity'. He added that:

> We have learned from the study of lives that beyond childhood, which provides the moral basis for identity, and beyond the ideology of youth, only an adult ethics can guarantee to the next generation an equal chance to experience the full cycle of humaneness – to become as truly individual as he will ever be, and as truly beyond all individuality.[73]

Unfortunately, by this time the reluctance to face up to this challenge was no longer confined to a small number of slothful parents or groups of zealous child-centred progressive educators. Adult ethics had acquired a superficial existence. Disconnected from the past, emptied of moral content, it existed as a series of 'how to ...' statements, instrumentally cobbled together from self-help books by professionals. Socialisation was increasingly perceived as a technique or a process that appeared independent of educating the young in the legacy of the past.

72 Erikson (1968) pp.29–30.
73 Erikson (1968) p.42.

Chapter 5: Socialisation and Its Counter-Cultural Impulse

As society became distanced from its past it became increasingly difficult for adults to figure out what values they ought to transmit to the younger generations. From the late 19th century onwards, adult authority over the process of socialisation was continually contested. Numerous social and professional movements insisted that only they possessed the expertise required for the socialisation of young people. Movements for Mental Hygiene, Social Hygiene, Eugenics and the Children's Bureau, along with networks of psychologists, social scientists and educators, contributed to the displacement of parental authority. They were joined by influential commentators and policy makers associated with the progressive movement in the US and with New Liberalism and Social Democracy in Europe.

Disparate concerns – reform politics, child saving, the race improvement agenda of eugenics, the technocratic impulse for the elimination of waste by industrialists – converged to call into question traditional forms of socialisation. Professional intervention in the domain of socialisation steadily grew in the 20th century.

The professionalisation of socialisation and its promotion of ideals drawn from social science, and particularly psychology, weakened the influence of traditional moral ideals. Before the term 'socialisation' gained currency, the process of inter-generational transmission of values was sometimes referred to as *moralisation*. In its early usage, socialisation was still depicted as an authoritative act of transmitting moral norms.[320] However, the traditional emphasis on conveying established moral ideals to children gave way to an approach that contested them. Socialisation slowly turned into what Danziger described as 'a matter of changing obsolescent individual attitudes'.[321] This focus on changing 'obsolescent' attitudes represented a challenge to the values that underpinned them and in an embryonic form unleashed a conflict that with the passing of time would crystallise into what today is referred to as 'culture war'.

The project of eliminating obsolescent attitudes should be conceptualised as a form of moral engineering. Many of its practitioners identified themselves as social engineers whose vocation was to transform society through reforming pre-

320 See Franklin Giddings' classic *The Theory of Socialization: A Syllabus of Sociological Principles for the Use of College and University Classes*, New York: Macmillan & Co. (1897).
321 Danziger (1976) p.25.

https://doi.org/10.1515/9783110708899-006

vailing attitudes. Unlike socialisation, which involves the transmission of pre-existing values, social engineering is devoted to gaining support for attitudes that as yet lack significant support in society. At the risk of simplification, this difference can be understood as one between mainly affirming prevailing attitudes (socialisation) and changing them (social engineering). The emphasis of social engineering, or what in the contemporary era is called 'Raising Awareness', on combating prevailing attitudes means that it self-consciously contests views that are associated with the older generations. The mission of raising awareness invariably results in cultural conflict.

With hindsight it appears that the Culture War began in the nursery and its battles were frequently directed at gaining control over the levers of socialisation. Movements of all shades of political opinion became drawn towards the project of training and educating children to become a New Man, a species of human whose physical and moral outlook was not distorted by the superstitions and irrational customs of the past. During the first three decades of the 20th century, political movements often invested their hopes in the figure of a New Man who, untainted by the distortions of the past, would serve to transform or revitalise society. Movements from left and right promoted their version of what a New Man would look like and achieve.

Leon Trotsky, one of the leaders of the Russian Revolution, projected a utopian vison of a new 'superman'. In his *Literature and Revolution* (1924), he wrote that

> Man will make it his purpose to master his own feelings, to raise his instincts to the heights of consciousness, to make them transparent, to extend the wires of his will into hidden recesses, and thereby to raise himself to a new plane, to create a higher social biologic type, or, if you please, a superman.[322]

Far right and fascist movements were also attracted to the myth of the New Man. The fascists idealised their New Man as virile, physically hard, forceful and committed to the taking of initiative. Adolf Hitler described the New Man as 'slim and slender, quick like a greyhound, tough like leather, and hard like Krupp steel'.[323]

The utopian vision of educating children to become the New Man of the future was not confined to radical far left or far right ideologues. Similar sentiments were often advocated by individuals associated with the technocratic and social engineering ambitions of liberals, eugenicists and progressives. The

---

322 www.marxists.org/archive/trotsky/1924/lit_revo/ch08.htm (accessed 17 February 2019).
323 See the discussion in www.britannica.com/topic/fascism/Volksgemeinschaft (accessed 23 March 2020).

behaviourist psychologist John B. Watson claimed to hold the key to the secret of creating a New Man through the application of science to the field of socialisation. In 1924, he asserted:

> Give me a dozen healthy infants, well-formed, and my own specified world to bring them up in and I'll guarantee to take any one at random and train him to become any type of specialist I might select – doctor, lawyer, artist, merchant chief, and yes, even beggar-man and thief, regardless of his talents, penchants, tendencies, abilities, vocations, and race of his ancestors.[324]

The convergence of techniques of socialisation with different political projects and versions of utopia highlighted the potential for the nursery to become a seed bed for cultural conflict. This idealisation of the New Man did not perish in the interwar era. It re-emerged in the 1980s to refer to a male who embraced anti-sexist attitudes and rejected outdated masculine values and the traditional male roles.[325] In contemporary times, gender-neutral and anti-sexist socialisation promises to produce young people who are not tainted by the heteronormative attitudes of the past. Today, these sentiments are constantly conveyed by those who promote the cause of 'raising awareness' of those who are still in the thrall of outdated attitudes.

Social engineering

Those who wished to liberate children from being dominated by the obsolescent ideas and attitudes of their parents customarily insisted that their critique was based on science. Danziger remarked that their approach appeared to 'show the influence of what might be called an ideology of social engineering'.[326] In the current era the term 'social engineering' – especially when attached to family life – conjures up images of a dystopian *Brave New World*. However, during the first half of the 20th century professionals involved in the field of socialisation-related activities frequently and enthusiastically referred to themselves as social engineers. Psychologists, in particular, unreservedly called for the application of techniques of social engineering to ensure that people developed personalities that would make them suitable members of their society.[327] By the 1930s, social

---

324 J.B. Watson (1924) *Behaviorism*, New York: People's Institute, p.82.

325 See www.bbc.co.uk/news/magazine-25943326.

326 Danziger (1976) p.17.

327 See S.R. Herman (1995) 'Alva Myrdal's campaign for the Swedish comprehensive school', *Scandinavian Studies*, 67(3), 330–359, at 78–79.

workers often referred to their activities as a form of social engineering. In 1936 a *Handbook on Social Work Engineering* asserted that 'through the practices of scientific social case work and social engineering, the contribution of social work to human happiness and public welfare may ... be considerable'.[328]

Mead, who played a pivotal role in the development of what is described as the 'scientific study of socialisation', regarded social engineering as essential for helping people acquire the right kind of personality traits. According to one study, 'Mead and her colleagues' believed 'strongly in the righteousness and efficacy of social engineering'.[329] Her commitment to social engineering was linked to her ambition to challenge American moral culture and ensure that the socialisation of children was conducted on a more enlightened foundation.[330]

Mead, like many leading American cultural anthropologists, was drawn towards the project of challenging the cultural norms and attitudes that prevailed in their societies. They also went a step further and argued for the necessity of engineering these attitudes and personality traits associated with them out of existence. They were enthusiastic about the potential for using psychology to achieve their objectives, and collaborated with psychologists and psychiatrists like Erikson, Fromm and Kurt Lewin. Mead drew on psychology to highlight differences based on culturally specific regimes of child socialisation. Her study, *Coming of Age in Samoa*, was subtitled, *A Psychological Study of Primitive Youth for Western Civilization*. The interwar era saw the emergence of what were referred to as 'culture-and-personality networks', which encouraged collaboration between cultural anthropologists and psychiatrists.

In the US, the Advisory Committee on Personality and Culture set up by the Social Research Council played a co-ordinating role in promoting research into the inter-relationship between personality and culture in the 1930s. Their objective was to harness their research to what a study of the Council described as a 'project of liberal social engineering', which 'aimed at reconstructing American culture so that it would foster the needs and mental health of the individual while adjusting the individual to group life'.[331] According to one of the committee's major reports, the aim of such cultural reconstruction would be the 'ulti-

---

328 P.J. Guild and A.A. Guild (1936) *Handbook on Social Work Engineering*, Richmond: Whittet & Shepperson, p.8.

329 W.L. Wall (2009) *Inventing the 'American Way': The Politics of Consensus from the New Deal to the Civil Rights Movement*, Oxford: Oxford University Press, p.90.

330 Wall (2009) p.93.

331 D. Bryson (2009) 'Personality and culture, the Social Science Research Council, and liberal social engineering: the Advisory Committee on Personality and Culture, 1930–1934', *Journal of the History of the Behavioral Sciences*, 45(4), 355–386, at 359.

mate control of the larger patterns of collective life'.[332] The adoption of cultural reconstruction as a goal was influenced by the perception that during the 1930s American society experienced an 'unprecedented sense of social and cultural disintegration'.[333] During the Depression years it appeared to many individuals that they had lost their place in the world and that their culture struggled to provide them with a sense of meaning in what appeared an increasingly insecure world. In these circumstances social engineering held out the promise of protecting 'the threatened personality of the individual by creating a culture geared towards their needs'.[334]

Mead's friend and colleague, the cultural anthropologist Ruth Benedict, explicitly called for social engineering to challenge what she held to be narrow-minded western values. Benedict believed that with the adoption of effective psychological techniques and policy, a new, more progressive personality could be created. She assumed that it was up to people like her – enlightened social engineers – to influence what society considered to be normal. 'The relativity of normality is important in what some day will come to be a true social engineering', wrote Benedict in 1934. Benedict claimed that since normality is 'man-made', there was no necessity for the future generations to accept the cultural normalities of the past; 'our picture of our own civilization is no longer in this generation in terms of changeless and divinely derived set of categorical imperatives'. She adopted a confident view regarding the possibility of re-engineering civilisational norms:

> No society has yet achieved self-conscious and critical analysis of its own normalities and attempted rationally to deal with its own social process of creating new normalities within its next generation. But the fact that it is unachieved is not therefore proof of its impossibility. It is a faint indication of how momentous it could be in human society.[335]

Benedict's optimistic vision of the potential of science to re-engineer what society considers normal and alter the personality traits of future generations resonated with the influence of scientism in the 1930s and 1940s. Scientism constituted a politicised view of science that advocated reliance on the authority of the expert to manage the institutions of public life. Its politicisation of science or the scientisation of politics possessed great appeal to social reformers and uto-

332 Bryson (2009) p.359.

333 Bryson (2009) p.358.

334 Bryson (2009) pp.359–360.

335 R. Benedict (2017) *An Anthropologist at Work*, London: Routledge, p. 179; see R. Benedict (1934) 'Anthropology and the abnormal', *Journal of General Psychology*, 10(1), 59 – 82.

pian ideologues alike. The conviction that society should be reformed through the application of scientific principles was directly applied in relation to the socialisation of young people.

Benedict and her colleagues' ambition was to displace traditional forms of socialisation with the techniques provided by social engineering. This ambition was by no means confined to a handful of marginal academics. By the 1930s, and especially during the Second World War, this approach had gained significant institutional support, and academics like Mead and Benedict played an important role in influencing the cultural politics of the American Government. Mead's influential classic, *And Keep Your Powder Dry* (1942), was commissioned by government. It emphasised the impact of culture on the formation of personalities and reflected the sentiments of the social engineering ambitions of Mead and her colleagues. This book was still used by schools in civic classes until the 1960s.

Typically, the cultural relativist advocates of social engineering did not elaborate a system of values or moral norms that would serve as the content of socialisation. 'The recognition of cultural relativity carries with it its own values, which need not be those of absolutist philosophies', wrote Benedict.[336] What Benedict and her co-thinkers advocated was the adoption of traits like flexibility, adaptability, a willingness to question prevailing norms, that they saw as consistent with relativity. In this way a new personality, freed from outdated moral norms, could flourish. Their aspiration to 'free' personality from the past appears as an end in itself.

Despite the articulation of ambitious society-wide reforms, the project of social engineering tended to be principally interested in influencing and managing the socialisation and education of children. As one study pointed out, their work was 'intimately connected with a human engineering agenda oriented toward the socialization and education of the individual'.[337]

The love affair of social engineering with the socialisation of the young developed first in the United States. Arendt linked the early development of cultural conflict over socialisation in the United States to the fact that this nation of immigrants showed an 'extraordinary enthusiasm for what is new'.[338] Erikson also reiterated this view. In a lecture delivered in 1973, he wrote of the 'shining newness of the American identity' and that 'faith in that newness which includ-

336 R. Benedict [1934] (1989) *Patterns of Culture*, Boston: Houghton Mifflin, p.277.
337 D. Bryson (2015) 'Mark A. May: scientific administrator, human engineer', *History of the Human Sciences*, 28(3), 80–114, at 88.
338 Arendt [1954] (2006) p.173.

ed the power to renew newness itself exists in all of us to this day'.[339] In addition to America's unique embrace of novelty, the ideal of progress through the application of science resonated with the relative optimism that prevailed in this society until the late 1960s.

Despite its historical celebration of rugged individualism, the United States proved unusually hospitable to the adoption of social engineering to manage change and to regulate the future development and behaviour of society. The American progressive movement adopted an explicit technocratic approach towards the education and socialisation of young people. Edward Ross, the progressive sociologist, eugenicist and economist, personified this outlook. In 1906, Ross emphasised the importance of 'moral experts' in order to manage the enormous power of 'public opinion'. He came to this conclusion because he was concerned that 'the judgments the average man passes upon the conduct of his fellow are casual, inconsistent and thoughtless'.[340] Unlike ordinary voters, whose behaviour was unreliable and dysfunctional, experts could be relied on to serve as rational decision makers.

Ross' enthusiasm for moral experts was shared by a significant section of the ruling elites, who looked to science and organisation to manage the unpredictable impact of change. The progressive social engineering ethos was adopted by prominent public figures across the political divide. This ethos was embraced by 'corporate capitalists who sought control of the market, physicians or scientists who claimed a special role in society by virtue of their expertise, and progressive reformers who sought control of the forces of change'.[341] Soon similar sentiments were being proclaimed in the UK by the New Liberals and sections of the recently formed Labour Party.

In its early phase, 1890–1930, the appeal of social engineering resonated with the widely held conviction that, through science, many of society's outstanding problems could be solved. Its promise of managing change through the application of new rational forms of management appealed to the industrial and cultural elites of virtually all shades of political opinion. As the author of *Machine Age Ideology: Social Engineering and American Liberalism, 1911–1939*, explained, the 'theory behind social engineering' argued that the world had become a very different place from the past and that 'politics as a governing device had become outdated'. It insisted that, instead of the wrangling and demagogic

339 Erikson (1974) p.32.

340 See Anonymous author (1906) 'The nation's need of moral experts', *Current Literature*, XLI(2), p.193.

341 S.J. Diner (1998) *A Very Different Age: Americans of the Progressive Era*, New York: Hill and Wang, p.7.

appeals to the masses, what was required was scientific management and administration oriented towards 'troubleshooting and problem solving'.[342]

Social engineering provided ideological support for the rule of expertise. This ideology contained an imperative to bring all dimensions of human experience – including personal and family life – under its spell. In 1901 H.G. Wells prophesised the passing of democracy as the inevitable consequence of the ascendancy of expertise. He wrote that 'at present the class of specially trained and capable people – doctors, engineers, scientific men of all sorts – is quite disproportionally absent from political life'. Nevertheless, he predicted that the 'forces are in active operation to drag it into the centre of the stage for all that'.[343]

On reading advocates of social engineering discussing their worldview, one is struck by their confident paternalistic conviction that they know what is in the best interest of the targets of their intervention. Speaking through one of his characters in the novel *The New Machiavelli*, H.G. Wells, who was sympathetic to this ethos, states;

> I became more and more convinced that the independent family unit of today, in which the man is master of the wife, and owner of the children, in which all are dependent on him, subordinated to his enterprises and liable to follow his fortunes up or down, does not supply anything like the best possible conditions. We want to modernize the family footing altogether. An enormous premium both in pleasure and competitive efficiency is put upon voluntary childlessness and enormous inducements are held out to women to subordinate instinctive and selective preferences to social and material considerations.[344]

In this instance the aim of modernising the family through promoting the eugenic policy of childlessness is conveyed through the promise of democratising the family. The aim of eliminating the man as a master of his family was coupled with the objective of enforcing 'competitive efficiency'. In this way a 'democratic' form of social engineering claimed to serve both as a mechanism of socialisation and also as a medium for realising social efficiency.[345]

Though the ethos of social engineering often projected a utopian vision of a world fundamentally transformed in accordance with scientific principles, its practice was often drawn towards the more modest objective of rationalising the process of socialisation. It was as if the rearing of children and their social-

342 J.M. Jordan (1994) *Machine Age Ideology: Social Engineering and American Liberalism, 1911–1939*, Chapel Hill: University of North Carolina Press, pp.6–7.

343 Wells (1901) *The Review of Reviews*, p.177.

344 Wells [1911] (2005) p.324.

345 For a discussion of democratic social engineering see W. Graebner (1986) 'The small group and democratic social engineering, 1900–1950', *Journal of Social Issues*, 42(1), 137–154.

isation proved to be the most promising field for the implementation of social engineering ideals. During the 1940s, the culture-and-personality school of anthropologists and psychiatrists declared that 'social scientists could redesign the character of a culture by modifying the child rearing of its future generations'.[346] Meyerowitz noted that the re-engineering of culture through the rationalisation of the socialisation of children 'lifted child rearing from the domain of parents and families (and pediatricians and therapists) and into the realm of group identity, national politics, and international relations'.[347]

The conviction that the re-engineering of socialisation held the key to a progressive future was enthusiastically promoted by the anthropologist Weston LaBarre in his address to the Annual Meeting of the National Committee for Mental Hygiene in 1948:

> Whether he knows it or not, man has the key to his own future evolution in his unwitting and unready hands, for through anthropological and psychiatric knowledge and control of the bringing up of our children, we are potentially able to shape almost any kind of human personality which an increasingly integrated world would seem to require.[348]

LaBarre concluded that the importance of modifying the way that future generations are socialised was 'potentially one of the greatest scientific discoveries of modern times', since the 'single most important thing in human cultural behavior is literally and specifically the way we bring up our children'.[349]

The transformation of socialisation into a project of social engineering continued to be actively promoted by the therapeutic professions in the post-Second World War era. In the UK, the Child Guidance movement looked to the Welfare State to provide an emotionally healthy environment and ensure the healthy development of society.[350] They, like their American counterpart, unhesitatingly assumed that socialisation and family life was an appropriate site for their intervention. For example, Murray Bowen, who was one of the leaders of the Family Therapy movement, perceived his role as that of an engineer. He stated in 1966 that:

---

346 Meyerowitz (2010) p.1086.

347 Meyerowitz (2010) p.1086.

348 W. LaBarre (1948) 'The age period of cultural fixation', an address presented at the 39th Annual Meeting of the National Committee for Mental Hygiene, Inc., 4 November 1948, New York City, p.185.

349 W. LaBarre (1949) 'The age period of cultural fixation', *Mental Hygiene*, 33, 209–221, at 211, 216.

350 J. Stewart (2011) '"The dangerous age of childhood": child guidance and the "normal" child in Great Britain, 1920–1950', *Paedagogica Historica*, 47(6), 785–803.

> In broad terms, the therapist became a kind of expert in understanding family systems and an engineer in helping the family restore itself to functioning equilibrium. The overall goal was to help family members become system experts who could know the family system and an engineer in helping the family restore itself to functioning equilibrium.[351]

The re-engineering of the family to assist the socialisation process has proved to be an extraordinarily resilient idea influencing expertise on this subject. Its practice is arguably far more expansive today than at any time in the past.

Socialisation – a site for cultural contestation

The social engineering ethos was zealously pursued by progressive social scientists, particularly educators and psychologists, who were determined to challenge and overturn prevailing cultural norms. Rather than leaving matters to chance, 'you want to organize a culture', argued one of Wells' social engineering-influenced characters.[352] Although they did not refer to their project as a Culture War, in all but name their aim was to vanquish cultural norms and attitudes that they regarded as archaic obstacles to the realisation of progress. As one study of progressivism and social democracy in Europe explained, 'they emphasized cultural change through education and democratization not because they trusted the popular will, but because they believed nothing less than a dramatic reorientation of values would suffice to accomplish their goals'.[353]

The focus of social engineering on cultural change led to an emphasis on assuming a dominant influence over children's education and socialisation. Educating children to internalise an orientation to life that was antithetical to those of their parents and ancestors was seen as the most effective way of achieving cultural change. Reformers often deployed an engineering-related metaphor to suggest that their campaign against traditional culture was in fact a technically neutral policy of ensuring that education and socialisation were conducted according to the principles of science and rationality. Even the domain of morality was subjected to this form of rationalisation. Dewey, the doyen of progressive education, regarded 'educational practice as a kind of social engineering'. Though in his 1922 essay, 'Education as engineering', Dewey complained that 'there is at

351 Cited in D. Weinstein (2013) *The Pathological Family: Postwar America and the Rise of Family Therapy*, Ithaca: Cornell University Press, p.41.

352 Wells [1911] (2005) p.277.

353 J.T. Kloppenberg (1986) *Uncertain Victory: Social Democracy and Progressivism in European and American Thought, 1870–1920*, New York: Oxford University Press, p.413.

present no art of educational engineering', he was optimistic that it was only a matter of time before this ambition would be realised.[354] As noted previously, he referred to the use of educational techniques as a form of 'moral engineering'.[355]

Dewey extolled the virtues of 'constructive social engineering', which relied on the adoption of the techniques of scientific inquiry in the classroom. As was the case with professionals drawn towards social engineering, Dewey's interest in education was reinforced by the conviction that children played a critical role in the realisation of social change. As one study explained, 'Dewey argued that the most fruitful breeding ground for social improvement was to be found in the relatively flexible and immature, rather than in adults whose "habits of thought and feeling" were more or less fixed, and whose environment was relatively rigid'.[356]

The famous Jesuit saying, 'give me a child until the age of seven and I will give you the man', appeared to be taken to heart by Dewey and other social engineers. This sentiment was recast in a secular and scientific hue by psychologists and curriculum engineers who advocated the view that human beings were malleable creatures, whose behaviour and attitude could be made better through the application of progressive techniques of education and socialisation. Consequently, the environment of children became an important target of intervention for them.

During the last decades of the 19th century there were numerous calls for the establishment and promotion of child-study. One of its British advocates claimed that college and schools should train their students in *paedology* – the science of the child – instead of wasting their time learning Greek, Latin or trigonometry. Writing in 1894, he praised Stanley Hall for the establishment of 'The National Association for the Study of Children' the previous year, and approvingly cited the prophecy that some of us 'will live to see the day when the Science of the Child will have taught the world more in fifty years about the child than the world learned during the preceding five thousand years'.[357] The explosion of interest in the study of children eventually led to the labelling of the 20th century as 'The Century of the Child'.

---

354 http://middlegradescurriculum.yolasite.com/resources/Education%20Engineering-Dewey.pdf (accessed 2 April 2019).

355 See the discussion in his chapter titled 'Reconstruction in moral conceptions', https://archive.org/details/reconstructionin00deweuoft/page/160 (accessed 12 April 2019).

356 M. Bergman (2015) 'Minimal meliorism: finding a balance between conservative and progressive pragmatism', *Action, Belief and Inquiry*, 2, 2–28, at 2.

357 See '"Paidology" – the science of the child', *Review of Reviews*, March 1894, p. 280.

In 1900, the Swedish social reformer Ellen Key published her book, *The Century of the Child.* This influential book – which was translated into English in 1909 – offered a coherent exposition of a worldview that promoted the child as the medium for the realisation of social and cultural change. It enthusiastically projected a vision of the malleability of human beings:

> While earlier days regarded man as a fixed phenomenon, in his physical and psychical relations, with qualities that might be perfected but could not be transformed, it is now known that he can re-create himself. Instead of a fallen man, we see an incompleted man, out of whom, by infinite modifications in an infinite space of time, a new being can come into existence. Almost every day brings new information about hitherto unsuspected possibilities; tells us of power extended physically or psychically.[358]

Key stated that what stood in the way of the creation of a 'higher type of man' was the influence of prevailing cultural norms. 'In no respect has culture remained more backward than in those things which are decisive for the formation of a new and higher race of mankind.'[359] The prerequisite for the emergence of a 'new and higher race' of people was the scientific education and socialisation of the child.

Outwardly, *The Century of the Child* comes across as an enlightened celebration of children, and most accounts of this text and its influence underline this interpretation of the text. To be sure, statements like 'the time will come in which the child will be looked upon as holy' – which are celebrated throughout the book – lend credence to this assessment. However, this book is much more than a sacralisation of childhood. In places, it reads like a soft social engineering version of Plato's *Republic.* It idealises the rule and authority of the expert and communicates a barely disguised sense of contempt towards the rest of society. Key's book is under the sway of eugenic ideals that called for the need for racial improvement. In her praise of Francis Galton, one of the founders of eugenics, 'the science of the amelioration of the race', she exhibits the paternalistic instincts associated with this movement.

Key was more restrained than some of the hard-core eugenicists who believed that before people could marry and become parents they needed permission from experts, but she nevertheless believed that people should behave in accordance with the laws of eugenics. 'Man must come to learn the laws of natural selection and act in the spirit of these laws', she wrote.[360] She was particu-

358 E. Key (1909) *The Century of the Child*, New York: G.P. Putnam's Sons, p.4.
359 Key (1909) p.5.
360 Key (1909) p.46.

larly scathing of parents who did not share her ethical outlook and miseducated their offspring, and denounced those who 'can transmit to their children all kinds of intellectual mutilation and bodily unsoundness' and who were 'without the slightest conception of that morality which will mould the new mankind'.[361] She cited with approval a statement attributed to Mary Wollstonecraft, to the effect that 'if children are not physically murdered by their ignorant mothers, they are ruined psychically by the inability of the mother to bring them up'.[362]

Key's focus on the child was to a significant extent influenced by the instrumental project of harnessing society's concern with children to achieve wider social and political objectives. Her outlook was widely shared by many would-be paidologists, who looked upon children as the instrument for the realisation of progress. Many of them embraced psychology as the medium for understanding children's problems, solving them and influencing them. This stance towards children was codified by the Mental Hygiene movement. One of the aims of this movement, which was originally founded in 1909, was the 'investigation of the psychological factors related to education',[363] During the decades to follow, the Mental Hygiene movement broadened its scope and developed the idea of positive mental hygiene, which aimed to assist children to develop healthy personalities. As one of its advocates explained in 1928:

> At the present time it might be said that mental hygiene is interested not only in the prevention of the various forms of maladjustment but in the development of the best possible type of personality. This aim might be called 'positive mental hygiene'.[364]

This movement called for early intervention in childhood since it found that human pathologies and 'maladjustments' could be 'traced further and further back into childhood and infancy'.[365] It advocated a science that stressed the importance of early socialisation. As one study observed, 'the mental hygiene paradigm originated with the premise that society could be perfected through the socialization of children'.[366]

In Britain, the tendency to invest in children and hopes about building a better world in the future also gained influence in the early decades of the 20th century. One historian of psychology pointed out that 'the promise of remaking man

361 Key (1909) p.55.
362 Key (1909) p.235.
363 www.ncbi.nlm.nih.gov/pmc/articles/PMC5287990/ (accessed 9 May 2020).
364 J.W. Bridges (1928) 'The Positive Hygiene movement', *Public Health Journal*, 19(1), 1–8, at 8.
365 Bridges (1928) p.8.
366 See Richardson (1989) p.2.

through a new education epitomised by Edmund Holmes' *What is and What Might Be* (1911), was attractive to those disenchanted by a socialism that was losing such a dimension'.[367]

The Child Guidance movement, which was founded in Chicago in 1906, shared many of the objectives of the Mental Hygiene movement.[368] Child Guidance swiftly spread to Britain and other parts of Europe in the aftermath of the First World War. This movement promoted psychological intervention in the process of socialisation in order to 'promote children's mental well-being'.[369] Given its interest in socialisation it reoriented its focus from 'the clinic to the school' and in the process contributed to the medicalisation of education.[370]

Arendt was certainly right when she reflected in 1959 that 'the idea that one can change the world by educating the children in the spirit of the future has been one of the hallmarks of political utopias since antiquity'.[371] This sentiment bound Plato's idealisation of an authoritarian city-state to the various social engineering projects initiated in the 20th century. It is worth noting that the premise that 'you can never intervene in childhood early enough' continues to dominate social policy to this day. Mental hygienists adopted this outlook and concluded that 'by the time children came to the attention of psychiatrists and social workers, it was too late'. They therefore claimed that 'in the interests of prevention it was critical to reach children before they became "problems"'.[372]

Gaining influence over the early years of a child became a central objective of social engineering. As Frank argued;

> It is now becoming evident that the process of early education of the child, which ordinarily takes place in the home and family, gives rise to the basic character structure as a persistent way of organizing and interpreting experience and reacting affectively toward life. To the extent that both clinical and experimental studies are showing how various cultural traditions and certain time-honored methods of rearing children tend to foster distortions of the

---

367 M. Thomson (2006) *Psychological Subjects: Identity Culture, and Health in Twentieth-Century Britain*, Oxford: Oxford University Press, p.118.

368 D.M. Levy (1968) 'Beginnings of the child guidance movement', *American Journal of Orthopsychiatry*, 38(5), 799–804.

369 John Stewart, 'The dangerous age of childhood: child guidance in Britain c.1918–1955', 2012, www.historyandpolicy.org/policy-papers/papers/the-dangerous-age-of-childhood-child-guidance-in-britain-c.1918-1955 (accessed 10 May 2020).

370 Thomson (2006) p.116.

371 See H. Arendt (2003) *Responsibility and Judgment*, New York: Schoken Books, p.197.

372 S. Cohen (1983) 'The mental hygiene movement, the development of personality and the school: the medicalization of American education', *History of Education Quarterly*, 23(2), 123–149, at 129.

> personality and persistent affective reactions, destructive to social order and to the individual, it would appear that in this area of early childhood education we have one of the most significant opportunities to modify the predominant personality difficulties and distortions characteristic to our society.[373]

Early childhood education was and remains to the present time the key instrument of social engineers determined to turn children into new and enlightened versions of adults.

Back in 1921, the American psychiatrist William Alanson White coined the phrase 'the golden period for mental hygiene' to refer to the early phase of childhood, when intervention could be most effective. For social engineers, the golden period of early childhood represented a moment when expert intervention could prevent the acquisition of various personality pathologies and ensure that young people adopted the right kind of values. Similar sentiments were voiced by progressive educators and child professionals. The influence of these pressure groups had a massive impact on education – first in the United States, then in other parts of the world. As one study of this movement explained, 'few intellectual and social movements of this century have had so deep and pervasive an influence on the theory and practice of American education as the mental hygiene movement'. According to its author, Sol Cohen:

> The mental hygiene movement provided the inspiration and driving force behind one of the most far-reaching yet little understood educational innovations of this century, what I call the 'medicalization' of American education. I mean by this metaphor the infiltration of psychiatric norms, concepts and categories of discourse – the 'mental hygiene point of view' – into virtually all aspects of American education in this century, epitomized in the idea of the school's responsibility for children's personality development.[374]

Through the medicalisation of education, schools became focused on the personality of the child. This reorientation of schooling was based on the premise that 'the personality development of children must take priority over any other educational objective'.[375]

The trend towards the medicalisation of education and socialisation should not be interpreted narrowly as representing merely a form of public health intervention. Its aim was the 'adjustment' of a child's personality, and to achieve this objective social engineers were determined to insulate young people from the negative influence of customs and values that prevented children from adjusting

373 Frank (1941) pp.623–624.
374 Cohen (1983) p.124.
375 Cohen (1983) p.124.

to the outlook they advocated. This was a cause which some of the leaders on the National Committee for Mental Hygiene fought as if it were a cultural crusade. One of the leaders of the NCMH, the psychiatrist Adolph Meyer, articulated this sentiment when he indicated that his organisation was waging an 'educative war' on behalf of mental hygiene.[376]

Outwardly this 'educative war' appeared to have little to do with competing ideologies. It often presented itself as a morally neutral form of therapeutic intervention in children's lives. However, these movements were not simply motivated about the need to improve the welfare of children – they were also deeply devoted to the task of re-socialising children to the point that they could serve as instruments for changing society. From their perspective, it was not only children who were maladjusted but also society.[377] Helping children to adjust was linked to the hope that society, too, would be cured of its sickness.

For social engineers, psychology promised to provide the most effective instrument for influencing and shaping the personality of children. That is why they have continually sought to offer psychological solutions for the educational problems of children. They were and remain relatively indifferent to the content of schooling and of socialisation, and instead concentrate on tackling the psychological obstacles to learning and the development of a healthy personality. Studies of the history of progressive education indicate that, through its concern for the psychological development of children, its greatest legacy was the medicalisation of education. According to one account, by the 1930s its psychological emphasis meant that the progressive movement's 'potential anti-intellectualism came to the fore'.[378] Leading progressive educators like William Kirkpatrick embraced mental hygiene and argued for the freeing of children from the 'artificial demands of subject matter requirements'. Kirkpatrick believed that shielding children from the imposition of a robust regime of disciplinary knowledge would prevent their 'personality maladjustment'.[379]

Mental hygienists possessed an unapologetic anti-intellectual stance towards schooling. As Cohen explained, they 'invariably depict the academic curriculum in pejorative terms: the "rigid curriculum," the "academic menu," the "old scholastic ideals of education," the "mere acquisition of knowledge"'. They also attacked 'the academic subject-matter-centred curriculum as a Procrustean bed, resulting in disaffection, failure, behavior problems, or personality maladjustment: "the reason for misfit children was a misfit curriculum", they ar-

376 Cited in Cohen (1983) p.132.

377 Thomson (2006) p.86.

378 Zilversmit (1993) p.12.

379 Zilversmit (1993) p.15.

gued'.[380] Typically, they 'urged teachers to de-emphasize content and subject-matter and pay more attention to the child's personality development as opposed to his intellectual development'.[381]

Hostility to academic subjects was pronounced among American curriculum engineers and psychologists. In the early 20th century, these subjects were not only denounced as irrelevant to the experience of children but also as positively harmful to their health. Stanley Hall criticised the 'ideal of knowledge for its own sake' and asserted that 'children's health and well-being were almost always jeopardized by traditional schools studies'.[382] The sentiment that traditional academic education actually undermines children's health and well-being was a re-occurring theme promoted by the medicalisers of the curriculum. It was in this vein that Caroline Zachary, a leading progressive pedagogue, dismissed the academic curriculum as a 'relic that no longer served any useful purpose and that impaired students' personal development'.[383]

The assertion that academic learning can have an adverse impact on children's well-being and on their mental health was based on the conviction that much of what children do in school is unnatural and therefore stultifies their personal development. Often the very formality of education was condemned for curbing children's natural inclinations and causing them mental distress. Such concerns have been regularly raised in relation to the alleged risks to children caused by homework. In 1900 Edward Bok, editor of *The Ladies' Home Journal*, launched a campaign against homework. He alleged that the 'mental health of American children was being destroyed' by it.[384] Others targeted discipline, rote learning and the inflexibility of the curriculum. Dewey stated that too much focus on literacy caused 'undue nervous strain' and he warned of a 'sad record of injured nervous systems and muscular order and distortions'. As far back as 1898, he denounced attempts to teach 6- and 7-year-old children to read because it 'cripples rather than furthers later intellectual development'.[385]

Dewey's pedagogy was opposed to what he described as the 'indoctrination' going on in schools. Writing in 1937, he commented that 'parents (especially those from upper classes) are often accomplices in such indoctrination and demand that the school system maintains the status quo and transmits the accept-

380 Cohen (1983) p.130.
381 Cohen (1983) p.130.
382 Cited in D. Ravitch (2000) *Left Back: A Century of Failed School Reforms*, New York: Simon & Schuster, p.70.
383 Cited in Ravitch (2000) pp.274–275.
384 Cited in Ravitch (2000) p.90.
385 Cited in Ravitch (2000) p.357.

ed social and moral values'.[386] Dewey's solution to this problem was not to explicitly challenge the values of the status quo but to rely on pedagogic and psychological techniques to encourage the 'healthy differentiation' of children 'from their families of origin'.[387]

For progressive educators like Dewey, the psychic distancing of children from their families and their cultural influences was one of the supposed benefits of the medicalisation of education. The psychic distancing of children from their parents was most systematically promoted by Swedish Social Democratic social engineers. The sociologist and prominent public figure Alva Myrdal was in no doubt that the goal of educational reform was to achieve children's early independence from parents.[388]

A study of the history of the medicalisation of education indicates that the growth of its influence paralleled that of social engineering. Stanley Hall boasted in 1908 that 'the doctor now follows the child into the school'.[389] In 1917, *Life Magazine* depicted the public school as a clinic, 'monitored by medical inspections, sanitized and charged with the mandate of "medical moralization"'.[390] Medical moralisation – with its emphasis on the mental health of the child – implicitly sought to undermine the influence of customs and values that it believed harmed a child. Invariably such customs and values were ones through which cultural continuity gained definition.

The medicalisation of education was not simply an intervention designed to assist the development of children's personalities. It was also implicitly directed against the cultural norms thought to be responsible for damaging and distorting children's personalities. Frank called for the 'critical scrutiny of the traditional ideas and beliefs about human nature, about human conduct, our ethical and moral teachings and an exposition of how these either block or actually threaten integrated personality development'. He stated that 'the prevailing practices of education of children call for similar examination and exposition of their consequences'. Concluding with a note of reassurance, he added that 'it might be sug-

---

386 J. Dewey (1937) 'Education and social change', *Bulletin of the American Association of University Professors*, 23(6), 472–474, at 472.

387 I. Pérez-Ibáñez (2018) 'Dewey's thought on education and social change', *Journal of Thought* 52(3–4), 19–31, at 19.

388 E. Herman (1995) *The Romance of American Psychology: Political Culture in the Age of Experts*, Berkeley: University of California Press, p.334.

389 S. Petrina (2006) 'The medicalization of education: a historiographic synthesis', *History of Education Quarterly*, 46(4), 503–531, at 505.

390 Petrina (2006) p.507.

gested that the psychiatrist is uniquely competent to tell us how to practice the Christian injunction to love little children'.[391]

The emphasis on the unique expertise of therapeutic professionals represented a call for bringing the socialisation of the young under their management. Parental incompetence in this domain was unfavourably contrasted with the expertise of psychiatrists and educational psychologists. This outlook was most systematically elaborated in the influential writing of Talcott Parsons, who claimed that each 'phase of the socialization process' was 'analogous to a therapeutic process'.[392] Parsons recognised the importance of the socialisation of children, but since he tended to view it as a technical process he assumed that its realisation depended on the quality of contribution of technical experts.

Targeting culture

From the 1930s onwards, arguments for the re-engineering of childhood often relied on the insights provided by cultural anthropologists with their emphasis on the variability of childrearing practices. They argued that childrearing played a central role in shaping the character of society at the same time as children's character was seen to be determined by their culture. Modifying or changing culture through the adoption of new techniques of socialisation was often advocated as the prerequisite for building an ideal democratic world. This issue preoccupied Mead, just as the US was about to enter the Second World War in 1942:

> we are faced with the problem of building a new world; we have to re-orient the old values of many contrasting and contradictory cultural systems into a new form which will use but transcend them all, draw on their respective strengths and allow for their respective weaknesses. *We have to build a culture richer and more rewarding than any that the world has ever seen* .... This can only be done through a disciplined science of human relations. (Emphasis added)[393]

Science was the medium for the realisation of cultural renewal. For Mead and her colleagues, the building of a rich culture required a fundamental reorientation of western values and norms, particularly as they pertained to the socialisation of the young.

---

391 Frank (1941) p.623.

392 T. Parsons and R.F. Bales (1956) *Family: Socialization and Interaction Process*, London: Routledge & Kegan Paul, p.60.

393 Cited in L.L. Langness (1975) 'Margaret Mead and the study of socialization', *Ethos*, 3(2), 97–112, at 104.

One of the first important studies that drew attention to the deficits of the childrearing practices of western society was John Dollard's *Frustration and Aggression* (1939). The frustration-aggression hypothesis of Dollard contained an implicit critique of the American regime of socialisation. It claimed that this regime made children frustrated, which in turn led to aggressive behaviour among the youth. Though written in an understated tone, *Frustration and Aggression* unfavourably contrasted the socialisation practices in America with the supposedly freer and more permissive childrearing styles of non-western cultures. This study became arguably the most important study on socialisation in the late 1930s and 1940s, and influenced discussion on the subject for years to come. Coinciding with the eruption of the Second World War, this book's claim that parenting was responsible for enhancing the frustration and aggression of their children found a ready-made audience among policy makers and commentators.

The study hinted darkly at the 'forbidding atmosphere of our patriarchal family' which was 'expressed in the precept "honor thy father and mother"'.[394] It asserted that 'this commandment alone is a warrant for a general aggressive parental program against the aggressive behavior of the child itself'.[395] What was significant about Dollard's argument was not merely his criticism of the American patriarchal family but his contention that there were cultures that did a much better job at raising their children.

Dollard pointed to cultures where the frustration-aggression pattern of adolescent development did not exist because they 'allowed relatively free expression of sex instigation that appears at maturation'. Drawing on the work of anthropologists, he concluded that where these 'ideal' conditions are present 'there is apparently little conflict at pubescence'.[396] He cited the work of Mead, 'who has conducted the most extensive studies of post-pubescent behaviour in primitive societies' and who reported that 'in Samoa free expression of the sex drive is uninhibited and there is a marked reduction of adolescent conflict'. Dollard also cited the work of the London School of Economics anthropologist Bronislaw Malinowski, 'who found that there is no neurotic behaviour among the Trobriand Islanders' – as opposed to neighbouring tribes where 'sexual activity is rigidly tabooed'.[397]

Remarkably, the objections that professional socialisers hurled against the traditions of the past did not apply to the very traditional cultures of non-western society. The studies based on the fieldwork of cultural anthropologists often

394 J. Dollard et al. (1939) *Frustration and Aggression*, New Haven: Yale University Press, p.78.
395 Dollard et al. (1939) p.108.
396 Dollard et al. (1939) p.108.
397 Dollard et al. (1939) p.108.

implied that the traditional values and customs of Pacific Island communities could serve as models for rapidly changing non-traditional western societies. There was something of a utopian naivety about Dollard's description of happy teen-agers enjoying a fulfilling life of sexual permissiveness in Pacific Islands. In part this gullibility towards exotic cultures was influenced by a mood of estrangement from western culture. The author even referred to a study, *Russia, Youth and the Present-Day World* (1934), to claim that in the Soviet Union youths have 'been given emancipation from sexual restraints', and have achieved responsibilities that go way beyond those enjoyed by their peers in the West.[398] The readiness with which Dollard naively accepted Soviet propaganda about its young people's emancipation from sexual restraints is itself worthy of study. Mead echoed Dollard, when she cited the 'spectacular experiment in Russia' as a possible culture to be emulated by America.[399]

The exoticism of Dollard was shared by many professional socialisers who were under the spell of the bowdlerised version of the Freudian theory of 'sexual repression'. In the 1930s, sexual repression prevailing in authoritarian families was perceived as the cause of neuroses and held responsible for the aggressive behaviour associated with fascism and related forms of pathological behaviour. This thesis was forcefully presented in the work of Wilhelm Reich, whose work on the rise of fascism in Germany 'diagnosed sexual repression by society as a major contributor to the political passivity – repression that instilled in the child a deep anxiety, insecurity, and the need to internalize society's prescriptions'.[400] In the US, advocates of the frustration-aggression thesis hoped that new cultural norms of child training would reduce children's frustration and thereby ultimately contribute to 'controlling aggression within modern society'.[401]

In contrast to repressed western communities, anthropologists found societies where sexual permissiveness appeared to create a culture that appeared to be free from neuroses. Often these romanticised accounts of non-western cultures served as the springboard for criticising the way western societies socialised their young. As one study observed;

---

398 See F.E. Williams (1934) *Russia, Youth and the Present-Day World*, New York: Farrar and Rinehart, p.76.
399 Cited in Jewett (2020) p.80.
400 F. Samelson (1986) 'Authoritarianism from Berlin to Berkeley: on social psychology and history', *Journal of Social Issues*, 42(1), 191–208, at 195.
401 Bryson (2015) p.103.

> Both Malinowski and Mead used the practices of 'primitives' to comment on the middle- and upper-class norms of their own societies. Malinowski implicitly applauded the Trobriand Islanders, who had 'no condemnation of sex or of sensuality as such,' and contrasted them with the British, whose 'repressions of the nursery ... especially among the higher classes' led to 'clandestine inquisitions into indecent things.' Likewise, Mead found that the Samoans' 'knowledge of sex and the freedom to experiment' contributed to their easy 'adjustment,' without the adolescent crises or adult neuroses that she thought marked her own society.[402]

Ruth Benedict barely disguised her contempt for some of the values she associated with western culture. She was critical of the selfish and individualistic outlook of her society, which she diagnosed as sick. 'Western civilization', she wrote, 'allows and culturally honors gratifications of the ego which according to any absolute category would be regarded as abnormal.'[403]

In one of the earliest cultural anthropological critiques of American culture, Edward Sapir observed in 1924 that 'it is perhaps the sensitive ethnologist who has studied the aboriginal civilization at first hand who is most impressed by the frequent vitality of culture in less sophisticated levels'. Sapir admired the 'well-rounded life of the average participant in the civilization of a typical American Indian tribe' and the 'creative' role that people play in the 'mechanism of their culture'.[404] His praise of the vitality of the culture of a 'less sophisticated' society contrasted with his disappointment with that of America. He wrote of the 'chronic state of cultural maladjustment' in the US, which has 'for so long a period reduced much of our higher life to sterile externality'.[405]

In Britain, the sentimentalisation of non-western culture was voiced by the Glaswegian psychoanalyst, Ian Suttie. He claimed that Freud's arguments about repression and the influence of patriarchy were 'distortions peculiar to Western civilisation'. Suttie drew on anthropological studies of the Arunta people of Australia to show that there were alternative forms of emotional and social regimes to the psychological distortions that prevailed in the West.[406]

On re-reading the socialisation literature of the 1930s and 1940s, it is difficult to avoid the conclusion that some of the contributors wished to convey the impression that, at least as far as childrearing was concerned, western cul-

---

402 Meyerowitz (2010) p.1064.

403 Cited in Meyerowitz (2010) p.1069.

404 E. Sapir (1924) 'Culture, genuine and spurious', *American Journal of Sociology*, 29(4), 401–429, at 414.

405 Sapir (1924) p.413.

406 See R. Hayward (2012) 'The invention of the psychosocial: an introduction', *History of the Human Sciences*, 25(5), 3–12, at 4.

tures were more damaged than others. Writing in 1973 and reflecting back on her motive for writing her first book, *The Coming of Age in Samoa* (1928), Mead noted that its aim was to show that there was a better way of socialising the young. She stated that she hoped 'it would be intelligible to those who might make the best use of its theme, that adolescence need not be the time of stress and strain which Western society made it; that growing up could be freer and easier and less complicated'.[407] As in the 1920s so almost 50 years later, Mead self-consciously adopted the cause of the adolescent as a point of departure for critiquing western culture.

The ease with which the discussion of the problem of socialisation moved on to a critique of western culture indicated that child development served as an ideal vehicle for the questioning of wider social norms. During the 1930s, as an officer with the General Education Board, Frank laid great emphasis on the reconstruction of culture as the 'primary route to the production of a pacified social order'.[408] He viewed 'the training and care of children' as 'the master technique of social progress'.[409] He suggested that through the application of social engineering, culture itself could be transformed. As Bryson wrote, for Frank 'what was needed ... was the redirection of culture with a view to producing wholesome, sane, and noncompetitive personalities':

> such a project would combine various approaches, including the critical re-examination and reinterpretation of cultural tradition by specialists and, most importantly, a series of programs aimed at the personalities and outlooks of adolescents, such as the reorienting of the curriculum of secondary education toward 'human relations' and the fostering of wholesome aesthetic experience among the nation's youth.[410]

Typically, Frank, like most professional socialisers, argued that it was the interest of the child that necessitated the forging of a new culture. In this way, their politicisation of culture appeared as an ideologically neutral doctrine of scientific socialisation.

The goal of establishing a new culture was integral to the social engineering projects of professional groups. The social engineering ambitions of anthropology were explicitly endorsed in 1948 by Bernard Mishkin, who noted that the 'new anthropology can reduce tensions all over the world'.[411]

---

407 M. Mead (1973) 'Preface' to *Coming of Age in Samoa*, New York: Wm. Morrow & Co., p.12.
408 Bryson (1998) pp.409–410.
409 Bryson (1998) p.413.
410 Bryson (1998) p.418.
411 Bernard Mishkin, 'Science on the march', *The New York Times*, 30 January 1949, p.82.

He hailed the 'new anthropology' as a 'branch of social engineering'. For their part, psychiatrists hailed the 'third revolution' of psychiatry, which boasted that it could cure not only individuals but also nations and societies. In April 1941, Robert Yerkes, who was a leading member of the US Government's wartime Emergency Committee in Psychology, stated that he was looking forward to 'a period of reconstruction during which innovations are likely to be the unescapable order of the day and the fashioning of a new civilization a necessity'.[412] This point was echoed by Mead, who wrote that 'we must see this war' as a 'prelude to a greater job – the restructuring of the culture of the world – which we will want to do, and for which, because we are also a practical people, we must realize there are already tools half forged'.[413]

The demand for a new culture, and its implicit condemnation of western values and customs, gained influence in the 1940s. Its ethos of scientific socialisation gradually acquired institutional support within the newly created international organisations such as UNESCO and the WHO, and among professional bodies promoting mental health and social and educational reform. It also enjoyed significant support among public administrators working in different branches of government in the US, Canada, Sweden, Britain and other parts of Europe.

Outwardly the newly established international organisations celebrated western democracy and way of life, and professional bodies tended to support the West against the Soviet Union in the unfolding Cold War. At the same time, they conveyed serious reservation about western culture, and often depicted it as a source of mental health pathologies. This sentiment was clearly communicated by the title of the book *Psychosocial Medicine: A Study of the Sick Society* (1948), authored by Glaswegian public health investigator James L. Halliday, who claimed that 'society itself was sick'.[414] The representation of society and its culture as sick continued to influence the outlook of sections of the therapeutic professions. The diagnosis of society as the patient was the focus of psychiatrist G.M. Carstair's BBC Reith Lecture in 1962.[415] He called for the adoption of new methods of socialisation and warned that 'our emotional

---

412 R. Yerkes (1941) 'Psychology and Defense', *Proceedings of the American Philosophical Society*, 84, 527–542, at 536.

413 M. Mead (1942) *And Keep Your Powder Dry: An Anthropologist Looks at America*, New York: William Morrow and Company, p.261.

414 Thomson (2006) pp.200–201.

415 See Editorial (1963) 'Diagnosis of a sick society', *British Medical Journal*, 1(5324), 97, pp.135–136.

attitudes are sometimes anachronistic and ill-adapted to the changing realities of our society'.[416]

From the 1940s the claim that western culture was sick and required the therapeutic intervention of experts was constantly asserted by members of the mental health lobby. Writing in 1968, the psychologist Abraham Maslow summed up this outlook when he stated that 'sick people are made by sick cultures'.[417] The term 'sick culture' conveyed the idea that its practices and values were responsible for people's mental health problems and character defects. This diagnosis suggested that before these problems could be put right, a sick culture needed to be transformed.

The targeting of the sick culture of the West frequently focused on challenging its morality, particularly its alleged deleterious impact on the socialisation of children. Along with other leaders of the newly established post-Second World War international organisations, Julius Huxley, advocate of 'reform eugenics', who became the first Director General of UNESCO, played an important role in gaining institutional support for the displacement of traditional morality by what he called 'scientific humanism'. Huxley and his colleagues dismissed morality as dogma and the exercise of moral judgment was denounced by them as the unthinking imposition of archaic values. Some went so far as to suggest that the idealisation of moral values during the process of the socialisation of young people was responsible for human conflict and the two world wars of the 20th century.

George Chisholm, Director General of the WHO, personified his era's ambitions of moral engineering. He asserted that people had to be re-socialised to reject their old-fashioned moral outlook. He attacked a moral outlook that relied on the 'concept of right and wrong' as the basis of child training. In a widely publicised lecture, delivered in 1946, he asked 'What drives people to war' before answering, 'Only one common factor – Morality'.[418] He denounced morality and its imposition on the younger generations.

Chisholm claimed that the task of an enlightened system of education was the 'eradication of the concept of right and wrong which has been the basis of child training'. He called for the 'substitution of intelligent and rational thinking for faith in the certainties of the old people'.[419] Liberation from the crushing bur-

416 See George Carstairs, 'The first years', Lecture 2, Reith Lectures, transmission, 18 November 1962, Home Service, pp.5–6.

417 Cited in C. Hoff Sommers and S. Satel (2005) *One Nation Under Therapy*, New York: St. Martin's Press, p.62.

418 Chisholm (1946) p.7.

419 Chisholm (1946) p.9.

den of making moral distinctions was presented as essential to overcome the 'poisonous certainties fed us by our parents, our Sunday and day school teachers, our politicians, our priests, our newspapers and others with a vested interest in controlling us', argued Chisholm.[420] Freedom from moralities was presented by parenting experts, educators and a growing body of therapeutic professionals as the foundation of an open-minded personality.

The main instrument adopted by moral engineers to diminish the influence of traditional morality was through the promotion of mental health. Mental health intervention was no longer simply focused on the individual but on culture as a whole. As Frank argued in 1950, 'mental health may thereby be given the larger meaning and inclusive significance of a community-wide goal'.[421] But the achievement of this goal demanded fundamental cultural change.[422] Frank's call for a cultural revolution required ridding society of its traditional views of human nature and morality. He was determined to '"clean up" the cultural environment' by getting people to rid themselves of old beliefs and replace them with 'more constructive' ideas. He was in no doubt that the adoption of mental health intervention as the new form of socialisation would lead to 'human development'.[423]

In effect what Frank offered was a form of a science-inspired religion:

> A community program for mental health, if it is to have meaning for people and is to draw on the strengths of our culture, must be presented as more than a psychiatric proposal; indeed, it must enlist much of what people mean by their religion. Viewed in these larger terms, we may regard mental health programs as the beginning of a self-conscious effort to reorient our culture and our social order in the light of the awareness, the insights, the understandings now becoming available, to help us advance toward the human dignity which is both the prerequisite to, and the product of, mental health.[424]

Though infused with optimism, this utopian vision of a new culture was short on detail on what kind of values would prevail. Other than uphold mental health as the foundational value of the new culture, it had little to say about what values serve as the inspiration for socialising children.

Socialisation, which had served as the main terrain for the practice of social engineering since the turn of the 20th century, soon became implicated in a wider conflict over culture. Establishing influence over the cultural values that would

---

420 Chisholm (1946) p.9.
421 Frank (1953) p.167.
422 Frank (1953) pp.167–168.
423 Frank (1953) p.171.
424 Frank (1953) p.177.

be internalised in childhood dominated the vision of the different groups of social engineers. In the narrative of social engineering, transforming culture required the reorganisation of socialisation on non-traditional and scientific principles. They believed that through the process of cultivating the development of healthy personalities, culture itself could be restructured for the good of society as a whole.[425] Socialisation had acquired a counter-cultural impulse.

425 Bryson (2009) pp.374–375, 379.

Chapter 6: Quest for Moral Authority

The imperative of social engineering sought to recast human relations as a technical issue, the solution to which lay in the domain of science. John Dewey and other progressive commentators justified this approach on the ground that new technology and rapid change had created a world where people's affairs were dominated by 'remote and invisible organizations' that were too complex to be apprehended by laymen.[426] What followed from Dewey's prognosis of mechanical forms of behaviour and interaction was the necessity for the project of human engineering. 'The age of human engineering is with us', declared one of Dewey's supporters, who stated that 'where it will take us no one may safely predict, but its changes promise to be more revolutionary than those science has recently introduced, and of vastly more importance for man.'[427]

The metaphor of engineering favoured by its advocates evoked a world where the application of science and technology would transform society and replace conflict and war with benevolent forms of management and administration. In practice, social engineering had the far more modest objectives of modifying behaviour and providing technical solutions to social problems. *Social Engineering* was the name of the journal of the League for Social Services. Launched in 1899, it conveyed the impression that social work and social engineering were synonymous. The self-conscious designation of social engineering for social work and family guidance continued into the 1950s.[428]

From its inception, the liberal sections of the self-identified social engineering movement believed that they were in the business of promoting democratic values. The historian Andrew Jewett refers to supporters of this movement as 'scientific democrats'.[429] Jewett ascribed the motive of supporting democracy to this movement, even though he recognises that many of its leading participants 'did not necessarily' possess a 'lofty view of the average citizen's cognitive capacities' or the 'potentialities of public deliberation as a political force'.[430]

426 J. Dewey (1954) *The Public and Its Problems*, Denver: Alan Swallow, p.98.
427 F.E. Andrews (1932) 'Human engineering', *North American Review*, 233(6), 511–518, at p.511.
428 See M.B. Sussman (1955), *Sourcebook in Marriage and the Family*, New York: Houghton Mifflin, for a discussion of applied social engineering.
429 A. Jewett (2012) *Science, Democracy and the American University: From the Civil War to the Cold War*, Cambridge: Cambridge University Press.
430 Jewett (2012) p.282.

https://doi.org/10.1515/9783110708899-007

From the outset, social engineering sought to de-politicise conflict and displace ideologically driven policy making with its apparently neutral scientific approach to public affairs. It sought to gain legitimacy on the ground that, unlike other institutions, it embodied disinterestedness. A key argument for its advocacy of the rule of experts was that it removed the main issues of the day from the grubby world of conflicting interests into the rational and disinterested sphere of science. One of the objectives of the turn of the 20th century progressives was to 'remove politicians from the center of action, replacing them with social scientists who control social structures after the manner of engineers taming raging rivers'.[431] The flip-side of their deification of the rule of unelected, disinterested expert was their low estimation of the value of democracy.

The radical liberal and progressive British philosopher Bertrand Russell's *The Scientific Outlook* (1919) offered a paradigmatic example of how an endorsement of the authority of science coexisted with a sceptical stance towards democracy. He explained that 'equality, like liberty, is difficult to reconcile with scientific technique' and that though 'democratic forms may be preserved in politics' they will have 'little content'. Russell indicated that since an 'ordinary man cannot hope to understand "technical questions", society would be ruled by experts'.[432] Though Russell was more sympathetic to democracy than most of his co-thinkers, he was in no doubt that eugenic scientific principles justified preventing 'unfit' parents from having children.[433] Moreover, his supposedly disinterested scientific point of view led him to predict that 'as time goes on we may expect a greater and greater percentage of the population to be regarded as mentally defective from the point of view of parenthood'.[434] Russell's paternalistic impulses were and continue to be shared by all the different strands – from left to right – of social engineers.

The failure to see an inconsistency between advocacy of a paternalistic form of expert authority and genuine democracy is characteristic of an important blind spot within the outlook of social engineering. They did not regard citizens as their equals but as targets of their intervention. Many scientific democrats embraced the metaphor of 'society as patient' and assumed that they – and only they – possessed the insights necessary for curing the diseases of culture. They believed that 'science could shape new kinds of citizens'.[435] To achieve

---

431 M. Bamta (1996) 'Review: *Machine-Age Ideology, Social Engineering and American Liberalism, 1911–1939* by John M. Jordan', *American Quarterly*, 48(1), 121–127, at 123.

432 B. Russell (1919) *The Scientific Outlook*, London: George Allen & Unwin Ltd, p.229.

433 Russell (1919) p.229.

434 Russell (1919) p.229.

435 Jewett (2012) p.21.

this objective, they adopted psychology as their main instrument and from the 1940s acted on the assumption that changing/altering/reforming/enlightening people's personality was the precondition for reforming society.

Promoters of scientism regarded global organisations as ideal institutions to promote their project. Post-Second World War international organisations – the WHO, UNESCO, World Federation for Mental Health – publicised the use of scientific expertise to solve the problems facing humankind. They declared that their disinterested science could ameliorate the condition of humanity. UNESCO, in particular, was devoted to the project of ridding the world of prejudice and authoritarianism. The Preamble of its Constitution stated that 'since wars begin in the minds of men, it is in the minds of men that the defences of peace must be constructed'.[436] The project of educating the 'minds of men' was, according to a study of UNESCO's founding ideology, 'effectively equivalent to an experiment in social engineering on a global scale'.[437]

Some social engineers assumed that they had the authority to mould and shape people's opinions. Edward Bernays, a leading pioneer in the field of public relations and propaganda, was unabashed in his advocacy of engineering consent. In his influential essay, 'The engineering of consent' (1947), he explained that governments need to use 'an engineering approach – that is, action based only on thorough knowledge of the situation and on the application of scientific principles and tried practices to the task of getting people to support ideas and programs'. He justified the need to use psychological techniques to engineer consent on the ground that governments could not wait until the public understood the wisdom of its proposals. He wrote:

> The average American adult has only six years of schooling behind him. With pressing crises and decisions to be faced, a leader frequently cannot wait for the people to arrive at even general understanding. In certain cases, democratic leaders must play their part in leading the public through the engineering of consent to socially constructive goals and values.[438]

Bernays' paternalistic sentiment towards the average American adult was based on two characteristic features of the ethos of social engineering: the assumption of the moral superiority of the scientific expert and a deeply held mistrust of de-

436 Cited in W. Stoczkowski (2009) 'UNESCO's doctrine of human diversity: a secular soteriology?', *Anthropology Today*, 25(3), 7–11, at 7.

437 Stoczkowski (2009) p.7.

438 E.L. Bernays (1947) 'The engineering of consent', *Annals of the American Academy of Political and Social Science*, 250(1), 113–120, at 114–115.

mocracy and of the 'average' person. Suspicion towards the politics of public life led to a preference for technical solutions to the problems facing society.

Social engineering, with its promise that science could solve the problem of human conflict, was widely disseminated in the media and institutions of education. The meaning of the term 'social engineering' was rarely elaborated upon. For example, in 1951 one source stated that 'social engineering is democratic and scientific problem solving'.[439] However, what was at stake was not simply the application of techniques of problem solving but of a veritable ideology for the management of society. In his influential bestseller, *The Organization Man* (1956), Whyte drew attention to the unstated and protean character of this ideology. He wrote of a 'popular ideology' that interlocked 'separate credos' and which was 'highly elastic'. Whyte highlighted *scientism* as one of the core components of this ideology.

Whyte drew attention to the widespread interest in the science of human relationships and human engineering. He was struck by the growing cohort of social engineers busy practising their craft in different sectors of economic and public life and the similar sensibility that they tended to display. He wrote that 'no matter what branch of social engineering a man is engaged in – "mass" communication, "the engineering of consent," public relations, advertising, personnel counselling – he can feel himself part of a larger movement'.[440]

Whyte commented that some social engineers possessed a utopian vision that energised them to regard 'science' as not 'merely a tool' but as the only path to salvation in a world where 'laymen have gone mad'.[441] As experts, they felt entitled to guide or manipulate the public. He concluded that the 'real impact of scientism is upon our values'.[442] Whyte highlighted how apparently politically neutral 'experts in human relations' succeeded in challenging prevailing values and replacing them with their own.

Numerous social commentators in the 1950s and 1960s – Whyte, David Riesman, Herbert Marcuse – sounded their concern about the diverse forms of psychological techniques used to manipulate public opinion. Vance Packard's bestseller, *Hidden Persuaders* (1957) offered a sensationalist account of the way consumers' desires were manipulated by the advertising industry. Although many of these commentaries went far too far in their evocation of the omnipotent

439 https://books.google.co.uk/books?id=mUpLAQAAMAAJ&q=%22social+engineering%22&dq=%22social+engineering%22&hl=en&sa=X&ved=0ahUKEwiJ3ZvxycnmAhXgQEEAHTE1BuE4ChDoAQgpMAA (accessed 7 September 2019).

440 W. Whyte (1956) *The Organization Man*, New York: Simon and Schuster, p.27.

441 Whyte (1956) p.27.

442 Whyte (1956) p.31.

forces of manipulation, there is little doubt that psychology was increasingly deployed – with varying degree of success – to manage public opinion.

'During this century we have learned to reject authority', stated the 1962 Reith Lecturer, the psychiatrist George Carstairs, who nevertheless seized upon the authority of science to declare that 'the explosive expansion of science' has introduced 'something new into human experience'; a 'mental climate favourable to new forms of political organization, world-wide in scope'.[443] Post-war scientism was drawn towards a globalist vision and often appeared to favour international institutions over national ones. Through outsourcing authority to international institutions, its advocates sought to de-politicise conflict and claimed to offer a superior alternative to the messy business of politics.

Although at times social engineers possessed an ambition to harness the power of science and technology to transform society, their main focus tended to be on the re-engineering of humans and the way they related to one another. For some of them, the vision of society as machine gave way to the person as machine. For social engineers, altering behaviour through techniques of behaviour modification appeared as the most promising way of achieving their objectives. That is why behaviourism and behaviourist psychology played such a central role in social engineering projects. The conviction that behaviour 'could be shaped to fit social goals by those who understood the nature of those goals and the means of achieving them' inspired social reformers and progressive activists.[444] Invariably, social engineers concluded that it was through early intervention in childhood that they could realise their objective of controlling people's behaviour. Hence the importance they attached to developing 'appropriate techniques of socialization' for engineering people's personality.[445]

The quest for authority

The transformation of social engineering into an ideology that relied on the authority of science and of experts was accomplished through the influence and activity of a variety of diverse interests and movements. In the first instance, social engineering and its promotion of scientism aimed to establish a new, for-

443 George Carstairs, 'The changing British character', Lecture 6, Reith Lectures, transmission 17 December 1962, Home Service.

444 See J.A. Mills (1998) *Control: A History of Behavioral Psychology*, New York: New York University Press, p.8.

445 Mills (1998) p.163.

ward-looking authority to replace the different forms of traditional moral authority, which appeared to be swiftly unravelling.

Challenging traditional forms of authority and moral norms, and projecting science as the legitimate foundation of authority, were high on the agenda of social engineering. Although the authority of science was frequently presented as amoral and value free, its representatives implicitly and often explicitly drew attention to its moral superiority over its competitors. This argument was eloquently outlined by the social theorist Robert Merton in his essay, 'A note on science and democracy'. Written in 1942, in the midst of the war against fascism, Merton presented science as a moral and cultural weapon to be wielded against anti-democratic forces. In what he characterised as the 'revolutionary conflict of cultures', Merton drew attention to the unique moral status of the scientist. He claimed that 'it is probable that the reputability of science and its lofty ethical status in the estimate of the layman is in no small measure due to technological achievements'. To reinforce this claim, he stated 'every new technology bears witness to the integrity of the scientist'.[446] For Merton, the normative foundation of scientific authority was constituted by its capacity to achieve results – it was true because it worked; its utility was its truth.[447]

At a time when traditional sources of legitimation appeared exhausted, science appeared to possess a singular capacity to provide society with an authoritative guide to the future. The vanishing of tradition was an invitation to the reconstitution of authority in a new form. In an era of scientific and technological progress, the project of reconstituting authority was drawn inevitably towards the status enjoyed by technical expertise and specialised knowledge. But unlike traditional authority, which touched on every dimension of the human experience, the authority of the expert was confined to that which could be exercised through reason. Joseph Raz writes that the 'authority of the expert can be called theoretical authority, for it is an authority about what to believe'.[448]

Raz observed that unlike political authority, which 'provides reason for action', theoretical authority 'provides reason for belief'.[449] However, while it is valid to draw a conceptual distinction between these two forms of authority, historical experience suggests that expertise easily becomes politicised. With the passage of time, the distinction between these two forms of authority becomes blurred, and the very fragility of political authority encourages a process where-

---

446 Merton, R. (1942) 'A Note on Science and Technology in a Democratic Order', *Journal of Legal and Political Sociology*, vol.1, no.12, pp.115–126, p.117.

447 Merton (1942).

448 J. Raz (1990) *Authority*, Oxford: Basil Blackwell, p.2.

449 Raz (1990), p.5.

by politicians outsource their power to experts. 'Governments find expert advice to be an indispensable resource for formulating and justifying policy and, more subtly, for removing some issues from the political domain by transforming them into technical questions', writes Stephen Hilgartner.[450]

Terrence Ball suggests that the potential for the politicisation of expertise can be understood through considering the distinction between epistemic and epistemocratic authority. Epistemic authority is 'that which is ascribed to the possessor of specialized knowledge, skills, or expertise'.[451] For example, this form of authority works through deference to doctors on medical matters and lawyers on legal affairs. Epistemocratic authority, 'by contrast, refers to the claim of one class, group, or person to rule another by virtue of the former's possessing specialized authority not available to the latter'.[452] Ball argues that:

> [E]pistemocractic authority is therefore conceptually parasitic upon epistemic authority. Or, to put it slightly differently, epistemocratic authority attempts to assimilate political authority to the non-political epistemic authority of the technician or expert.[453]

Ball claims that the conceptual distinction between political rule and expert authority in modern society becomes 'blurred if not meaningless'. In effect, the epistemocratic imperative extends the claim of expertise to the domain of political and public life, assimilating moral and political issues to 'the paradigm of epistemic authority' and asserting that 'politics and ethics are activities in which there are experts'.[454] The influence exercised by epistemocratic authority today is shown by the constant slippage between scientific advice and moral and political exhortations on issues as diverse as public health and childrearing. The influence of managerial and technocratic ideals on public life indicates that the epistemocratic ideal is one 'to which political reality in some respects increasingly corresponds'.[455]

Reservations about the influence that expertise could exercise over public life coexisted with the conviction that its authority was indispensable for maintenance of order in a modern society. Many supported expertise because of its capacity for transforming moral questions into impersonal, technocratic ones.

450 S. Hilgartner (2000) *Science on Stage: Expert Advice as Public Drama*, Stanford: Stanford University Press, p.146.

451 T. Ball (1987) 'Authority and conceptual change', in Pennock, J.R. and Chapman, J.W. (eds) *Authority Revisited*, New York: New York University Press, p.48.

452 Ball (1987) p.48.

453 Ball (1987) p.48.

454 Ball (1987) p.51.

455 Ball (1987) p.51.

In this way scientism – the politicisation of science – promised to de-politicise the question of authority. One of its consequences was to undermine the moral foundation on which adult authority rested, which in turn had the effect of unleashing a dynamic that would turn socialisation into a *site of permanent cultural conflict.* The quest for a new foundation for authority was the point of departure for the eventual surfacing of the crisis of identity and its subsequent politicisation.

The re-engineering of the normative foundation of society

One of the impulses that motivated the promotion of the authority of science was the aspiration to develop a new normative foundation for human society. William I. Thomas, a leading American sociologist, declared that once 'we have a science of rational control', then 'we can establish any attitudes and values whatever'.[456] Social scientists possessed a firm conviction that 'science could itself provide norms for the reconstruction of human life'.[457] Social engineering was in all but name *moral engineering.*

Dewey wrote of 'the technique of social and moral engineering', which relied on the natural sciences acquiring a normative content.[458] He hoped that in this way the ethical value of science would form the foundation for human moral conduct. Moral life comes to resemble the pursuit of science. 'It is rendered flexible, vital, growing', argued Dewey.[459] Thus, moral reasoning turns into a species of scientific inquiry that can be tested, modified and re-engineered. For Dewey, the scientific method is the moral method used for investigation of the 'engineering of mind'. For Dewey, the reconstruction of morality was conterminous with science acquiring a status previously accorded to religion. Decades later, one of Dewey's disciples, the philosopher Richard Rorty, declared that his goal was to revive Deweyan 'social engineering', conceived as the 'substitute for traditional religion'.[460]

---

456 Cited in D. Ross (1994) 'Modernist social science in the land of the new/old', in Ross, D. (ed.) *Modernist Impulses in the Human Sciences, 1870–1930*, Baltimore: Johns Hopkins University Press, p.187.
457 Ross (1994) p.187.
458 Dewey (1920) p.174.
459 Dewey (1920) p.175.
460 Cited in T. Pangle (1993) *The Ennobling of Democracy: The Challenge of the Postmodern Age*, Baltimore: JHU Press, p.63.

The search for the 'science of rational control' invariably led progressive social engineers to the conclusion that 'science, guided by expert minds, would enable the control of social phenomena, primarily by adjusting people to their changing environment'.[461] This was to be achieved by drawing on the resources provided by psychology, a science that held out the promise of adjusting people to adopt the ethos of social engineering. Burnham depicted psychology as the scientific wing of the American progressive movement, which held the view that human beings were malleable and under the guidance of experts 'could make and remake' their world.[462] American psychology was permeated with a technoscientific attitude that stressed the twin goals of knowledge and application, of science and practice, often employed in the service of increased order, efficiency, rationalisation and control.[463] Psychology's technoscientific attitude encouraged it to acquire a 'social engineering function', which to a greater or lesser extent persists to this day.[464]

In the interwar decades, the quest for order and control also often possessed a utopian dimension. Leading behaviourist psychologists like Watson and Skinner sought to 'win a cultural battle' against views that they regarded as obstacles to progress. Watson in particular promoted ideas regarding childrearing and family life with a view to bringing about social and cultural change.[465]

From the outset, social engineering deployed its ideology of scientism to undermine and discredit traditional cultural norms. Scientism relies on the well-earned prestige enjoyed by the sciences. However, it inappropriately expands its application to the resolution and management of problems in the moral, social and political spheres. The most effective instrument that scientism had at its disposal was psychology. Psychology offered a scientific equivalent to what was in the 19th century referred to as moral therapy. Unlike moral therapy, which conveyed explicit normative and value- related assumptions, psychology presented itself as a value-neutral science that was freed from traditional morality. Brinkmann points out that psychology sought to instrumentalise morality. For exam-

461 J.G. Morawski (1982) 'Assessing psychology's moral heritage through our neglected utopias', *American Psychologist*, 37(10), 1082–1095, at 1090.

462 J.C. Burnham (1960) 'Psychiatry, psychology and the progressive movement', *American Quarterly*, 12(4), 457–465, at 458.

463 A. Rutherford (2017) 'BF Skinner and technology's nation: technocracy, social engineering, and the good life in 20th-century America', *History of Psychology*, 20(3), 290–312, at 291.

464 Rutherford (2017) p.291.

465 R.F. Rakos (2013) 'John B. Watson's 1913 "Behaviorist Manifesto": setting the stage for behaviorism's social action legacy', *Revista Mexicana de Análisis de la Conducta*, 39(2), 99–118, at 102.

ple, the 'early methods of personality re-formation called "moral therapy" were transformed into the value neutral notion of "psychotherapy"'.[466] The shift from moral therapy to a 'nonmoral psychology' helped to reduce morality to psychology, which meant that over time the 'value of anything' came to be determined by its psychological function.[467] Commenting on the historical development of this trend, Justman stated that 'nothing has done more to discredit the very language of morality than psychology'.[468]

In his study of the history of psychology, Danziger underlines the shift from this profession's focus from character to personality. As Danziger explains, character, with its 'moral overtones', gradually gave way to a focus on personality. He suggests that 'the decisive factor favouring the emergence of "personality" as the description of a twentieth-century psychological object was probably its preceding medicalization'.[469] Unlike character, which was a moral accomplishment and was associated with ideals like, duty, courage and integrity, personality could be discussed in terms of scientifically validated traits that psychologists could treat. Psychological concepts did not merely displace moral ones; they were also deployed to pathologise forms of behaviour influenced by strongly held moral sentiments. As Justman pointed out, 'not only' does psychology 'efface moral issues and unwrite the very language of moral judgment, it intimates that such judgment is a hindrance to human emancipation, even a disease'.[470] In recent decades the diseasing of judgment has gained powerful cultural validation to the point that it has become the cultural norm.[471]

Psychology's displacement of moral authority had a profound impact on the authority of religion. As Rieff wrote, for more than a century now, theologians have been 'screening psychologists in the hope of finding one who could rescue theology for them'.[472] The Anglican Bishop, Frank Russell Barry was hopeful and yet ambiguous about the Church's relation with psychology. In his *Christianity and Psychology* (1923), he wrote of 'the terrific strain to which all were subjected, and from which we have none of us as yet fully recovered' and which 'forced the mind back, as it were, upon itself, and created an unprecedented interest in the

466 Brinkmann (2010) p.9.

467 Brinkmann (2010) p.36.

468 S. Justman (1998) *The Psychological Mystique*, Evanston: Northwestern University Press, p.127.

469 Danziger (1997) p.125.

470 Justman (1998) p.128.

471 See F. Furedi (2020) *Why Borders Matter and Why Humanity Must Relearn the Art of Drawing Borders*, London: Routledge, ch. 1.

472 Rieff (2006) p.64.

specifically mental sciences, as well as in spiritism and similar cult'. He asserted; 'We are all psychologists today.'[473] Gradually Christian theologians in the Anglo-American world came to regard psychology as an ally, that could help them to respond to a need which religion alone could not fulfil.[474]

Written three years before his death, Stanley Hall's 'The message of the Zeitgeist' (1921) served as a call to arms for psychology to assume its role as the principal instrument for civilisational renewal. For Hall, psychology was not an instrument simply for curing individual illness but also society as a whole. In line with one of the main tenets of the ideology of social engineering, Hall called for a break with 'the reckoning of the past'.[475] Striking a modernist tone, he wrote that

> there is a new discontent with old leaders, standards, criteria, methods and values, and a demand everywhere for new ones, a realization that mankind must now reorient itself and take its bearings from the eternal stars and sail no longer into the unknown future by the dead reckonings of the past.[476]

He wrote of a world that was ill and required a 'great physician for its soul'.[477] Stalin, who referred to his favourite novelists as 'engineers of human souls', was clearly on the same page as Hall.[478]

Hall wrote of the need for the 'psychological pedagogue' to become an 'engineer in the domain of nature',[479] and referred to psychologists as a 'sort of high priest of souls', who were 'not content merely to fit men for existing institutions as they are to-day' but would 'develop even higher powers, which gradually molt old and evolve new and better institutions or improve old ones'.[480]

Hall's utopian vision was to be overseen by scientific experts and intellectuals:

> Henceforth, as never before, progress is committed to the hands of the intellectuals and they must think harder, realizing to the full the responsibilities of their new leadership. Sci-

473 F.R. Barry (1923) *Christianity and Psychology*, London: Student Christian Movement, p.16.
474 See the discussion in G. Richards (2000a) 'Psychology and the churches in Britain 1919–39: symptoms of conversion', *History of the Human Sciences*, 13(2), 57–84.
475 S. Hall (1921) 'The message of the Zeitgeist' *Scientific Monthly*, 13(2), 106–116, at 107.
476 Hall (1921) p.107.
477 www.theguardian.com/books/2011/aug/19/engineers-of-the-soul-review (accessed 5 April 2019).
478 See the discussion in www.theguardian.com/books/2011/aug/19/engineers-of-the-soul-review (accessed 5 April 2019).
479 Cited in Morawski (1982) p.1085.
480 Cited in Morawski (1982) p.1085.

> ence in its largest sense is from this time forth to rule the world. The age of laissez faire is ended and research, discovery, investigation, and invention, which have done so much already, must now take the helm and be our pioneers in this new era. In everything it is the expert who must say the final word.[481]

Hall appointed the university as the 'chief shrine' and 'powerhouse' of the spirit of social engineering. He described the university as the 'new church of science', where intellectuals with a calling are 'smitten with the passion of adding something to the sum of the world's knowledge.[482] Nodding in agreement, the psychologist James McKeen Cattell stated 'scientific men should take the place that is theirs as masters of the modern world'.[483]

It is evident that their claim to scientific objectivity notwithstanding, these high priests of the soul often strayed into the domain of morality and their psychological language communicated values in a medicalised form. Erikson's conceptualisation of identity crisis is instructive in this respect. He recognised that the crisis of identity had an important normative dimension. He wrote at length of a 'normative identity crisis' facing adolescents and, as some commentaries have indicated, some of the case studies he uses in his *Childhood and Society*, read 'like a handbook of dos and don'ts for raising children'.[484] Though his normative assumptions are conveyed in a medicalised psychological vocabulary, it is evident that his arguments aim to promote objectives that are value and politics related. As Giorgi contends, 'at societal level, the objective is to promote "social health", "cultural solidarity" and "the reduction of economic and political prejudice which denies a sense of identity to youth"'.[485]

The re-engineering of the moral foundation of society was and continues to be pursued through the medicalisation of human experience. In 1975, the theologian and philosopher Ivan Illich captured this trend with the phrase 'medicalization of life' to draw attention to the relentless 'proliferation of medical agents', which perversely had the effect of 'decreasing, the organic and psychological coping ability of ordinary people'.[486] Sol Cohen has argued that the 'post-World War II climate was especially favourable' to the promotion of psychologically informed cultural norms. He wrote that 'the mental hygiene point of view became part of the common stock of knowledge, the "conceptual small change

481 Hall (1921) p.113.
482 Hall (1921) p.116.
483 Cited in Morawski (1982) p.1091.
484 Giorgi (2017) p.50.
485 Giorgi (2017) p.50.
486 I. Illich (1975) 'The medicalization of life', *Journal of Medical Ethics*, 1(2), 73–77, at 77.

of the mass media," celebrated on the musical stage, in the movies, and in literature, a language which had deeply penetrated the zeitgeist of the country'.[487]

As an influential cultural force, medicalisation was first institutionalised in the domain of socialisation and particularly in education. In his study of the medicalisation of American education, Cohen convincingly argues that during the interwar era progressive educators and psychiatrists advocating the ethos of mental hygiene succeeded in replacing traditional disciplinary pedagogy with a therapeutic one. They targeted 'three sources of stress in the school that had to be rectified: failure, the academic subject-matter-centred curriculum, and disciplinary procedures'.[488] To realise their aim of re-engineering children's personality, they argued for the de-emphasis of academic subject matter. A study on progressive education theory concurs with this assessment and draws attention to its 'intense concern for the psychological development of children'.[489] Educating the personality of children also coincided with the agenda of the business community, who believed that the acquisition of traits like adaptability and flexibility would help enhance the quality of the workforce.

The crusade to transform the purpose of education towards the goal of promoting the mental health of children was ratified in 1950 at the historic Mid-Century White House Conference on Children and Youth. The conference took as its slogan 'A Healthy Personality for Every Child'. This conference concluded with the statement that 'the school' must 'assume the primary responsibility for the healthy development of the whole personality of each child'.[490]

Students of educational reform have argued that it takes several generations before its ideals become institutionalised. The diffusion of reforms into everyday classroom practice can take up to half a century.[491] The time scale for the diffusion of therapeutic education was far more rapid. Moreover, from the mid-20th century its presence in the classroom increased decade by decade. Raising self-esteem, teaching emotional literacy, resilience, grit, wellness and mindfulness are some of the therapeutic fads adopted by schools in recent decades.

The constant expansion of the medicalisation of education has a significance that goes way beyond its impact on the school curriculum. Compulsory education provided a ready-made target audience for the project of socialising young people to internalise therapeutic values. As Cohen concluded, 'the body of ideas bequeathed' to education 'by the mental hygiene movement are now

487 Cohen (1983) p.139.
488 Cohen (1983) p.130.
489 Zilversmit (1993) p.12.
490 See Cohen (1983) p.139.
491 See Cohen (1983) p.139.

part of our "common-sense"'.[492] Moreover, this common sense has over the decades become integral to the way that western culture gives meaning to human experience. The medicalisation of education has played a significant role in the transmission of therapeutic cultural norms throughout society.

The main reason why the imperative of medicalisation did not become a subject of serious deliberation until the 1970s is because its normative ideological ambitions were rarely made explicit. It is difficult to give the movement devoted to the re-engineering of socialisation a name. Cohen's characterisation of this movement is apposite in that it

> can best be understood if treated not as an autonomous medical or scientific discipline, but as an ideology with a social function, the more effective because of the assumed neutrality of the medical profession and by virtue of its scientific sounding language of health and disease.[493]

Its scientific rhetoric, along with its claim of professional neutrality, coincided with a 'psychiatric vision of salvation' from the regime of traditional attitudes and values that allegedly distorted children's personality. In the 21st century, the ethos of medicalisation is communicated in a more downbeat language but, if anything, it exercises a far greater influence over western culture than it did during the previous century.

Displacing the political

Political ideologues and capitalist entrepreneurs alike looked to the authority of science for advancing their cause. Milovan Djilas, the prominent dissident in communist Yugoslavia, wrote in his *New Class* (1957) that 'being very practical men, the Communist leaders, immediately establish cooperation with technicians and scientists, not paying attention to their "bourgeois" views'.[494] Even the Nazi Government in Germany sought to legitimate is policies on the basis of its racial science. Habermas observed that in the post-war period, technology and science worked as a quasi-ideology: he wrote of the 'scientization of political power' and argued that politicians had become increasingly dependent on professionals.[495]

492 Cohen (1983) p.139.

493 Cohen (1983) pp.141–142.

494 M. Djilas (1957) *New Class*, London: Thames and Hudson, p.134.

495 Habermas [1967] (1987) *Toward a Rational Society*, London: Polity Press, p.63.

For businessmen, social engineering promised efficiency and harmonious relations with labour. For reformers, it held out the possibility of taming the conflicts associated with mass society and competing political interests. Scientism and moral engineering appeared as a powerful antidote to the irrational ways of traditional customs. They also served as instruments for de-politicising public life and insulating the ruling elites from the constant pressure exerted by the mass electorate. Although the aspiration for control transcended the ideological divide, the politicisation of science and its transformation into the quasi-ideology of scientism was most systematically pursued by American progressives, British New Liberals and Swedish Social Democrats. These movements sought to offer an apolitical alternative that acclaimed science the supreme authority for managing society.[496]

Already in the early decades of the 20th century, social psychology in the guise of a scientific analysis had served as the basis for a political critique of the irrational emotions that apparently surface in a mass democracy. The new elitist psychologists claimed that 'democracy, equality, and liberty alike were incompatible with human nature and its instinctual crowd propensity'.[497] In the decades to follow, their explicit elitist disdain for democracy became more muted. However, in one important respect their critique of democracy anticipates a recurring theme in political psychology. They constantly draw attention to the disposition of people towards the acceptance of authoritarianism.

Towards the late 1930s, because of its endorsement by authoritarian regimes, social engineering lost some of its explicit appeal. Karl Popper noted that 'the term "social technology"' and 'even more the term "social engineering" is likely to arouse suspicion and to repel those whom it reminds of the "social blueprints" of the collectivist planners, or perhaps even of the "technocrats"'. Popper opted to add the word 'piecemeal' to his form of social engineering in order to 'off-set undesirable associations'.[498] During the 1960s the term 'social engineering' often tended to invite negative connotations. In a series of essays written in the 1960s titled *The End of Ideology*, Daniel Bell indicated that the idea of a new utopia of social harmony realised through social engineering had little appeal for intellectuals.[499] In more recent decades, the term 'social engineering' has suffered from its association with the failure of planning in com-

496 Diner (1998) p.7.

497 R.N. Soffer (1969) 'New elitism: social psychology in prewar England', *Journal of British Studies*, 8(2), 111–140, at 115.

498 K. Popper (1986) *The Poverty of Historicism*, London: Ark Paperbacks, p.65.

499 Cited in B. Carlson (2005) 'Social engineering, 1899–1999: an odyssey through The New York Times', *American Studies in Scandinavia*, 37(1), 69–94, at 81.

munist societies and the loss of legitimacy suffered by large-scale social programmes of the welfare state.

Nevertheless, social engineering has retained its influence, albeit in a more implicit and less utopian form than in the past. Its persistence has been underwritten by the continued demand for control. The liberal economist Friedrich Hayek, one of the most forceful critics of scientism, wrote in the early 1950s that 'the universal demand for "conscious" control or direction of social processes is one of the most characteristic features of our generation', for 'it expresses perhaps more clearly than any of its other cliches the peculiar spirit of the age'.[500] Hayek claimed that the 'engineering point of view, is much greater than it is generally realized' and that the desire 'to apply engineering technique to the solution of social problems has become very explicit'.[501] In this respect, Hayek proved to be prescient.

Back in the late 1960s, writing about the 'scientization of politics and public opinion', the political philosopher Jürgen Habermas wrote that, as an ideology, scientism permeated all social institutions, leading to the 'depoliticization of the mass of populations'.[502] Since Habermas wrote those words, the scientisation of political life has gone much further than at any time during the modern era. The past 40 years has seen the institutionalisation of a form of technocratic governance that justifies its legitimacy on the ground that it eschews all ideology and that its policies are evidence based. The very fragility of political authority encourages a process whereby politicians outsource their power to experts.

A radical illustration of the outsourcing of decision making to science occurred during the Covid pandemic, when governments constantly asserted that their policies were 'following the science'. The representation of scientific activity as a stand-alone The Science constitutes an important development in the narrative of scientism. The rhetorical mutation of science into what is referred to as The Science highlights the ideological turn towards scientism. Unlike genuine science, which subscribes to the ethos of open-ended experimentation, 'The Science' is an ideological and political construct. The placing of a definite article, 'the', before science represents a slippage from a scientific fact that can be questioned to an unanswerable moral dogma.

Though in theory technocratic governance presents itself as apolitical and untainted by moral assumptions, its ideological preference becomes exposed whenever its theory is put into practice. Take the science of parenting and of so-

---

500 F.A. Hayek (1952) *The Counter-revolution of Science: Studies on the Abuse of Reason*, Glencoe: Free Press, p.87.

501 Hayek (1952) p.94.

502 Habermas [1967] (1987) pp. 75, 81.

cialisation and its claim of professional disinterestedness. Experts constantly claim that their science entitles them to be the authoritative voices on issues that were hitherto perceived as strictly pertaining to the domain of personal and family life. From their perspective, childrearing, education and relationships needed to be reorganised in accordance with the latest finding of scientific research. However, these experts possessed a powerful crusading ethos that went way beyond the findings of scientific research. Kessen wrote that:

> Critical examination and study of parental practices and child behaviour almost inevitably slipped subtly over to advice about parental practices and child behaviour. The scientific statement became an ethical imperative, the descriptive account became normative.[503]

Nor did experts merely provide advice. Often with the backing of official institutions they could impose their policies on schools and directly influence the conduct of family life. As against the authority of science, the insights and values of ordinary people enjoyed little cultural valuation.

Decades of parental advice of a scientific and psychologically informed pedagogy have failed to live up to their promise of producing well-adjusted children with healthy personalities. Indeed, the medicalisation of socialisation has had the perverse effect of intensifying the sense of emotional disorientation among young people and creating the conditions for the flourishing of a crisis of identity.

Backlash against moral engineering

The project of social engineering, which was devoted to providing a scientific solution to the problem of control and order, frequently strayed into the domain of moral norms. The politicisation of expertise rarely confined itself strictly to technical matters. From the outset of its emergence in the 19th century, expert authority claimed a moral status that was superior to the rest of society. 'Precisely because there were truths that no honest investigator could deny, the power to make decisions had to be placed in the hands of experts whose authority rested on special knowledge rather than raw self-assertiveness, or party patronage, or a majority vote of the incompetent', wrote Haskell.[504] The work of science was

503 Kessen (1979) p.818.
504 T.L. Haskell [1977] (2000) *The Emergence of Professional Social Science: The American Social Science Association and the Nineteenth-Century Crisis of Authority*, Baltimore: Johns Hopkins University Press, p.87.

often associated with the 'purity of the scientist' and a 'refined moral sensibility'.[505]

The case for affirming the unique moral status of the expert was clearly stated by E.A. Ross in 1906, when he wrote of the need for moral experts on the ground that the 'judgments' of 'the average man' are 'inconsistent and thoughtless'.[506] During the decades following Ross' call for moral expertise, many psychologists rose to the occasion. Some, like B.F. Skinner, argued that behavioural engineers are the one group of scientists whose purview includes making value judgments. He asserted that scientists like biologists and physicists may not have more wisdom than their fellow citizens but 'behavioural scientists apparently do'.[507] Unlike Skinner, most social engineers eschewed to explicitly adopt the role of moral expertise. However, in practice, through their critique of traditional morality, they contributed to its de-legitimation.

Chisholm took pride in his profession's refusal to acquiesce to the demands of traditional morality. 'The fact is that most psychiatrists and psychologists and many other people have escaped from these moral chains and are able to observe and think freely from the magic fears of our ancestors'.[508] Calling on his profession to accept its responsibility 'to remodel the world', Chisholm sought to create a new moral order. To realise this objective, people had to be taught 'to put rational thinking in place of obsolete concepts of right and wrong'.[509] The casual manner with which Chisholm indicted moral values with which he disagreed indicated that he was no less a moralist than those who he accused of promoting values he opposed. He was a fervent advocate of world government and world citizenship, which he perceived as morally superior to a national one.[510] He was also a 'naïve moralist', who according to one of his critics considered his 'own system of values not morality but rationality'.[511]

---

505 C.V. Eby (1994) 'Thorstein Veblen and the rhetoric of authority', *American Quarterly*, 46(2), 139–173, at 152.

506 E.A. Ross (1906) 'The nation's need of moral experts', *Current Literature (1888–1912)*, vol. XLI, p.93.

507 H. Kuhlmann (2005) 'Walden Two: a behaviorist utopia', in *Living Walden Two: B. F. Skinner's Behaviorist Utopia and Experimental Communities*, Urbana-Champaign: University of Illinois Press, p.30.

508 Chisholm (1946) p.9.

509 A. Kardiner (1946) 'Western personality and social crisis: a psychiatrist looks at human aggression', *Commentary* 2, 436–442, at 436.

510 J. Farley (2009) *Brock Chisholm, the World Health Organization, and the Cold War*, Vancouver: UBC Press, p.18, n.55.

511 T. Szasz (1989) *Law, Liberty and Psychiatry*, Syracuse: Syracuse University Press, p.3.

The authority of science, particularly through the influence exercised by psychology, proved relatively successful in gradually eroding the influence of traditional morality. Its cultural appeal first emerged in higher education and among the professions, and gradually expanded to elite cultural institutions. From the 1930s onwards it came to dominate school pedagogy, and through the media its influence over popular culture increased incrementally. Even sections of the Church were prepared to give way to psychology's promise of moral authority. In October 1919 a Protestant Pastor, Dr William Rosecrance Prince, informed his audience at New School of Christian or Applied Psychology in Los Angeles that with 'perfection of psychology mankind will reach the perfection predicted for the millennium'.[512]

The challenge that moral engineering posed to the way of life of most people was frequently remarked on by commentators who were uncomfortable with this development. It was in the domain of religion and in schooling that the introduction of anti-traditionalist practices and norms periodically provoked a backlash. In Britain, religious leaders attempted to forge an amicable relation with psychology, until it became clear that they were expected to make most of the concessions. It was only when 'some hardline psychoanalysts adopted an explicitly anti-religious stance' that Church leaders became wary of psychology's impact on their authority.[513] In 1939, Reverend J.C.M. Conn of Kelvinside Old Parish Church, Glasgow, sounded the alarm:

> Make no mistake, contemporary psychology, in some of its forms, has taken the field as an enemy of the Christian religion, making the boldest tremble for his faith in spiritual reality, and offering its own cures for moral ills. The greatest issues of faith are being decided on this front. Is theology or psychology to have the last word as the supreme authority in matters of faith and morals?[514]

As it turned out in the decades to follow, theology came under the influence of psychology far more than the other way around.

It was in education, particularly in the United States, that the backlash against the mounting challenge against traditional values and modes of socialisation was most noticeable. Schooling became the terrain where the earliest traces of what would crystallise into the culture wars of the late 20th and 21st centuries can be located. In American education, the ideology of social engineering through the progressive invisible pedagogy had acquired an authoritative status

---

512 'Devil and Hell are mere superstitions: pastor declares age-old idea has outlived usefulness', *Los Angeles Times*, 13 October 1919.

513 Richards (2000a) p.57.

514 Cited in Richards (2000a) p.58.

within the teaching profession. The invisibility of its pedagogic influence was important because through its practice it could substantially alter the regime of socialisation without appearing to directly challenge pre-existing norms. As Zilversmit's study of progressive educational theory indicates, its prescription 'led to an unattractive reliance on manipulation' of children in the classroom. So-called 'child-centred learning' meant that though children were 'supposedly making their own choices' what they ended up doing was determined in advance; 'the hand of authority was there but so disguised that it could not be readily recognized'.[515]

Through the application of the invisible pedagogy, progressive teachers sought to shape the personality of children in accordance with their own attitude and values. At times sections of the teaching profession became so confident of their authority that they lectured parents not to interfere in the education of their children because they might actually harm them.[516] To many it seemed that progressive education was not only undermining the traditional ethos of socialisation but was also 'Un-American'. During the Cold War in the early 1950s a backlash against progressive education meshed with a wave of anxiety about the influence of communism over American cultural institutions. In response to hostility provoked by progressive education, many of its supporters changed their language and began to refer to it as 'modern education'.[517]

Though the backlash against progressive educated resonated with millions of people it failed to dent its influence over the field of pedagogy. Despite the hostility of successive Republican Governments in the US and of Conservative ones in the UK, in all but name some version of a psychologically informed invisible pedagogy retained influence over the teaching profession.[518] With hindsight, one is struck by the flexibility and adaptability of this pedagogy. For over a century educational psychology held out the promise of the certainty of science and the claim that it could transform children's personality, and make them more adaptable and efficient. Its utilitarian objectives have resonated and continue to resonate with sections of the Establishment concerned about creating a skilled labour force. Others are interested in using invisible pedagogy to alter cultural attitudes in society through cultivating personality traits that distance children from the values of the past. In this way a marriage of convenience

515 Zilversmit (1993) pp.175–176.

516 Zilversmit (1993) p.170.

517 Zilversmit (1993) p.110.

518 An illustration of this continuity is Justman's discussion of teaching literature as a form of therapy that promotes psychological values to children. See S. Justman (2010) 'Bibliotherapy: literature as exploration reconsidered', *Academic Questions*, 23(1), 125–135.

between a technocratically driven skills agenda and a psychologically informed promotion of therapeutic values had succeeded in establishing a hegemonic influence over the socialisation of children in schools.

Moral engineering through the application of a rationalised and medicalised ethos has successfully weathered periodic backlashes to its authority. In part its success has been underwritten by the weakening of other sources of authority and the de-politicisation of public life. Yet, though its outlook exercises a powerful influence over society, its inability to offer a coherent normative foundation for society ensures that it will be continually contested. In spite of considerable efforts, it has failed to become a moral authority in its own right. This was a point that Max Weber, one of the founders of sociology, clearly understood. He approvingly cited the Russian writer Leo Tolstoy: 'Science is meaningless because it gives no answer to the question, the only question important to us: "What shall we do and how shall we live?"'[519]

---

519 M. Weber [1919] (1958) 'Science as a vocation', in Gerth, H. and Mills, C.W. (eds) *From Max Weber: Essays in Sociology*, New York: Oxford University Press, p.143.

Chapter 7: Inventing Authoritarian Personalities

Since its discovery as an important issue for society, deliberations surrounding socialisation were motivated by a variety of different concerns. Childrearing was seized upon as a problem confronting the healthy development of society. At times it was also depicted as the solution to the problems of society. Proponents of a utopian vision of creating a new enlightened humanity through a scientific approach to socialisation competed with those who were interested in the more modest project of limiting the damage caused by incompetent parents. During the 1940s, the more utopian and reformist approaches to socialisation tended to give way to a growing body of opinion that regarded the prevailing regime of childrearing as the cause – direct or indirect – of global conflicts and the rise of authoritarian movements. Preventing children from developing authoritarian personalities permeated the discussion on socialisation in the 1940s.

The Second World War concentrated the mind, and the events surrounding it – before, during and after – reinforced the interest of policy makers, academics and professionals in influencing and reforming the prevailing methods of education and socialisation. In the UK a significant section of the political and cultural Establishment had come around to the view that addressing this problem was of the utmost urgency. This attitude also influenced members of the public, who had become influenced by claims widely disseminated by psychologists to the effect that incompetent forms of parenting were not only responsible for a variety of social problems but also for the scourge of authoritarianism.

According to one account, 'by the end of the war, British men and women had become acutely concerned about the long-term effects of authoritarian, undemocratic, and "affectionless," environments on personality development'.[520]

Long-standing expert opinion that portrayed such family environment as the underpinning of totalitarian societies gained a wider hearing through the media, and influenced post-war public opinion.[521] Psychologists argued for a preventive interventionist approach that would thwart the development of aggressive personalities. To realise this objective, mental health activists demanded that psychology should have an expansive brief; one that would not only deal with individual but also with society-wide pathologies. Representatives from the British

520 T. Chettiar (2013) *The Psychiatric Family: Citizenship, Private Life, and Emotional Health in Welfare-State Britain, 1945–1979*, Ann Arbor: Northwestern University Press, p.103.
521 Chettiar (2013) p.103.

https://doi.org/10.1515/9783110708899-008

Medical Council, the Royal College of Physicians and the Royal Medico-Psychological Association insisted that psychological medicine should break new ground. Their 1945 Report on the *Future Organisation of the Psychiatric Services* stated, 'where psychiatry begins and ends has not been settled. Within the development of preventative medicine its borders will become less rather than more definite.'[522]

In the United States, the campaign to get hold of and reform the regime of socialisation was, if anything, more influential than in the UK and other western societies. After the war, experts 'attributed major troubles in American society to underlying emotional problems, including insecurity, immaturity, and imbalance'.[523] Emotional maladjustment was often linked to the incompetent and misguided way that children were socialised. The emotional problems, whose causation was attributed to socialisation, were portrayed as a threat to social cohesion and were even diagnosed as a danger to democracy.

Benjamin Spock's social engineering approach towards parenting was influenced by his perception of the upheavals of the late 1930s and the catastrophic world war that followed it. The arguments contained in Spock's *Baby and Child Care* were developed against a background of European dictatorship; it was written during the course of the world war. Graebner noted that for Spock 'the child could all too easily come to participate in this tragedy, whether as a timid follower or a charismatic leader-dictator'.[524]

There emerged alongside an unprecedented political interest in mental health, a narrative of anxiety concerning identity and its crisis. Soon, the crisis of identity became one of the narratives through which the deficits surrounding socialisation were discussed. In the decades to follow, this narrative would become increasingly politicised to the point that identity became coupled with politics, and the refrain, the 'Personal is Political' acquired great cultural influence.

In the 1940s psychology and its social engineering ambitions gained widespread currency as policy makers and institutions looked for an antidote to conflict, aggression and war. With the rise of the nuclear age, it was generally assumed that an era of anxiety had arrived and that the mental health of citizens would become a significant issue. As one study outlined, 'by then, many in industry, government, education, medicine, and the media had concluded that life was wellnigh impossible without the guidance of experts in mental

---

522 Cited in R. Hayward (2009) 'Enduring emotions: James L. Halliday and the invention of the psychosocial', *Isis*, 100(4), 827–838, at 829.
523 M. Vicedo (2012) 'Cold War emotions: mother love and the war over human nature', in Solovey, M. and Cravens, H. (eds) *Cold War Social Science*, New York: Palgrave Macmillan, p.4.
524 Graebner (1980) p.613.

health'.[525] A study on 'democratic social engineering' points out how a 'significant contingent' of 'American reformers' turned to social psychology to find a solution to the threat they identified.[526]

The threats identified ranged from the disease of fanaticism that erupted in the 1930s to a variety of personality traits that supported aggressive and intolerant behaviour. In particular, traits associated with an authoritarian personality and a psychological disposition towards conformism and prejudiced behaviour were targeted as the condition requiring mental health intervention. Psychology provided scientific authority for 'the transformation of human beings in line with the prescriptions of theory', noted Justman.[527] His argument, that psychology 'falls into the category of ideology as an argument produced to defend given interest', is an important one for understanding some of the key cultural-political developments during the decades leading up to the current era.

The aim of activists relying on the warrant provided by psychology was not merely to diagnose and treat certain emotional states but also to transform people's personality in accordance with a distinct – if often unacknowledged – political outlook. As we shall see, advocates of social engineering were not simply targeting authoritarian personalities but mobilising psychology against the political ideas they opposed.

The most influential case for the pursuit of political therapy was elaborated in one of the most prominent social science texts of the post-Second World War era, *The Authoritarian Personality*. This text – a product of a major research project undertaken in collaboration between Theodor Adorno and like-minded academic social engineers – was underpinned by the ideological conviction that 'they were not only in the right but scientific, their opponents not only wrong but sick'.[528] Their key opponent was the 'potential fascist', who could be anyone whose personality was disposed towards prejudice and authoritarian behaviour. The marker for becoming a fascist was certain personality traits that were formed through socialisation. Adorno and his colleagues noted that the 'major influence upon personality development arises in the course of child training as carried forward in a setting of family life'.[529] The logical conclusion that followed

525 I. Dowbiggin (2011) *The Quest For Mental Health: A Tale of Science, Medicine, Scandal, Sorrow, and Mass Society*, Cambridge: Cambridge University Press, p.101.

526 Graebner (1980) p.629.

527 Justman (1998) p.40.

528 Justman (1998) p.40.

529 T.W. Adorno et al. (1969) *The Authoritarian Personality*. New York: W.W. Norton & Company, p.2.

from this assessment was that social engineers needed to pay special attention to what was going on in the nursery, the family home and in schools.

In a similar vein, Mead defended her emphasis on childrearing practices by drawing an analogy, appropriate for wartime,

> between the production of children and the production of machines: just as one way of understanding a machine is to understand how it is made, so one way of understanding the typical character structure of a culture is to follow step by step the way in which it is built into the growing child.[530]

The re-engineering of childrearing was one of the key objectives of Mead and her circle of anthropologists, psychologists and policy makers.

It is useful to highlight two important features of the politics of social engineering. It always cloaked its political ambition in the guise of scientific and technical neutrality. To use a contemporary phrase, 'it was following the science'. It worked most effectively as a silent or invisible ideology. Pierre Bourdieu's important reflections on what he called the 'hidden curriculum' are apposite in this respect.[531] Political therapy worked in a similar indirect fashion through the recasting of its ideological objectives through the language of health.

Secondly, despite its stated emphasis on protecting democracy from fanaticism, social engineering was and remains inspired by an undemocratic paternalistic temper of regarding its target audience as morally inferior. This sentiment was unambiguously asserted by Chisholm in a radio interview in 1956. In response to the question of whether he believed that the public's will was the best guarantee of a strong democracy, Chisholm replied:

> No! The public's will is no guarantee of a strong democracy. If there are enough weak, dependent, faithful, obedient, immature, irresponsible, superstitious or hating people, or people who want to be followers in a population, a 'strong man' will be what they want, until they get one, and then they cannot get rid of him.[532]

Chisholm's list of undesirable personality traits summed up his notion of the 'average man', who 'does not trouble to inform himself to be able to vote intelligently'.[533] This contemptuous characterisation of the electorate, which endures

---

530 Cited in R. Handler (1990) 'Boasian anthropology and the critique of American culture', *American Quarterly*, 42(2), 252–273, at 261.

531 P. Bourdieu and J.C. Passeron (1990) *Reproduction in Education, Society and Culture*, London: Sage.

532 Farley (2009) p.173.

533 Cited in Farley (2009) p.173.

to this day, is wedded to the belief that the health of society depends on the authority of social engineers and experts.

Adorno shared Chisholm's sentiments towards the working of democracy. He was in no doubt that the electorate could not be relied on to make the right decisions. He declared that it was 'thoroughly acknowledged throughout the ages' since oligarchy arose in Greece, 'that the majority of the people frequently act blindly in accordance with the will of powerful institutions or demagogic figures, and in opposition both to the basic concepts of democratism and their own rational interest'.[534] Political therapy rather than the electorate ensured that rational decisions were taken to protect the interests of society.

The pathology of socialisation

As we noted previously, the conventional critique of socialisation focused on the use of supposedly outdated methods by incompetent parents and teachers. Adult authority was criticised on the ground that it tended to miseducate children and thwart their healthy development. Gaining control over the socialisation of the young was the ambition of many professionals. This goal was most forcefully pursued by Social Democratic governments in Sweden, which from the 1930s onwards sought to turn socialisation into a responsibility of the state.

The Swedish social scientist Gunnar Myrdal, and his partner, the politician and social scientist Alva Myrdal, developed a social democratic, social engineering paradigm that sought not only to direct the socialisation of young people but also to use children to assist the project of re-socialising their parents. Their objective was to create a universal system of nurseries and after-school care to facilitate the realisation of their objective of neutralising the influence of parents over their children. The Myrdals sought to replace the 'influence of their parents' with those of professional socialisers.[535]

The Myrdals insisted that professional control over socialisation was the precondition for creating 'worthy citizens'. They assumed that the upbringing of children was a public duty rather than the private responsibility of parents. Alva Myrdal possessed a low opinion of the capacity of parents to socialise their children. As a study of her ideas explained, 'The child was in a sense

534 T.W. Adorno (1950) 'Democratic leadership and mass manipulation', in Gouldner, A. (ed.) *Studies in Leadership: Leadership and Democratic Action*, New York: Harper & Brothers.

535 L. Lucassen (2010) 'A brave new world: the left, social engineering, and eugenics in twentieth-century Europe', *International Review of Social History*, 55(2), 265–296, at 269.

the project of a nursery teacher or of a parental educator like Myrdal. The goal of parental education was the children's early independence from parents.'[536]

The intervention of the state and of child professionals under the supervision of Swedish Social Democratic Governments was more thoroughgoing and went much further than in other societies. However, the premise on which Swedish policies were based – particularly the claim that the socialisation of children needed to be professionally managed and that parental influence over their children had to be diminished – was widely echoed by policy makers in other parts of the western world.

The problem of socialisation and the necessity for professional intervention in the cultivation of a healthy personality was a frequently discussed political topic during the Cold War. In 1950, at the Mid-Century White House Conference On Children and Youth, the ideas of leading child psychologists like Erikson and John Bowlby and of parenting expert Benjamin Spock were widely echoed by the delegates.[537] Similar high-profile conferences organised in the decades to follow served to promote the ethos of professional socialisation to an ever-widening audience.

During the 1940s and 1950s, the pre-existing critique of parental incompetence gave way to a much darker narrative about the problem of socialisation. Increasingly, the focus of concern shifted towards the moral status of the family itself. The family was often portrayed as the source of many of society's ills. As the historian Fred Matthews argued, by the 'mid-1940s the doctrine that the family was the key to social problems ... had become conventional wisdom among the helping professions'.[538] The family was frequently diagnosed as sick and was seen to contribute to 'soldiers' breakdown, fascism, prejudice, homosexuality, and most pertinent for family therapists, delinquency and schizophrenia'.[539] This sentiment was captured by the question 'What's wrong with the family?', which Margaret Mead posed in *Harper's* in the spring of 1945. This question, which would be repeated with increasing frequency in the decades to follow, would invite the answer 'just about everything'.

The diagnosis of the family as source of illness was associated with the behaviour and dysfunctional childrearing techniques of mothers and fathers. Some psychologists blamed strict, authoritarian fathers; others targeted overbearing, suffocating mothers. Adorno and his colleagues criticised both and asserted

536 Herman (1995) p.334.

537 Vicedo (2012) p.238.

538 Cited in D. Weinstein (2004) 'Culture at work: family therapy and the culture concept in post-World War II America', *Journal of the History of the Behavioral Sciences*, 40(1), 23–46, at 24.

539 Weinstein (2004) p.24.

that an 'idealization of motherhood and strict fatherly authority yielded rigid personalities prone to antidemocratic tendencies'.[540] Erikson was critical of American mothers for 'standardizing and overadjusting children'.[541] The common premise of all the different theories was that the solution to all the negative consequences of socialisation relied on altering the early experience of childhood.

The professional consensus on family life was that, on balance, the prevailing modes of socialisation tended to encourage authoritarian, prejudiced and anti-democratic personality traits. These sentiments, which were already in currency in the 1930s, gained powerful momentum in response to the threat posed by the Nazis and other totalitarian movements during the Second World War. Often the appeal of anti-democratic sentiments to sections of the public was interpreted as the outcome of distinct personality traits acquired during the process of socialisation. In numerous accounts the family was portrayed as the source of prejudice and anti-Semitism, and was frequently held responsible for Hitler's rise to power.[542]

Though attacks on customary family practices were politically motivated, their authors claimed that they were merely guided by the science of psychology. The experts associated with the studies that led to the publication of *The Authoritarian Personality* placed great emphasis on what they presented as the rigorous empirical survey that underpinned their study. Yet, though presented as a work of objective scientific research, *The Authoritarian Personality* should be interpreted as a moral critique of traditional forms of socialisation. In particular, its research and arguments appear to be founded on the *a priori* assumption that authority distorts personality development.[543] On inspecting the content of the studies associated with *The Authoritarian Personality*, it becomes evident that their authors were hostile towards family values and practices such as the exercise of parental discipline, the valuation of obedience and the close identification of children with their parents. Their sentiments, which pre-dated the 'research', were then recast through the language of science.

The study's chapter on parents and children by Else Frenkel-Brunswik comes across as a moral critique of family life communicated through the jargon of psychology. Its argument is based on the simplistic assumption that strict parenting breeds authoritarian personality types, who then turn out to be potential

540 Vicedo (2012) p.236.

541 Vicedo (2012) p.236.

542 See C. Lasch (1977) *Haven in a Heartless World: The Family Besieged*, New York: Basic Books, pp.85–96.

543 Adorno et al. (1969).

fascists. According to this model, authoritarianism in the family serves as the functional equivalent of authoritarianism in public life. As in the case of medieval theories of authority, the authority of the parent mimics the political authority of the ruler.

The approach adopted by the authors of *The Authoritarian Personality* was to establish a model where a variety of negative traits were associated with those who score high on their F scale (F is the abbreviation for 'fascist'). They couple more attractive personality traits with liberal autonomous individuals, who are obviously low scorers on the F scale. According to the thesis advanced in this text, 'conformist and conventional idealisation of parents and a sense of obligation and duty for parents' is a marker for a high score on the F scale.

The study draws a contrast between the tendency towards '*idealization of the parents*' as opposed to what it characterises as '"*Objective appraisal*" of parents by unprejudiced subjects'. It concludes that those who score low on the F scale are likely to be 'more critical and realistic about their parents'.[544]

Authoritarian and extremist personality traits are depicted as a function of dysfunctional family life. Ethnocentrism and authoritarianism are represented as a response to rigid parental discipline. The aim of the authors of this study was to modify the behaviour of individuals with prejudiced and authoritarian personality traits. To realise this objective, the study argues that those likely to score high on the F scale should be subjected to a form of political therapy that relieves them of their uncertainties. It noted that:

> In our present-day struggle to achieve a strengthening of the tolerant, liberal point of view we may have to avoid presenting the prejudiced individual with more ambiguities than he is able to absorb and offer instead, in some sphere at least, solutions which are constructive and at the same time serve the general need for avoidance of uncertainties.[545]

A few observers have criticised what they see as the strongly politicised agenda that underpinned *The Authoritarian Personality.* Social critic Christopher Lasch argued that, by equating mental health with left-wing politics and associating right-wing politics with an invented 'authoritarian' pathology, the book's goal was to eliminate authoritarianism by 'subjecting the American people to what amounted to collective psychotherapy – by treating them as inmates of an insane asylum'.[546]

---

544 Adorno et al. (1969) p.340.
545 Adorno et al. (1969) p.486.
546 C. Lasch (2013) *The True and Only Heaven: Progress and Its Critics*, New York: Norton, p.44.

The preference of the study for subjects who are critical and 'realistic' about their parents was consistent with the pre-existing ethos of professional socialisers who regard the widening of the psychic distance between parent and child as indispensable for the cultivation of desirable personality traits. The introduction of the concept of 'objectivity' into what is a highly subjective and emotional parent–child relationship sought to encourage an instrumental regime of calculation and rationalisation into family life.

Throughout the study parental discipline is qualified by the term 'rigid' and its usage conveys a negative connotation. It constantly targets parental discipline. The study highlights its finding that families of 'prejudiced subjects' conduct their relations on the basis of 'rather clearly defined roles of dominance and submission in contradistinction to equalitarian policies'. It artificially contrasts the 'faithful execution of prescribed roles and the exchange of duties and obligations' with the 'exchange of free-flowing affection' displayed in 'democratic families'.[547] In a roundabout way, duty and obedience within the family are rebranded as a form of mindless submission to parental authority, which in turn encourages a disposition towards prejudice. The study draws a moral contrast between those who submit to parental authority and those who adopt the stance of 'principled independence'. The latter is depicted as morally superior to those who submit to parental authority.[548]

The Authoritarian Personality assigns a key role to the non-threatening father for producing a non-prejudiced individual. Such a father will allow the son to develop a soft version of masculinity. In this model of father–son relations the de-throning of paternal authority is crucial. The study argues that 'the unprejudiced man did not as a rule have to submit to stern authority in his childhood; in his later life, therefore, he neither longs for strong authority nor needs to assert his strength against those who are weaker'.[549] What is interesting about this characterisation of father and son interaction is that certain forms of emotional behaviour are causally inscribed a political value. A child who does not partake in the 'conscious criticism of the parents' is, by implication, ethnocentric. Someone who is intimidated by a 'threatening father figure' is likely to turn into a 'prejudiced man'.[550]

The approach adopted by *The Authoritarian Personality* retains considerable influence to this day. In effect, psychology and personality have become politicised, and early intervention in the socialisation of young children was and con-

547 Adorno et al. (1969) p.482.
548 Adorno et al. (1969) p.350.
549 Adorno et al. (1969) pp. 364–365.
550 Adorno et al. (1969) p.482.

tinues to be presented as the instrument for combating prejudice and authoritarian inclinations. Writing in this vein, George Lakoff divided the US electorate into two groups – those who adhere to a strict father family and those to a nurturant parent family. According to Lakoff's schema, populists embody the outlook of the strict father family. It is their 'strict authoritarian values' that 'motivate them to enter the voting booth'.[551] By contrast, progressives are imbued with the 'nurturant parent worldview' and are inspired by the values of 'empathy and responsibility'.[552] The project of representing people's voting behaviour as a personality issue rather than a matter of political choice assigns a fatalistic influence to socialisation. Parental determinism is the pivot around which this fatalistic representation of political behaviour turns.[553]

In Britain, policy makers and psychologists linked with the Labour Party echoed the approach of Adorno and his colleagues. Evan Durbin, a leading Labour Party intellectual, argued that the 'emotional education of children' was the 'real source of democracy'. The psychologist John Bowlby concurred, and claimed that 'social and international relations would greatly benefit' if 'children were brought up more freely'.[554]

It is unlikely that millions of people read and studied the numerous psychological texts on *The Authoritarian Personality.* However, from the 1940s onwards the public was exposed to arguments advanced by a variety of parenting experts, whose views conveyed an approach similar to that of Adorno and his colleagues. Benjamin Spock, whose 1946 book *The Common Sense Book of Baby and Child Care* went on to sell over 39 million copies, echoed some of the arguments advanced by contributors to *The Authoritarian Personality.* In turn, Spock's call for a more collaborative anti-authoritarian and democratic family life resonated with prevailing cultural trends.

Unlike Adorno and his colleagues, Spock advocated the cultivation of disciplined children. One of his concerns was to reconcile discipline with the task of avoiding patterns of authoritarian behaviour. As Graebner explained:

> To achieve discipline without risking an authoritarian response, Spock developed what might be called a 'democratic' model of child rearing. Its components were firm yet friendly

---

551 So argues Don Hazen, editor of Alter Net, in his Introduction to G. Lakoff (2014) *Don't Think of an Elephant! Know Your Values and Frame the Debate*, White River Junction: Chelsea Green Publishing, p.xiii.

552 Lakoff (2014) pp.11–12.

553 The concept of parental determinism is elaborated in chapter 3 of F. Furedi (2008) *Paranoid Parenting*, London: Continuum Press.

554 Bowlby and Durbin are cited in J. Nuttall (2005) 'Labour revisionism and qualities of mind and character, 1931–79', *English Historical Review*, 120(487), 667–694, at $$251$$.

> leadership of the child by the adult, avoidance of obvious confrontation and conflict, and limited, but conceptually important, participation by the child in its own upbringing.[555]

Debates about how far to go with the contraction of discipline and the exercise of parental authority continue to this day. But the tendency to de-authorise the role of parents in the process of socialisation remained and still remains an important dimension of the professional narrative. Many child experts veered towards a form of socialisation that regarded a trading off of discipline for what they perceived as the realisation of the psychological health of the child as the way forward. In more radical versions of this approach, the precondition for the successful socialisation of children was to distance them from the influence of their parents and the moral values they upheld.

Although the psychological narrative that linked socialisation to authoritarian patterns of behaviour emerged in response to the specific political challenge posed by anti-democratic totalitarian movements, many of its features constituted a continuity with the objections raised by professionals in previous times. The concern that, left to its own devices, socialisation would lead to the cultivation of a personality with authoritarian traits offered a justification for long-standing arguments about the need to intervene in family life. Claims about the incompetence of parents and their negative influence over the process of socialisation have served to promote the constant expansion of intervention in family life. The analysis of socialisation outlined by psychologists and social scientists involved in the development of the concept of the authoritarian personality often bears an uncanny resemblance to the ideas discussed in the interwar period. For example, the personality trait of conformism – supposedly a marker for the prejudiced personality – had already been identified by the founders of political psychology in their accounts of the mob, herd mentality and mass society at the turn of the 20th century.

With the passing of time the professionalisation of socialisation expanded from children towards re-educating parents. Mead hoped that socialisation would soon assume a form where adults not only learnt from their ancestors and peers but also their children.[556] In this way, the pre-existing notion that parents had little to teach their children was supplemented by the assertion that parents could and should learn from their children. In some instances, since the 1970s, some educators have encouraged children to wean their parents away from outdated prejudices and to adopt the latest wisdom provided by ex-

555 Graebner (1980), p.622.
556 Mead [1970] (1972).

pert authority. The outcome of this development is the encouragement of *socialisation in reverse.*

Socialisation in reverse is the logical outcome of the pathologisation of socialisation. This approach is often promoted in schools and institutions of higher education. The British sociologist of education Basil Bernstein, arguably the most profound thinker on this subject, developed the concept of *invisible pedagogy* to account for the way that some schools distance children from their parents. Invisible pedagogy relies on implicit forms of teaching and indirect instruments of control. He saw it as 'progressive and revolutionary' but also a 'colonising movement in its relationship to parents' as the child becomes 'abstracted from his family'.[557] Invisible pedagogy not only distances children from their parents, but in more recent times has encouraged young people to re-educate their parents. Historically the use of schools to re-socialise parents was focused on immigrant children and their families in North America.[558] Since the 1980s teachers have sought to motivate children to encourage their parents to alter their behaviour in relation to the environment, healthy living and eating, and a variety of other concerns.

Arguably the most significant outcome of the pathologisation of socialisation and its professionalisation is its impact on adults and their capacity to transmit values and models of grown-up behaviour to the younger generation. Lack of clarity on these matters, and in particular on how to motivate children to gain independence and acquire the habits of a mature adult, are often experienced as a problem of identity or an identity crisis. That identity is a significant challenge facing young people is recognised by child and socialisation professionals and by the authors of *The Authoritarian Personality.* However, for them this problem is not that parents do too little socialising but that they are too involved in it and interfere with the healthy development of the child.

The Authoritarian Personality addresses the problem of identity in the following terms:

> The lack of an internalized and individualized approach to the child, on the part of the parents, as well as a tendency to transmit mainly a set of conventional rules and customs, may be considered as interfering with the development of a clear-cut personal identity, in the growing child. Instead we find surface conformity without integration, expressing itself in a stereotyped approach devoid of genuine affect in almost all areas of life.[559]

557 B. Bernstein (1977) *Class, Codes and Control*, vol. 3, London: Routledge & Kegan Paul, pp.122–123.
558 See Arendt [1954] (2006) pp.172, 174.
559 Adorno et al. (1969) p.370.

It is paradoxical that the transmission of conventional rules and customs is held responsible for the problems associated with child development rather than the absence of clarity about the content of socialisation. Yet, it is the bond forged through socialising children into a common world of values that provides the seed bed for the cultivation of identity.

The psychological critique of the authoritarian personality is guilty precisely of the criticism that it hurls at parents. Its formulaic model of personality types tends to rob individuals of the complexity of their behaviour and attitudes. They are given labels and reduced to the sameness of being low-scoring or high-scoring subjects. Hannah Arendt's comment on the instrumental use of psychology is apposite in this respect. She commented on the 'monotonous sameness and perverse ugliness so highly characteristic of the findings of modern psychology and contrasting so obviously with the enormous variety and richness of overt human conduct'.[560]

Adorno and his Frankfurt school colleagues developed the concept of 'ticket mentality', an 'all-or-nothing' personality that suggests that 'if one agrees to one policy idea of a political party, one must agree with all'.[561] The ticket mentality is one drawn to an ideological package that regards a people such as Jews or individuals through a system of fixed stereotypes. And yet, the stereotype of the personality of the would-be fascist has all the hallmarks of the very same ticket mentality. Its mechanistic flattening out of personality unwittingly encourages the formation of prejudice towards those who are diagnosed with the wrong kind of personality traits. If we jump ahead to the current era, it becomes evident that ticket mentality has taken on a variety of conflicting forms around the disputes over identity.

Identity crisis and its relationship to the professionalisation of socialisation

The conceptualisation of identity and its crisis occurred in the context of the discussion regarding the rise of authoritarianism and the personality traits that supported it. The first published linkage of the problem of identity and its relation to the development of authoritarian personalities is to be found in Fromm's *Escape From Freedom* (1941). Although Erikson is rightly attributed the pioneer theoret-

---

560 Arendt is cited in Justman (1998) p.141.

561 See discussion in E. Oberle (2018) *Theodor Adorno and the Century of Negative Identity*, Stanford: Stanford University Press, p.194.

ician of identity, it is in *Escape From Freedom* that we encounter the first attempt to elaborate the issue of identity as a central dilemma facing the human condition. For Fromm, the need for identity leading to the submergence of the self to a greater whole served as a psychological explanation for the rise of Hitler.[562]

During the first half of the 20th century, criticism of traditional methods of socialisation implicitly, and often explicitly, repudiated the customs and traditions that guided the lives of previous generations. Yet, many commentators who decried the influence of traditional customs and attitudes on the socialisation of the younger generation were also aware that there was no meaningful alternative with which to replace them. In some instances, they concluded that the breakdown of community and of tradition has a disorienting impact on individuals to the point of creating personalities that threaten democracy. Fromm believed that individuals require a sense of belonging in order to gain a feeling of security through which they can cultivate their identity. According to his thesis, the loss of the sense of belonging weakened the self, which in turn encouraged people to develop an obsessive interest in cultivating an identity.

The loss of a sense of belonging was also the point of departure of Erikson's concept of identity crisis. Following Fromm, Erikson perceived identity 'as an extension of culture'. He stated; 'in traditional cultures, identity is the equivalent of maintaining a traditional role; in modern societies it is weighed towards self-invention'.[563] Erikson believed that in a mass modern society the identities which people inherited from 'primitive, agrarian, feudal, and patrician cultures' are threatened, leading to an explosion of fear about their loss. He wrote that 'in this emergency masses of people become ready to seek salvation in pseudo identities'.[564] The pseudo-identities that Erikson and Fromm were particularly concerned about were ones that encouraged the adoption of anti-democratic traits.

Fromm attempted to link the phenomenon of what he described as 'the authoritarian character' with 'the loss of self'. He offered an analysis that provided a springboard for the subsequent formulation of Erikson's identity crisis and Adorno's authoritarian personality. Fromm's formulation of the intense state of insecurity and doubt brought on by the loss of self, leading to a loss of identity, was imaginatively elaborated through references to literary figures like Pirandello and Franz Kafka. Fromm referred to the 'sense of utter futility and helplessness' of the main character of Kafka's *The Castle* to highlight the predicament

---

562 For the pioneering contribution of Fromm to the development of the concept of identity, see Izenberg (2016) p.111.

563 Oberle (2018) p.197.

564 E.H. Erikson [1950] (1993) *Childhood and Society*, New York: W.W. Norton & Company p.413.

of the loss of self.[565] He stated that 'in order to overcome the panic resulting from such loss of identity, he is compelled to conform, to seek his identity by continuous approval and recognition by others'.[566] Fromm argued that in response to loss of identity individuals become 'ready to submit to new authorities which offer [them] security and relief from doubt'.[567]

Fromm, like many psychologists and social scientists, tended to portray the willingness of the masses to submit to authority as the main driver of authoritarian politics. In their discussion they failed to pay attention to the conceptual distinction between authority and authoritarianism and often seemed to imply that the latter flowed on from the former. Yet, at the same time, many contributors to the development of the concept of the authoritarian personality were aware that the loss of identity was in part a consequence of the loss of moral authority. The dangerous personality traits that they identified emanated from the loss of community and of traditional authority.[568]

Fromm treated authority and the need for it as a psychological pathology, particularly in relation to paternal authority. Although Fromm made a distinction between what he characterises as 'rational' as opposed to 'inhibiting' authority, in practice he ascribed negative and oppressive characteristics to the term. In his discussion of the character structure that is drawn towards Nazi ideology he cojoined the sado-masochistic character with that of an authoritarian one. He justified the use of this terminology 'because the sado-masochistic person is always characterized by his attitude toward authority'. Fromm added, 'he admires authority and tends to submit to it, but at the same time wants to be an authority himself and have others submit to him'.[569] To reinforce his argument, Fromm indicated;

> The Fascist systems call themselves authoritarian because of the dominant role of authority in their social and political structure. By the term *authoritarian character* we imply that it represents the personality structure which is the human basis of fascism.[570]

In effect, people's support for fascism was conceptualised as a psychological problem, a widely shared character flaw that is in part a consequence of the pressure to conform. Fromm's construction of an authoritarian character antici-

565 Fromm [1941] (1969) p.132.
566 Fromm [1941] (1969) p.203.
567 Fromm [1941] (1969) p.203.
568 Graebner (1980) p.626.
569 Fromm [1941] (1969) p.162.
570 Fromm [1941] (1969) p.162.

pates Adorno's invention of an authoritarian personality. Moreover, it does so without the aid of a massive empirical research project utilised by the authors of *The Authoritarian Personality* to legitimate their findings.

Both Fromm's and Adorno's arguments about the pathology of conformism were a restatement of the approach that informed the interwar project of professionalising the socialisation of young people. By the 1930s, conformity had become a serious cause of concern among social commentators and scientists. Boas and other cultural anthropologists worried about standardisation and a desire to 'be like everyone else'. Often, parents were blamed for the aspiration to conform.[571] In 1932, the radical left-wing novelist Alice Beal Parsons raised concern about the importance now attached to 'fitting in' that led parents to conform in order to guarantee their 'popularity'.[572] Commentators complained that parents were far too focused on getting their children to 'adjust' at 'any age'.[573]

In *Escape From Freedom*, the perennial condemnation of dysfunctional socialisation reappears in the more threatening form of conformism, which in turn leads to a loss of identity. After noting 'how our culture fosters' the 'tendency to conform', Fromm claims that the 'suppression of spontaneous feelings, and thereby of the development of genuine individuality, starts very early, as a matter of fact with the earliest training of a child'. Drawing on Freud, Fromm underlines the decisive influence that the 'early experiences of the child' have on the 'formation of its character structure'.[574] It is at this point that acting as the personification of society and behaving in accordance with its values, parents mould children to internalise the characteristics that society expects its members to possess. He writes that parents

> apply the educational patterns of the society they live in, but also that in their own personalities they represent the social characters of their society or class. They transmit to the child what we may call the psychological atmosphere or the spirit of a society just by being as they are – namely representatives of this very spirit. *The family thus may be considered to be the psychological agent of society.*[575]

Fromm regards the personality structure transmitted to the child as the main source of the emotional disposition to find refuge in the group and in mass anti-democratic movements.

---

571 I.T. Thomson (1997) 'From conflict to embedment: the individual–society relationship, 1920–1991', *Sociological Forum*, 12(4), 631–658, at 634.
572 Alice Beal Parsons (1932) 'Shall we make our children common- place', *Harper's*, 164.
573 I.L. Smith (1933),'We modern parents', *The Atlantic*, 152.
574 Fromm [1941] (1969) p.285.
575 Fromm [1941] (1969) p.285.

Although Fromm was principally interested in accounting for the rise of fascism and in explaining the susceptibility of the German middle class to Nazism, his approach towards the problem of socialisation and of identity claims to have a wider relevance. He delves back to the Renaissance to discover the modern man alienated from his self and frequently gives the impression that the problem of identity is at the heart of the human condition. Jumping from the Renaissance, to the Reformation, to the French philosopher Descartes, Fromm declared that:

> The identity of the individual has been a major problem of modern philosophy since Descartes. To-day we take for granted that we are we. Yet the doubt about ourselves still exists, or has even grown. In his plays Pirandello has given expression to this feeling of modern man. He starts with the question: Who am I? What proof have I for my own identity other than the continuation of my physical self? His answer is not like Descartes' – the affirmation of the individual self – but its denial: I have no identity, there is no self excepting the one which is the reflex of what others expect me to be: I am 'as you desire me'. This loss of identity then makes it still more imperative to conform; it means that one can be sure of oneself only if one lives up to the expectations of others. If we do not live up to this picture we not only risk disapproval and increased isolation, but we risk losing the identity of our personality, which means jeopardizing sanity.[576]

In this passage, the historical process of individuation, leading to the loss of the self, incites the impulse to conform. Conforming to the expectation of others turns into the predicament of the human soul. In Fromm's later publications, this ahistorical rendition of the fear of losing identity becomes more pronounced.

In *The Sane Society* (1955), Fromm proposes the thesis that 'the need to feel a sense of identity stems from the very condition of human existence, and it is the source of our most intense strivings'. He adds that 'behind the intense passion for status and conformity is this very need, and it is sometimes even stronger than the need for physical survival'.[577] This passion leads people to risk their lives and give up their freedoms 'for the sake of being one of the herd'. In this study, the pathology of conformism and the willing embrace of herd-like mentality acquires a life of its own and ceases to have any connection with a historically specific regime of socialisation.

As was the case with Mead and her colleagues, in *The Sane Society* Fromm calls for cultural change to solve the problem of socialisation and of identity. His proposals for changing culture are vague and are directed towards reforming education and adopting a more co-operative style of work and management. He

576 Fromm [1941] (1969) p.253.
577 Fromm (1955) p.64.

was positive about the social engineering approach adopted by the 1950s Labour Party towards the nationalisation of industry and workers' co-operation. Unlike subsequent counter-cultural figures, Fromm at least attempted to formulate an – albeit vague – alternative. His alternative called for a 'humanistic communitarianism' that was prepared to share work and experience.[578]

For Fromm, identity was a problem to be overcome through a new cultural ethos of solidarity and co-operation. In this sense, his approach was very different from that of Erikson and his co-thinkers, who regarded identity as a goal to be achieved. Consequently, in one sense Fromm's version of the problem runs counter to the way that supporters of identity culture and politics have conceptualised it from the late 1960s onwards. In another sense, through his invention of the concept of social character, Fromm provided the foundation for identity's shift from an individual to a group accomplishment.

Fromm developed the concept of social character in 1931 and elaborated it at length in his *Escape From Freedom*. Social character refers to that part of the character that is common to most members of society. These are '*the essential nucleus the character structure of most members of a group, which has developed as the result of the basic experiences and mode of life common to that group*'.[579] Society thus possessed a character structure – acquired through socialisation – which distinguished the behaviour patterns of one culture from another.

Fromm's concept of social character, like Mead's character structure of a culture, assumed that there are similarities in personality among people who share a common culture. In effect, in all but name they possess a shared identity. The internalisation of group norms by individuals led to a 'new era of scientifically respectable study of national character' and by the 1950s the 'science of national character' gained widespread influence in the social sciences.[580]

According to Gleason, with the development of this new science, the term 'character' gradually gave way to that of 'identity'. Gleason argued that Erikson's chapter in his *Childhood and Society* (1950), titled 'Reflections on the American identity', marked a 'milestone in the semantic history of identity because it was the first major publication in which the expression "American identity" was used as the equivalent of "American character"'.[581] Since that point, the use of terms like 'social character', or 'national' or 'cultural characteristics' to refer to group personality characteristics has tended to be displaced by that of identity. Gleason

578 Fromm (1955) p.313.
579 Fromm [1941] (1969) p.276.
580 Gleason (1983) p.193.
581 Gleason (1983) p.926.

believed that this shift occurred in part because identity was 'ideally adapted to talking about the relationship of the individual to society'.[582] This merging of individual identity with that provided with a group would from the 1970s onwards become a key site not only for political affiliation but also for conflict. Since that point, the identities that matter have been those between groups rather than between individuals. Individuals tend to be conceptually flattened out once they personify a group identity. Once these differences are politicised group identities tend to become absolutised.

Politics of prevention

Even before the term 'identity crisis' became a widely recognised public issue, identity was in crisis. According to the innovators of this concept, the loss of the self, leading to a search for identity, led to distorted and potentially dangerous personality structures. The solution to this problem could not confine itself to individual therapy but culture itself required serious modification. The justification for a culture war against the prevailing regime of socialisation was that it was the precondition for fighting prejudice and preventing children from cultivating anti-democratic personalities.

In the first instance this culture war was to be promoted through what the political psychologist Harold Lasswell characterised in 1930 as 'preventive politics'.[583] Through the use of experts, social conflict would be attenuated through 'reducing the level of strain and maladaptation in society'. Preventive intervention to improve mental health required using experts to re-engineer childrearing and education. This objective was explicitly outlined in the Foreword to the *Studies in Prejudice* series inaugurated by Adorno and his colleagues. Editors Max Horkheimer and S.H. Flowerman declared that 'our aim is not merely to describe prejudice but to explain it in order to help in its eradication'. The editors pointed out that 'eradication means reeducation scientifically planned on the basis of understanding scientifically arrived at'.[584]

One of the ways in which the re-education and the re-engineering of socialisation would proceed was through promoting values through the language of mental health in order to create what Eleanor Roosevelt described as a 'mentally healthy democracy'. Though calls to re-engineer socialisation through preventive

---

582 Gleason (1983) p.926.

583 See H.D. Lasswell (1930) *Psychopathology and Politics*, Chicago: University of Chicago Press.

584 Cited in P. Gottfried (2002) *Multiculturalism and the Politics of Guilt: Toward a Secular Theocracy*, Columbia: University of Missouri Press, p.92.

intervention were often advocated on the ground that it would assist the establishment of a mentally healthy democracy, it is evident that this movement was selective in its commitment to the ideal of democracy. Its advocates often appeared instinctively no less authoritarian than the personality traits they despised.

In his study *Mental Hygiene and Preventive Medicine*, the Scottish psychiatrist Hugh Crichton Miller, founder of the London-based Tavistock Clinic, went so far as to blame too much freedom and choice as the source of mental illness. At one point he suggested that in dictatorships, a loss of freedom may be compensated for by better mental health outcomes:

> Only a sense of social responsibility can save civilised man from himself. I find confirmation for this belief in the spectacle of the 'dictator' countries, where man's freedom of choice is largely restricted. He may resent such restrictions, but they make for an ultimate simplification of life that is nearer to mental health than the freedom that only accentuates the embarrassments of choice. I believe that these countries will presently show a reduced incidence of insanity and psychoneuroses, while the free countries will gradually deteriorate.[585]

Though written before the consequences of authoritarian dictatorship became abundantly clear during the Second World War, similar impulses driving preventive interventions continued to influence social engineers.

For example, a group of academics, concerned with what Adorno described in 1950 as 'Vaccines Against Authoritarianism', assumed as given that the main site for immunising society against authoritarianism was through cultivating the right kind of personality. They were in no doubt that they possessed a warrant to promote a programme of mass vaccination against the diseases of authoritarianism. Adopting this stance, the sociologist Jeremy Wolpert concluded that 'since personality is nourished incipiently in the family situation, and the attitudes toward authority gain their contours from this processing, a family atmosphere and structure which would generate such attitudes would seem to be an important point of attack'.[586] The use of the metaphor of a war suggests that what was at stake was a call to arms against the prevailing culture of family life. At times the project of professionalising socialisation became intertwined with a silent war against traditional family culture.

585 Cited in Thomson (2006) p.193.

586 J.F. Wolpert (1950) 'Towards a sociology of authority', in Gouldner, A. (ed.) *Studies in Leadership: Leadership and Democratic Action*, New York: Harper & Brothers, p.700.

The dynamic that drove activists to describe their project of eliminating personality traits and cultural attitudes through the public health language of mass vaccination often relied on a medicalised and psychological language to express its value and political preferences. The different actors promoting this project were careful to avoid the appearance of being ideological. Goals such as strengthening professional authority to hostility towards cultural values that contradicted their own through to anxiety about the behaviour of the masses were rarely elaborated into a coherent ideological system. Advocates of re-engineering human personality were wary about being explicit in challenging long-held cherished beliefs and attitudes.

Wolpert's priority was to gain influence over the more well-off and educated families, who were likely to respond more favourably to the advice of political psychologists and professional socialisers. He understood that

'the middle-class is much more receptive to changes in child rearing than lower-income groups and can be persuaded to make changes in this area'. He believed that it was pointless to attempt to influence the 'lower income groups' because they 'do not have the leeway to pay attention' to professional advice on how they should modify their behaviour. Wolpert believed that new cultural values could gain a foothold by first gaining the commitment of the elites and educated middle class and then using these groups to transmit them to others.[587]

A vaccine against authoritarianism is best understood as the politicised version of the public health ideal of preventive medicine. Ellen Herman has argued that the 'mantra of prevention' was presented as 'the only effective means of safeguarding democratic potential and averting a menacing epidemic of blind conformity and authoritarianism'. At least as an 'explicit public ideal and purpose of government ... experts would have to manufacture democratic personalities because U.S. social institutions had failed to produce people who could be trusted with democracy's future'.[588] In effect, the underlying premise of the politics of prevention was that paternalistic methods had to be used by experts in order to create the conditions for the flourishing of democratic personalities. Today, this sentiment is voiced by the 'aware' through the mantra of 'raising awareness'.

587 Wolpert (1950) p.700.
588 Herman (1995) p.81.

Chapter 8: Towards a New Personhood

From the standpoint of moral engineering the cultivation of a healthy personality required cultural change. Idealistic scientific democrats regarded science as an effective instrument for challenging and transforming culture. It seemed to them that science held out the promise of 'thoroughgoing cultural change, rather than simply the augmentation of the nation's knowledge base'.[589] Although often unstated, the ambition to transform culture is an intrinsic feature of moral engineering. The pursuit of cultural change relied on the resources provided by psychology. The values and attitudes promoted through psychology gradually developed into a distinct ethos that some commentators characterise as therapeutic or therapy culture. The influence of this ethos became evident in the 1960s, when the values of the so-called 'Counter-culture' were legitimated by the authority of psychology. Under the spell of psychology, members of the counter-culture prided themselves on being 'emotionally aware individuals', who were 'getting their heads together', 'expressing their feelings' and 'self-actualising'.

From character to personality

The premise of the project of using science to create new kinds of people was the conviction that humans were malleable. This belief was supported by an understanding of human nature that regarded it as both changeable and susceptible to the guidance of scientific professionals. This guidance was directed at the individual's personality. During the first decade of the 20th century, psychologists reconstructed the meaning of personality so that it conveyed connotations that were very different from pre-existing ways of imagining the self.[590]

The corollary of psychology's adoption of personality as a key site of its activity was the tendency to gradually abandon the use of the term 'character' when referring to the individual self. The type of subjectivity expressed through character presupposed a form of conduct bound up with the fulfilment of duties and responsibilities expected from members of a moral community. Samuel Smiles' bestselling *Character*, published in 1871, idealised 'truthfulness, chaste-

589 Jewett (2012) p.10.
590 See S. Cohen (1990) 'Review: the triumph of the therapeutic', *History of Education Quarterly*, 30(3), 371–379.

https://doi.org/10.1515/9783110708899-009

ness, mercifulness and with these integrity, courage, virtue, and goodness in all its phases'.[591] These were ideals expressed in the language of morality and for someone deemed to possess a good character they were non-negotiable.

Whereas the building of character occurred in the context of conforming to a 'set of public virtues', personality heralded 'the calculated and freely chosen participation in a diversified public sphere in which obligations towards public institutions are dependent upon a cost–benefit calculus'.[592] Personality is not composed of a fixed set of attributes but develops through the cultivation of the self and the realisation of individuality. Freed from its deep moral connotation, personality provided an ideal form of subjectivity for the science of psychology. In the early 1920s, the psychologist Gordon Allport played an important role in deepening the distinction between a seemingly normatively neutral personality and a value-laden character. His aim was to exclude the evaluation and study of character from the science of psychology.[593] The displacement of character by personality is illustrated by the decision of the scientific journal *Character and Personality* to rebrand itself as *Journal of Personality* in 1945. This rebranding exercise sought 'to avoid the moral connotations of the concept of character'.[594]

The attempt to frame personality as an objective and value-free concept required that its historical meaning be redefined. Historically, the term 'personality' had been used in a manner that was far more fixed than in the 20th century: 'personality is what makes a man to be himself, can never be divested ... nor interchangeable with that of any other creature', wrote the philosopher Abraham Tucker in 1777.[595] The 20th century version of personality still refers to the 'quality or collection of qualities which makes a person a distinctive individual', but compared with that of Tucker, claims to be far more fluid and open to change and adjustment.[596]

Originally, the concept of personality 'belonged to theology, law, and ethics, where it designated the moral aspects of the individual'.[597] That it lost its moral connotations and became increasingly medicalised was strikingly confirmed by

---

591 Cited in Thomson (2006) p.44.

592 H. Hendrick (2016) *Narcissistic Parenting in an Insecure World: A History of Parenting Culture 1920s to Present*, Bristol: Policy Press, p.13.

593 See K. Banicki (2017) 'The character–personality distinction: an historical, conceptual, and functional investigation', *Theory & Psychology*, 27(1), 50–68, at 54.

594 Brinkmann (2010) p.70.

595 A. Tucker (1777) *The Light of Nature Pursued*, 1st edition, 1768–1777, vol. 3, pt 1, London: W. Oliver, p.353.

596 See *OED*.

597 Brinkmann (2010) p.73.

the title of the French psychologist Théodule Ribot's study on *The Diseases of Personality* (1885).[598] Since that point, medical discourses on personality disorders and personality traits have constituted an important focus for psychological research. By the 1940s, personality had 'become an entrenched category of psychological investigation'.[599]

In its medicalised form, personality could be measured, broken down into typologies and distinct traits, and treated as an objective phenomenon. From the standpoint of the ideology of scientism, personality needed to be freed from its 'unwelcome moralistic background' in order to offer 'a realistic prospect of quantitative empirical research'.[600] Devoid of the normative connotation of character, moral issues that surrounded it could be 'redefined as scientific questions treatable by scientific methods'.[601]

The displacement of character by personality signalled the emergence of a new conception of the self. In the form of personality, the self was freed from having to conform to predetermined moral norms and living with moral duties and responsibilities. Personality was malleable, adaptable, flexible and expressive. It was something that could be developed and adjusted. To many, its 'appeal lay in the lightness of its moral load'.[602]

Throughout most of the 20th century, the most important focus of moral engineering was the human personality. During the interwar era, the preconditions for the realisation of a variety of different important projects – from radical reform to the maintenance of social control – were associated with the task of shaping and readjusting personality. At the same time, numerous social problems were interpreted as the outcome of personality deficits, such as the failure of individuals to adjust to the demands of a rapidly changing modern society. The most influential body promoting this outlook was the Social Science Research Council's Advisory Committee on Personality and Culture in the 1930s. During the Great Depression, this network of prominent social scientists, clinicians and administrators advocated the reconstruction of culture in order to create the conditions for the healthy development of individual personality. The long-term legacy of their activity was to render the boundary between culture and personality porous so that culture itself acquired a personality.

598 T.A. Ribot (1910) *The Diseases of Personality: Authorized Translation*, Chicago: Open Court Publishing Company.

599 I.A. Nicholson (1998) 'Gordon Allport, character, and the "culture of personality" 1897–1937', *History of Psychology*, 1(1), 52–68, at 52.

600 Banicki (2017) p.54.

601 Nicholson (1998) p.56.

602 Nicholson (1998) p.57.

Leading social engineering thinkers regarded prevailing culture and its norms as a drag on social progress. They believed that the persistence of outdated cultural beliefs prevented people's personalities from adjusting to change. They constructed a strong causal connection between 'personality disorders and social disorganizations'.[603] From the 1930s onwards, politics, too, became increasingly informed by psychology. Freedom from neurosis became a key political objective of the personality and culture school. L.G. Frank depicted the social scientist as a 'doctor working to remedy cultural diseases' and characterised 'society' as 'the patient'.[604]

One of the outcomes of the close connection drawn between culture and personality was the development of concepts that highlighted the community or national origins of distinct personality types. The decade of 1940 to 1950 saw a growing interest in the 'typical personality of a group' and its relation to its culture. Notions such as 'basic personality structure' and 'national character' were developed during this period in time.[605] Mead and Benedict played a pivotal role in the development of the concept of a national character. Their earlier interest in the relationship between psychological traits and group norms encouraged them to embark on a mission to 'discover how group norms and attitudes were stamped on the personalities of individuals belonging to different cultures'.[606] A series of publications on Russian, German, American and Japanese national characteristics held out the promise of a new science that could assist the task of cultural reconstruction in the post-Second World War era.

One of the most important legacies of the forging of the culture–personality axis was the growing tendency to de-individualise the concept of personality and to interpret it in group terms. These studies sought to capture the 'distinctive adult personalities found in particular nations'.[607] They often unwittingly fell into the trap of elaborating national personality traits which were little more than a rebranded version of ethnic stereotypes. Once personality traits were represented as cultural rather than simply individual accomplishments, they tended to be perceived as fixed. The original idea of a malleable personality sat uneasily alongside its representation as the personification of pre-existing national characteristics. Whereas initially the emphasis was on the malleability of personality, during the post-Second World War era it was often treated as an established fact.

603 Jewett (2012) p.283.
604 Jewett (2012) p.285.
605 Bryson (2009) p.356.
606 Gleason (1983) p.924.
607 Meyerowitz (2010) p.1077.

People could be categorised as possessing either an authoritarian or an open or a variety of other personalities.

The notion of a group personality emphasised the imperative of culture over self-created traits and characteristics. It was the conversion of this sensibility that led to the development of group-based identities in the 1960s. Erikson, who was in close contact with the cultural anthropologists involved in the development of the concept of a national character, made an important contribution to refocusing interest from personality to identity and from national character to national identity. During the decade to follow, identity became adopted as a group signifier of a variety of cultural communities. One reason why the notion of group personality came to be conveyed through the vocabulary of identity was because the latter facilitated the synthesis of individual, group and cultural consciousness. Personality continued to provide an important focus for moral engineering and worked alongside an increasingly expansive identity concept. But we are jumping ahead of ourselves!

Until the 1970s, personality trumped other psychological idioms for the presentation of the individual self. But, according to Brinkmann's analysis of the *PsycInfo* database, since the 1970s the concept of identity has gained greater and greater importance as a term reflecting issues to do with the self. Since that time, and especially from the 1990s onwards, identity has often done the work that psychologists previously assigned to personality. This point was underlined by Brinkmann, when he stated that 'identity, in short, has become a central problematic for human subjects today, something that defines them as individuals, in a way that character and personality did in earlier times'.[608]

Cultural critique masquerading as diagnosis

Although at times science necessarily enters the domain of moral and political life, most scientists rightly reject the idea that they have a legitimate role in the provision of normative guidance. In contrast, scientism has tended to adopt a more expansive view of the authority of science. Scientific democrats believed that science should not be detached from politics and morality, and claimed that it had an important and positive influence on the development of human values. Other sections of scientism tended to be less explicit and were either unaware or unwilling to acknowledge their predilection for straying beyond the boundaries of value neutrality.

608 Brinkmann (2010) p.68.

Despite the claim that the concept of personality was objective and devoid of moral content, it was always subject to (generally unacknowledged) normative assumptions about its healthy development. As a medicalised version of the self, it was interpreted through a vocabulary which allowed normative judgments to be recast in the language of health. Rieff was not far off the mark when he referred to psychology as the 'new science of moral management'.[609] The diagnosis of a healthy personality is not simply a medical but also a normative statement about morally desirable traits. For example, Frank's definition of a healthy personality highlighted the possession of culturally sanctioned values, such as 'self-confidence, courage, and the ability to conduct his interpersonal relationships with generosity and dignity'.[610]

Scientism through the form of medicalisation has gained widespread institutional support for an ideology that asserts that the issue of health is not simply a problem of the individual but of society. According to this outlook, finding a cure for a 'sick society' is as important as dealing with the illness of the individual. That is why 'raising awareness' and changing people's customs and behaviour are integral to the activities of moral engineering. Since its founding, the WHO has constantly sought to politicise health to achieve its objective of changing people's behaviour and curing a sick society. From its inception, the WHO has attempted to widen the meaning of health. The founders of the WHO believed that health should not be defined simply in physical terms as the absence of disease or disability. It also referred to the mental and social dimensions of a person's life. At its founding, the WHO defined health as a 'state of complete physical, mental and social wellbeing and not merely the absence of disease or infirmity'.[611] Such a broad definition of health left a lot to the imagination. In practice it led to a shift in focus from problems that were susceptible to medical solutions to ones that required cultural and social interventions. Once health becomes detached from the condition of an individual it can acquire a normative and a political dimension.

Changing people's minds was a key objective of UNESCO and the WHO. Their ambition quickly led to the politicisation of personality. As our previous discussion on *The Authoritarian Personality* indicated, the diagnosis of this personality disorder implicitly constituted a political judgment. Critics of people possessing an authoritarian personality not only claimed that they were sick but also on the wrong side of history. Some of the contributors to *The Authoritar-*

609 Rieff (2006) p.41.

610 Frank (1953) p.168.

611 www.who.int/about/who-we-are/constitution (accessed 16 May 2021).

ian Personality asserted that attitudes towards science could be used to serve as a marker for distinguishing healthy from unhealthy personalities. They suggested that a reliable way to distinguish a fascist from a democratic scientist was to see if they 'lauded simple empiricism (these were the fascists) or if they believed that science involved an active mind and the tolerance of ambiguity (these were the believers in democracy and the true scientists)'.[612]

When politics works as a form of diagnosis soon personality becomes politicised. Monographs were and continue to be published on topics such as a supposed communist and post-communist personality, fascist personality, capitalist personality and, of course, a democratic personality. Numerous researchers in psychology have published studies that contend that there is a close correlation between citizens' personality and their politics. To take a representative example: researchers at the University of Toronto 'discovered' that 'the psychological concern for compassion and equality is associated with a liberal mindset, while the concern for order and respect of social norms is associated with a conservative mindset'.[613]

In his study of Cold War political culture, Ron Robin suggested that psychology became an alternative to ideology as both an explanation and as a tool for dealing with competing arguments.[614] During this period the imperative of psychologising radical opponents transcended the conventional political divide. Unlike Adorno and his colleagues, who confined their discussion of authoritarianism to right-wing behaviour, political psychologists began to medicalise all forms of radicalism. Both left- and right-wing radicalism tended to be diagnosed as possessing important psychological deficits. In effect, such a diagnosis served as a form of moral condemnation.

According to the historian Michael Heale, during the 1960s'both political extremes tended to be dismissed as deluded'. Communists 'found themselves represented as psychologically impaired, whether as soulless automatons or as monomaniacal zealots'. He added that '60s students were disparaged as "emotionally immature"', 'feminists too were still vulnerable to crude insinuations rooted in Freudian theories about hysteria or penis envy'.[615]

---

612 See J. Cohen-Cole (2014) *The Open Mind: Cold War Politics and the Sciences of Human Nature*, Chicago: University of Chicago Press, p.147.

613 See ScienceDaily, 10 June 2010.

614 See R. Robin (2001) *The Making of the Cold War Enemy: Culture and Politics in the Military-Intellectual Complex*, Princeton: Princeton University Press.

615 M.J. Heale (2005) 'The sixties as history: a review of the political historiography', *Reviews in American History*, 33(2), 133–152, at 138.

One of the most interesting developments that came into play with the evolution of the social engineering of personality was its crusade against conformist behaviour during the Cold War era. The authors of *The Authoritarian Personality* played a pioneering role in the pathologisation of conformist personality traits. Frenkel-Brunswik associated the conformist idealisation of parents with a high score on the F scale. She cited the 'tendency towards conventionality' as a marker for a prejudiced personality. In contrast, a low scorer on the F scale tended to 'judge people more on the basis of their intrinsic worth than on the basis of conformity to social mores'.[616]

Whereas in previous times conformity to social and cultural norms was thought to be normal and encouraged, a growing body of social commentators condemned conformism as a form of cultural malaise. Until the unexpected explosion of youth radicalism in the 1960s, conformism was frequently diagnosed as a serious problem facing western societies. Social critics such as Riesman, Whyte and C.W. Mills were concerned that American culture was 'yielding conformist individuals and stifling individual agency'.[617] Numerous commentators in Britain raised concern about the apathy of the younger generations. A new genre of literature criticising conformism and apathy emerged, and this became a recurrent topic of concern among intellectuals and cultural commentators. Often criticism of authoritarian personalities seamlessly merged with the condemnation of conformist behaviour.

The cultural critique of conformist personalities was particularly widespread within academia. Academic critics often raised concern about the stifling consequences of homogenous and conformist behaviour. Being different and exhibiting non-conformist personality traits was the new cultural ideal. Academics perceived people possessing authoritarian personalities as very similar to one another, whereas those who were free of such personality traits were very different from one another.[618] A survey on American culture in 1959 indicated that variety and 'heterogeneity' had become 'one of America's new values'.[619] It was something of an understatement, when in 1958 a psychologist wrote that 'American psychology has become increasingly concerned with problems revolving around social conformity'.[620]

---

616 Adorno et al. (1969). See chapter X on parents and children by Frenkel-Brunswik, pp. 339, 340, 483.

617 Morawski and St Martin (2011) p.1.

618 Cohen-Cole (2014) p.40.

619 Cohen-Cole (2014) p.38.

620 M.L. Hoffman (1958) 'Conformity, conviction, and mental health', *Merrill-Palmer Quarterly*, 4(3), 145–150, at 145.

Conformist personality types were assumed to be closed minded and therefore by implication likely to possess authoritarian inclinations. Distinctions between conformism and non-conformism and between an open and closed mind conveyed important moral and political differences. It was suggested that these differences corresponded to the distinction between the left/liberal and the right/conservative. Psychology was harnessed to legitimate the claim that the concerns of conformist right-wing people were largely an expression of emotional 'status anxiety'. During the Cold War, leading American liberal commentators such as Richard Hofstadter and Lionel Trilling claimed that conservatism did not need to be taken seriously since it had no serious argument. Hofstadter's student Dorothy Ross recalled that the prevailing sentiment among fellow academics was that conservatives 'had no mind'.[621]

The politicisation of personality tended to direct its fire against those possessing conservative psychological traits. University of Pennsylvania psychiatrist Kenneth Appel stated that conservatism was itself a personality disorder. The liberal political commentator Arthur Schlesinger, Jr insisted that American conservatives were guilty of 'schizophrenia'. Leading social scientists such as Riesman and Hofstadter 'defined conservatism as a problem of abnormal psychology, a failure of intolerant, uninformed, and uneducated individuals to adjust to the complex modern world'.[622]

In his fascinating study, *Cold War Politics and the Sciences of Human Nature*, Jamie Cohen-Cole argues that the diseasing of conformism was paralleled by the goal of cultivating healthy anti-authoritarian personality types. The psychological condemnation of conformism was allied to the promotion of idealised personality traits. The defining feature of a positive personality type was creativity, a 'trait taken to be interchangeable with autonomy, rationality, tolerance, and open-mindedness'.[623] Cohen-Cole has described the campaign to cultivate a creative personality as one that was underpinned by a political agenda. It sought to 'politicize personhood' in order to legitimate the values that it upheld and to discredit those it opposed.[624] Political psychology and its ideological use of personality research acquired a powerful moralising impulse during the Cold War. Typologies of personality traits also represented moral statements about different kinds of people. Not surprisingly, one researcher discovered that 'scientists were creative and nonconformist, while the opposite held true for military offi-

621 Cohen-Cole (2014) p.51.
622 Dowbiggin (2011) pp.138–139.
623 Cohen-Cole (2014) p.35.
624 Cohen-Cole (2014) p.36.

cers'.[625] The drawing of distinctions between people which were previously expressed through a moral vocabulary was communicated through a diagnosis.[626]

Through the promotion of a non-conformist creative personality, a scientifically validated narrative on ideal attitudes was forged. This narrative allowed political moral judgments to be communicated in a neutral, scientifically informed language. That this was a flourishing enterprise is demonstrated by the publication by the mid-1990s of over two thousand studies on authoritarianism. Cohen-Cole has rightly drawn the conclusion that 'the lauding of mental attributes such as a penchant for open-minded inquiry or flexibility was a partisan endeavour, even if it did not always travel under an explicit banner of political activity'.[627] Scientism is rarely explicit about its political objectives, which is why its role as an ideology is so rarely visible and recognised.

During the Cold War, the reaction against conformism and the embrace of creativity were in part a response to the need to retain a techno-scientific edge against the Soviet Union. However, it is more useful to interpret hostility to conformism as a reaction to the values, forms of behaviour, cultural institutions and practices to which people were conforming.

Those who conformed to their community's expectations became an object of derision, decades before psychology diagnosed it as a problem. Psychology's discovery of the pathology of conformism illustrates how pre-existing cultural attitudes are often recycled as science-informed statements.

The stereotype of the conformist as a small-minded and easily manipulated individual was widely circulated through novels, short stories and essays during the 1920s and 1930s. Sinclair Lewis' powerful satirical novel, *Main Street* (1920) exuded contempt towards small-town America and the conformist personalities that inhabited it.[628] The narrow-minded community it depicted is riddled with shallow materialism and conformist hypocrisy. The individual with a conformist personality is also strikingly featured in Lewis' powerful novel, *Babbitt* (1922). The novel's main protagonist, George F. Babbitt, is totally overwhelmed by the conformist community that he inhabits. The stifling pressure to conform controls Babbitt to the point that he is both unable and unwilling to express views that deviate from what he thinks is right to think and feel.[629]

---

625 Cohen-Cole (2014) p.45.

626 See P. Bourdieu (2010) *Distinction: A Social Critique of the Judgment of Taste*, London: Routledge.

627 Cohen-Cole (2014) p.60.

628 S. Lewis (1920) *Mainstreet*, New York: Harcourt.

629 See S. Lewis [1922] (1996) *Babbitt*, Harmondsworth: Penguin.

Sinclair Lewis' novels made an important contribution to the construction of the pathology of conformism. Even before Lewis, other writers – such as Edgar Lee Masters, H.L. Mencken and Sherwood Anderson – had challenged the insular conformity of small-town America. However, none of them had the public impact of *Main Street* and *Babbit*. Lewis' assault on the provincial mentality of conformist America represented 'the beginning of a decade of literary revolt that would challenge every accepted value', wrote the literary critic Mark Schorer.[630] Sinclair's literary crusade against conformism caught the mood of the era. By the time he received the Nobel prize for literature in 1930 – the first American writer to receive it – the narrative of anti-conformism had become the ideal to which the cultural elites were expected to conform.

During the interwar era, Americans were often criticised by their culture elites for their 'herd instinct' and reluctance to think for themselves. By the 1930s, conformity had become a serious cause of concern. According to a survey of this development, mass production and large corporate bureaucracy were blamed for the standardisation of people. And as usual 'contemporary philosophies of education and child rearing' were identified as the 'culprits'.[631] Parsons complained that such significance was attached to 'fitting in' that parents are making their children 'commonplace' in order to ensure their 'popularity'.[632]

The widespread circulation of anti-conformist critiques in the pre-Second World War era indicates that they emerged independently of Cold War concerns. It also preceded the psychologically informed pathology of conformism. The psychological critique of the conformist personality and its valuation of the open-minded personality offered a scientifically framed version of pre-existing criticisms. These criticisms were already in circulation in the late 19th century, when what Soffer characterised as the New Elites in Britain sought to distinguish their superior rationality and individuality from the 'herd instincts' of the masses. Conformism to public opinion was portrayed as the typical behaviour of the non-thinking person who was incapable of acting rationally.[633]

The condemnation of conformism and the politicisation of personality invariably turned its attention towards influencing and re-engineering the mode of socialisation. Consequently, from the 1950s onwards, and especially during the 1960s, professionals involved in the sphere of socialisation sought to channel it in anti-conformist directions.

---

630 M. Schorer (1961) 'Main Street', *American Heritage*, 12(6), p.75.
631 Thomson (1997) p.634.
632 Cited in Thomson (1997) p.634.
633 See Soffer (1969).

Historically the aim of socialisation was to ensure that children grew up to conform to the prevailing values of society. Citing Durkheim's claim that the 'personality is the individual socialized', Lasch remarked that 'every society reproduces its culture – its norms and underlying assumptions, its modes of organizing experience – in the individual in the form of personality'.[634] In the 1950s and 1960s, an important shift occurred in the practice of socialisation; a turn from gaining conformity to customary values and practices to conforming to the values proposed by psychological experts.

At this point in time parenting experts, educators and psychologists proposed a new idealised type of personality to be cultivated through the process of socialisation. Pointing to this turn, Morawski and St Martin indicate that 'through the 1960s the ideally socialized person' was 'becoming flexible, capable of handling the societal changes as well as the multiple roles expected of them across the life span'.[635] This socialised person was not only flexible, creative and autonomous but also open minded and emotionally expressive. These were personality traits that had become widely promoted in American educational institutions, particularly in universities in the late 1950s and 1960s. The focus on the cultivation of an open mind did not necessarily lead to the flourishing of a genuine openness to new experience, but merely encouraged students to understand 'that there were no "right" answers'.[636] As I discuss elsewhere, the valuation of an open personality coexists with the devaluation of judgment.[637] Judgment, or being judgy, is a trait associated with a closed-minded personality. For psychologists, a closed-minded personality is problematic not simply because they are deemed to be set in their ways but also because they are not open to their advice and guidance.

The validated child

The most important initiatives designed to re-engineer people's personality occurred in the sphere of education. As we discussed in the previous chapter, educating the personality of children received the backing of sections of the business community on the ground that society required young people who were flexible, adaptable and capable of self-expression. Professionals and middle-class parents were in the forefront of supporting a movement that sought to en-

634 Lasch (1979) p.34.

635 Morawski and St Martin (2011) p.20.

636 See Cohen-Cole (2014) p.205 and ch. 7.

637 See Furedi (2020) chs 2 and 3.

sure that the psychological development of children was taken seriously by their schools. Since the 1920s, this therapeutic turn in education has ceaselessly gained importance in the schools of western societies.

During the 1930s there were clear signs that the project of educating children's personality had begun to resonate with academics and the helping professions. In her monograph on 'The modern American family' (1932), Helen Lynd was hopeful that the tide in favour of this project was beginning to turn: 'there is beginning to be some recognition of the fact that education solely or dominantly intellectual in emphasis, leaving out of consideration all emotional and other aspects of personality, may be as inadequate for a teacher, a lawyer, a business executive, or a bond salesman as for a parent'.[638]

Around this time, educational issues such as discipline and behaviour were often discussed in relation to their effect on children's personality. Educators complained that the new psychological theories of education had not gone far enough in the classroom. They emphasised the need to create an environment that allowed children to express themselves and demanded that teachers relaxed their technique of control and cease demanding obedience from their pupils. In 1931, Goodwin Watson, a Professor from Columbia University Teachers College, succinctly outlined this approach:

> The good teacher plans to exercise most of her influence on small children by the way she acts rather than by what she says. She never preaches. She is generous with approvals, and renders each child more attention when he needs to grow into intellectual and emotional awareness of these patterns. As a rule he should progress without advice from the counselor. The counselor asks questions, and when necessary gives experience. The pupil draws his own conclusions.[639]

The pedagogy outlined by Watson placed a premium on the use of psychology to validate children's personality. The previous emphasis in schooling on the provision of disciplinary knowledge gave way to the goal of cultivating children's capacity for self-expression.

In effect, the pedagogic approach outlined by Watson was one that was consistent with a psychologically informed narrative of socialisation by validation. Unlike in previous regimes of socialisation, the role of parents was not so much to transmit values as to validate the feelings, attitudes and accomplishments of their children. Teachers, too, were 'generous with approvals' and often saw their task as the cultivation of healthy personalities.

---

638 Lynd (1932) p.201.
639 G. Watson (1931) ['No title'], *Journal of Education*, 114(2), p.28.

Progressive educators supporting therapeutic education frequently complained about the lack of receptivity to their ideas. Their promotion of child-centred teaching methods frequently provoked a backlash from parents and sections of the teaching profession. Nevertheless, despite occasional setbacks the pedagogy of validation succeeded in steadily gaining ground.[640]

By the middle of the 1950s, therapeutic education and the emphasis on the management of the adjustment of children's personality acquired a dominant influence in pedagogic theory. A 1956 review by Goodwin Watson and his colleagues of 83 textbooks on educational psychology provided compelling evidence of the steadily growing interest of educators in children's personality. The review stated that 'increased attention to personality, mental hygiene, unconscious motivation, counseling, and psychotherapy represent the outstanding development' of the period between 1920 and 1956.[641] It pointed to the growing importance attached to the promotion of personality adjustment, which led to the transformation of school guidance from providing advice 'based largely on tests to more concern with emotional life'.[642] Watson also pointed to the 'spate of studies' on the personal syndrome called 'the authoritarian personality', which challenged the 'rigidity' of prevailing forms of character education.[643]

Watson and his colleagues drew attention to a new preoccupation of educational psychology, which was the importance of validating young people's identity. They wrote;

> To choose only one more among many other social factors, contemporary literature and psychotherapy agree that a pervasive problem within our culture is that of personal identity and finding valid meaning in life. Existentialism has arisen to meet a deep need. The psychological analysis of this demand and the educational implications awaits research.[644]

The identification of personal identity as a 'pervasive problem within our culture' was a new development within educational psychology. It was at this point in time that many of the issues linked to personality adjustment began to be interpreted through the narrative of identity and of an identity crisis. In wider culture, the phrase 'quest for identity' gained currency. A quest suggested that identity had to be discovered – it implied a psychological condition that had

640 Ravitch (2000) p.276.

641 G. Watson et al. (1956) 'Twenty-five years of educational research', *Review of Educational Research*, 26(3), 241–267, at 243.

642 Watson et al. (1956) p.243.

643 Watson et al. (1956) p.245.

644 Watson et al. (1956) p.245.

to be subjectively cultivated and achieved. Supporting this quest became one of the explicit objectives of socialisation through validation during the decades to follow.

A small group of educators regarded the programme of socialisation through validation as an irresponsible evasion of the duty of adults for transmitting their values to children. At the 1958 meeting of the Child Study Association of America some of them complained that techniques of personality adjustment insulated children from pressure and led to the lowering of educational standards and expectations. They called upon adults to become 'clearer and more confident about their own standards and ideals'.[645] Two years later, in 1960, the educational theorist Fred Kerlinger argued that the pedagogy of validation had the perverse consequence of diminishing the independence and sense of resilience of children.

Kerlinger noted that the introduction of what he called 'permissiveness' in education led to 'the manipulation of pupils'. He claimed that since emotional education tends to encourage a preoccupation with feelings, children lose their grounding in a stable and objective environment and become easily prey to manipulative techniques. 'When the central emphasis is on feelings, especially feelings toward other persons, objectivity, independence and autonomy become difficult to learn and to achieve', argued Kerlinger.[646]

Sixty years ago, Kerlinger had identified trends which would eventually crystallise into the mental health crisis that pervades western, and especially Anglo-American, education in the 21st century. Decades before the word 'snowflake' began to convey the connotation of fragility and vulnerability of the young, it was evident to some prescient observers that techniques of validation encouraged sections of young people to become inward looking, powerless and confused about their identity. However, though their reservations resonated with sections of the public, their sentiments were marginalised by the principal professional institutions dealing with the socialisation of young people. Socialisation through validation reflected the attitudes and concerns promoted by the cultural industries, whose views played an important role in the constitution of the public opinion of the late 20th century.

645 'Experts challenge adults to set ideals for young', *The New York Times*, 25 May 1958.
646 F.N. Kerlinger (1960) 'The implications of the permissiveness doctrine in American education', *Educational Theory*, 10(2), 120–127, at 125.

The re-engineering of personhood

The medicalisation of the self, with its emphasis on a psychologised notion of personality, entered the mainstream of society by the 1960s. During the decades to follow, the influence it exerted coincided with the gradual transformation of the meaning of personhood. Personhood is one of those taken-for-granted concepts which is rarely discussed and whose meaning is seldom elaborated. The first interesting academic reference to it that I found through my research was in a review article of a book on George H. Mead's educational theories in the *American Journal of Sociology*, in 1944. Samuel Strong, the author of this review, used the term 'personhood' to refer to the normative dimension of what it means to be a human; pointing in particular to the way that education plays a role in the cultivation of personhood. Strong wrote that 'the purpose of education is the development of personhood', which affords 'a clear conception on the part of the individual of his relation to society'. Through this process of the 'development of the self', 'the individual incorporates into his conduct the meanings and role that exists in the community'.[647] Personhood is thus shaped by meanings and normative expectations that a community communicates to individuals.

One reason why this important term, which refers to the normative dimension of being an individual human being, has remained relatively underdeveloped is because many social science commentators and psychologists are likely to be wary of the term's moral connotations. So, although widely discussed in psychology, given the moral properties that touch on the meaning of being human, science finds it difficult to clarify or engage with the concept of personhood. An article in the journal *Personhood and Health Care*, titled 'The failure of theories of personhood', draws attention to psychology's estrangement from this concept.[648]

Personhood is closely related to the idea of *moral identity*, which Kenneth Gergen associates with the definition of 'a worthy and acceptable individual by the standards inhering in one's relationship'.[649] The cultural script through

---

647 S. Strong (1944) 'A review of a book on the educational theories of George H. Mead's approach to behaviourism by A.S. Clayton', *American Journal of Sociology*, 50, 7–11, at p.9.

648 T.L. Beauchamp (1999) 'The failure of theories of personhood', in *Personhood and Health Care*, International Library of Ethics, Law, and the New Medicine, vol. 7, Dordrecht: Springer; see also Frank Furedi, www.spiked-online.com/2017/12/13/turning-childhood-into-a-mental-illness/.

649 K.J. Gergen (2005), 'Narrative, moral identity, and historical consciousness: a social constructionist account', www.researchgate.net/publication/298103687_Narrative_moral_identity_and_historical_consciousness_A_social_constructionist_account (accessed 25 April 2021).

which a community's moral identity is conveyed is intimately linked to the sense of the past and to its long-standing customs and traditions. The cultural and historical sensibility through which moral identity is constructed into a settled sense of personhood requires the support of ethnopsychology. Ethnopsychology, a concept drawn from anthropology, refers to the culturally variable narratives of the meaning of selfhood and the emotional attitudes appropriate to a community.[650] It provides a common-sense emotional narrative that offers members of a community guidance about how they should perceive their existence, how they should feel and react to the challenges they face, and the kind of emotions that are appropriate in the different circumstances they confront.[651] The ethnopsychology that prevails at any one time has a significant influence on the emotional dimension of personhood as it indicates a community's expectations of how individuals are expected to respond to their predicament.

One of the most durable and significant achievements of the project of moral engineering and its hegemonic influence on socialisation is the slow and steady but ultimately radical shift in the meaning of personhood. A vivid manifestation of this development – which occurred gradually over the 20th century – is the shift from valuation of self-reliance and stoicism to the celebration of help seeking. The person, as a seeker of help and professional support, is idealised as an open-minded, emotionally honest individual who understands that self-reliance should not be taken too far.

The contemporary ideal of personhood stands in sharp contrast to the one that prevailed during the first half of the 20th century. The classical ideals of rugged individualism, such as self-help, self-reliance and self-discipline, have become conspicuously marginal to the cultural life of the 21st century. Instead, personhood has turned inward, focused on the inner self, especially the importance of maintaining self-esteem through the respect and approval of others. Most striking of all is the shift from the ideal of self-determination to an emphasis on people needing 'support' from experts, therapists and public agencies. Help seeking has become an act of virtue in a culture that posits dependence on professional guidance as the precondition for the education of a healthy personality. The institutionalisation of help seeking is pervasive in the domain of childrearing, schools and universities. Implicit in the elevation of help seeking as a personal virtue is the premise that since the normal state of personhood

---

650 A. Frawley (2020) 'Self-esteem, happiness and the therapeutic fad cycle', in Nehring, D., Madsen, O.J., Cabanas, E., Mills, C. and Kerrigan, D. (eds) *The Routledge International Handbook of Global Therapeutic Cultures*, Abingdon and New York: Routledge.

651 See J.P. Hewitt (1998) *The Myth of Self-Esteem: Finding Happiness and Solving Problems in America*, New York: St. Martin's Press, p.21.

is helplessness, the act of seeking professional help is an admirable display of courage and honesty.

The pedagogy of validation, and its counterpart in the spheres of socialisation and childrearing, is justified on the ground that human emotions and personality require professional help and intervention. Through the medicalisation of the self and the conceptualisation of personality as a site of fragility and disorder, personhood itself has become psychologised. Alongside the medicalisation of the self, society, too, is frequently perceived as sick and damaged. Back in the 1930s, social commentators suggested that the United States was a 'sick society' in need of cure. The 1932 anthology *Our Neurotic Age* and Karen Horney's 1937 book *The Neurotic Personality of Our Time* associated the personality disorder of the individual with illness of society: 'there is a growing realization among thoughtful persons that our culture is sick, mentally disordered, and in need of treatment'.[652] During the decades to follow, the tendency to perceive the problems of everyday life through the prism of mental illness gained traction.

When in 1965 Berger wrote that 'psychoanalysis has become part of the American scene', he could be sure that his audience would treat his statement as a matter of fact. Berger remarked that psychoanalysis had become a cultural phenomenon that influenced the American legal system, religion, literature and popular culture. He claimed that at least three areas of everyday life – sexuality, marriage and childrearing – had been 'significantly' affected by it.[653] During the same year, Paul Halmos published the first systematic investigation of the impact of this phenomenon on British society and concluded that its influence was 'in a process of rapid growth'.[654] A year later the American sociologist Philip Rieff announced *The Triumph of the Therapeutic*. Discussion of the growing impact of the therapeutic ethos was not confined to the Anglo-American world. Serge Moscovici in France and Thomas Luckmann in Germany testified to the impact of the same trend in continental Europe.[655]

Alongside the emergence of therapy culture, the ethnopsychology of the West has also dramatically altered.[656] This shift can be seen in the growing ten-

652 Cited in Meyerowitz (2010) p.1073.

653 P. Berger (1965) 'Towards a sociological understanding of psychoanalysis', *Social Research* 32(1), 26–41.

654 P. Halmos (1965) *The Faith of the Counsellors*, London: Constable, p.37.

655 See S. Moscovici (1961) *La Psychoanalyse – Son Image et Son Public*, Paris: Presses Universitaires de France;and T. Luckmann (1967) *The Invisible Religion: The Problem of Religion in Modern Society*, London: Macmillan.

656 On therapy culture, see F. Furedi (2004) *Therapy Culture: Cultivating Vulnerability in an Anxious Age*, London: Routledge.

dency to represent vulnerability and emotional fragility as the defining feature of the human condition.[657] Implicitly, personhood is defined through the paradigm of vulnerability. The fatalistic narrative of vulnerability signals powerlessness and loss of agency, which fosters a cultural climate where people perceive themselves as not the subjects but the objects of history. In this new emotional landscape, the consciousness of being victims of circumstance permeates our version of personhood.

The positing of people as victims of circumstance reflects western cultural sensibilities towards the uncertainties confronting 21st century society. These uncertainties are conveyed through the colloquial usage of the discourse of trauma, anxiety and stress. Such an orientation sensitises people to regard a growing range of their experiences as emotionally harmful and damaging. The expanding list of conditions coupled with the state of vulnerability mirrors a diminishing significance attached to people's potential for resilience. This attitude informs the work of professional socialisers, who since the late 1970s have ceaselessly encouraged the perception that childhood faces a mental health crisis.[658]

In recent decades there has been a proliferation of medicalised conditions through which children's behaviour is diagnosed as a form of illness. Confused and insecure children are sometimes diagnosed as depressed or traumatised. Energetic or disruptive youngsters are presumed to be suffering from attention deficit hyperactivity disorder (ADHD). Kids who give their teachers a hard time or argue with adults might even find themselves labelled victims of 'oppositional defiant disorder'. Shy pupils are offered the diagnosis of social phobia. Children who really hate going to school might have 'school phobia'. Pupils worried about exams are diagnosed as suffering from 'exam stress'. Everyone who has been a child or who understands children will know that they are often concerned about how they will perform in exams, of course; but what is different today is that this is rebranded in the therapeutic language of 'exam stress'.

Through the passing of time, young people who are socialised to see their experiences through the prism of mental health internalise elements of this narrative. Unlike children who went to school 40 or 50 years ago, today's schoolchildren readily communicate their problems in a psychological vocabulary, using words like 'stress', 'trauma' and 'depression' to describe their feelings. Robert Merton elaborated the concept of 'self-fulfilling prophecy' to describe the way that initial assumptions and beliefs about a situation can play a significant

657 F. Furedi (2007) 'From the narrative of the Blitz to the rhetoric of vulnerability', *Cultural Sociology*, 1(2), 235–254.

658 See Frank Furedi, www.spiked-online.com/2017/12/13/turning-childhood-into-a-mental-illness/.

role in its outcome.[659] Justman writes of the 'nocebo effect'; the way that the expansion of medical diagnosis invites people to feel ill.[660]

The representation of existential problems as medical ones has an important influence on the way individuals perceive their health. The relationship between the medicalised narrative of well-being and its impact is a dialectical one, in that it does not simply frame the way people are supposed to feel and behave; it also constitutes an invitation to being 'not well'. That is why the sensibility of being 'not well' has today become part of many people's identity.

The 21st century version of a help-seeking personhood communicates a narrative that continually raises doubts about people's emotional capacity to deal with physical and emotional harms. The transformation of distress into a condition of emotional injury has as its premise the belief that people are likely to be damaged by unpleasant encounters and the setbacks thrown up by everyday life. In this context, 'trauma' has become an all-purpose term to describe the individual's state of mind in the aftermath of an adverse experience. In contemporary culture, distress is not something to be lived but a condition that requires treatment. From this standpoint the integrity of the person is threatened through exposure to adversity.

Commentators often interpret the emergence of therapy culture as if it were the natural outcome of prosperity, the rise of individualism, consumerism or obsession with the self. No doubt some of these trends, such as self-awareness and the greater availability of choice, have played a part in the emergence of a new, psychologised sense of personhood. However, the main cultural driver of the association of vulnerability with personhood was and remains the displacement of socialisation as a medium for transmitting values by a form of intervention oriented towards validation. As generation after generation of young people have gone through this regime of validation, they have acquired the disposition of perceiving issues that were hitherto seen as problems of existence through the prism of psychology. Without the support of moral bonds and values to provide young people with guidance and a sense of belonging, many of them become willing recipients of therapeutic intervention.

That the cultural changes promoted through a psychologically informed ethos of socialisation have had important implications for the meaning of personhood is shown by its gradual institutionalisation in the adult world. Since the 1990s, human resource professionals have introduced these medicalised ide-

---

659 R. Merton (1948) 'The self-fulfilling prophecy,' *Antioch Review*, Summer, 193–210.

660 S. Justman (2015) *The Nocebo Effect: Overdiagnosis and Its Costs*, New York: Palgrave, pp.x–xi.

als into the public and private sector. Validating employees and insulating them from emotional distress is now – at least rhetorically – accepted as 'best practice' by large and influential corporations. At the same time these sentiments are widely circulated and authorised by professional and cultural institutions, including the medium of popular culture. An ever-expanding industry devoted to the promotion of these sentiments influences all aspects of life. In his analysis of this 'caring industry' in the US, Dworkin estimated that there are approximately 100,305 clinical psychologists, 1.2 million clinical social workers and counsellors, 405,000 nurse psychotherapists and social workers and 17,500 life cultures working in 'just about every organized unit of state and society' in the US.[661]

The project of re-engineering socialisation did not simply intensify a disposition towards vulnerability but also called into question the normative foundation of what was traditionally termed 'moral identity'. Moral identity touches on normativity, sense of community and what Gergen described as a historical narrative. In his essay 'Narrative, moral identity, and historical consciousness', Gergen draws an important connection between a sense of historical continuity and the achievement of individual identity. He argues that 'historical narratives serve as a foreground for achieving moral identity within relevant historical communities'. He emphasises this point when he states that 'my capacity to achieve moral identity today is intimately linked to my relationship with the narratives of the past'.[662]

As we discussed in chapter 4, the loss of the sense of the past is intimately intertwined with scientism's critique of tradition and the distancing of society from its past. The anti-conformist turn of socialisation has played a critical role in weakening the individual's relationship to a narrative of the past. Despite its enormous implication for the achievement of moral identity, the significance of the loss of the sense of the past is rarely recognised by commentaries on the crisis of identity. In some cases, the liberation of the individual from the past is applauded as a positive development. In educational and cultural settings adults and children are encouraged to choose their identity. The implication of such a voluntaristic approach is that either children possess the moral and intellectual resources to construct their identity or alternatively that identities are ready-made goods that people can choose or reject. Experience indicates that identities that are not organically linked to an individual's past or cultural values possess a

661 https://nationalaffairs.com/publications/detail/the-politicization-of-unhappiness (accessed 6 July 2020).

662 Gergen (2005), 'Narrative, moral identity, and historical consciousness: a social constructionist account', www.researchgate.net/publication/298103687_Narrative_moral_identity_and_historical_consciousness_A_social_constructionist_account (accessed 25 April 2021).

fragile connection to the self. Instead of resolving the crisis of identity it leads to a dead end as individuals get trapped in their quest for identity. Without a historical narrative, identities fail to satisfy an individual's search for meaning.

The separation of identity from constitutive moral norms does not mean that it is morally neutral. As we saw with the case of personality, not all identities are equal. Just as some personalities are said to be damaged and sick, so some identities are perceived as inferior to others. Through the conceptual linkage of identity to grouphood, the consciousness of individual and group distinctiveness became indissolubly linked.

The psychological reframing of concepts like personality and identity provided the intellectual resources for the reshaping of the perception of the self and its relation to culture. That these concepts quickly became integrated into everyday language and acquired a commanding role in the narrative of personhood was made possible by the influence that socialisation through validation exercised on successive generations of young people. The most significant legacy of the medicalisation of human existence leading to the valorisation and institutionalisation of a therapeutic sensibility is the radical revision of the meaning of personhood. The ascendancy of this therapeutic sensibility illustrates the significant role that psychology has played in the modification of the meaning of personhood. Brinkmann wrote that 'the psychological ways of thinking about people have not just served as passive representations of human subjects, but have in fact deeply influenced how humans think and feel, and indeed influenced human subjectivity itself'. Moreover, 'since the birth of psychology, humans have increasingly come to think about themselves in light of psychology's concepts and categories, and their lives have become dependent on psychological technologies such as tests and therapies'.[663] Psychology's concepts and categories are as normal to us as the use of religious precepts and idioms in the pre-modern era.

663 Brinkmann (2010) p.57.

Chapter 9: Cultural Turn to Identity

Psychology's capacity to generate a cultural script projecting a series of values and a distinct sensibility indicates that it worked not merely as a science but also as an ethos. By the 1960s it was evident that this ethos guided sections of society to develop a distinctive understanding of their selves. It also instructed people how to feel, respond to problems, conduct relationships and present oneself in public. Therapy culture did not encompass the totality of western culture and the public was confronted with a variety of competing cultural claims. But by the 1960s a psychologically informed version of personhood was in the ascendancy and all but enjoyed a hegemonic status over young people – soon to be known as the baby boomers. This was the first generation to be thoroughly socialised by validation and those of its members who went to colleges and universities were likely to have become exposed to the arguments that underpinned the therapeutic cultural script.

The ascendancy of the new regime of socialisation was illustrated by its influence over the use of language. Language 'is the principal means by which an individual is socialized to become an inhabitant of a world shared with others and also provides the means by which, in conversation with these others, the common world continues to be plausible to him', explained Berger.[664] The proliferation of therapeutically informed words and terms and their growing usage – consciousness raising, raising awareness, self-actualisation, self-realisation, self-expression, uppers and downers, support groups, encounter groups – signalled the arrival of a new cultural sensibility. This language, which gradually drifted into the everyday vernacular, idealised a person who was 'getting his head together' and was emotionally expressive, unlike those who were 'uptight' or 'hung up' and who refused to deal with their 'issues'.

Though it would take a couple of decades for the ideals expressed through 1960s pop psychology to become institutionalised, at the time most serious observers of society knew that they were going through an era of profound cultural change. At this point there was not yet talk of a mental health crisis among children, post-traumatic stress disorder was not used in everyday conversation and the explosion of psychiatric diagnostic categories had not yet occurred.

664 P. Berger (1966) 'Identity as a problem in the sociology of knowledge', *European Journal of Sociology/Archives Européennes de Sociologie/Europäisches Archiv für Soziologie*, 7(1), 105 – 115, at 108.

https://doi.org/10.1515/9783110708899-010

A lot more was at stake than the influence of a psychologically informed sensibility. The Marxist historian Eric Hobsbawm described it as a 'cultural revolution'.[665] Decades later, the Italian writer and philosopher Umberto Eco recalled that 'even though all visible traces of 1968 are gone, it profoundly changed the way all of us, at least in Europe, behave and relate to one another'. He added that 'relations between bosses and workers, students and teachers, even children and parents, have opened up' and therefore 'they'll never be the same again'.[666] Eco's focus on the transformative impact of cultural change on the conduct of human relationships captured the essence of the events of 1968.

The generational conflict of the 1960s served as a conduit for a thoroughgoing process of cultural realignment. Suddenly, the trends discussed in the previous chapters – loss of the sense of the past and of adult authority, the detachment of society from its tradition, the idealisation of non-conformism, the displacement of a moral narrative by a psychological one, the medicalisation of society, the institutionalisation of socialisation through validation – gathered pace. The cultural changes that had been set in motion decades previously unexpectedly acquired sufficient power and assertiveness to self-consciously declare itself as a counter-culture. The discovery and institutionalisation of adolescence in the 19th century was consummated in the 1960s.

Outwardly the rise of the 1960s counter-culture appeared to represent the antithesis of the ambitions that usually accompany social engineering. Radical students lashed out against what they saw as the machine-like attitudes of leaders of the corporate world and displayed unreserved suspicion towards projects of social engineering. Their hostility towards science often went so far as to call into question scientific reasoning itself. Theodor Roszak's influential text *The Making of a Counter Culture* articulated these sentiments in an unambiguous anti-modernist fashion. Roszak described industrial society as 'fatally and contagiously diseased'. He condemned 'technocracy's essential criminality', which, he claimed, 'insists, in the name of progress, in the name of reason, that the unthinkable become thinkable and the intolerable become tolerable'. He added that the youthful counter-cultural activists refuse 'to practice such a cold-blooded rape of our human sensibilities' which is why generational conflict 'reaches so peculiarly and painfully deep'.[667] The approach outlined by Roszak explicitly called into question the ideals of Enlightenment modernity. He dis-

665 E. Hobsbawm (2020), *The Age of Extremes: 1914–1991*, Hachette UK, p.327.

666 Eco is cited in J.W. Muller (2013) *Contesting Democracy: Political Ideas in Twentieth Century Europe*, New Haven: Yale University Press, p.200.

667 T. Roszak (1970) *The Making of a Counter Culture: Reflections on the Technocratic Society*, London: Faber & Faber, p.47.

missed technocratic assumptions about science and intellect and argued that 'nothing less is required than the subversion of the scientific world view, with its entrenched commitment to an egocentric and cerebral mode of consciousness'. In its place, he demanded that 'there must be a culture in which the non-intellective capacity of the personality – those capacities that take fire from visionary splendour and the experience of human communion – become arbiters of the good, the true, and the beautiful'.[668]

Roszak's anti-modernist sentiments, which were widely shared by the so-called '60s generation', were in fact entirely consistent with some of the earlier modernist cultural criticism of a 'sick society' that emanated from the tradition of moral engineering. Though it was anti-science it was in the thrall of the psychological sensibility of scientism! Roszak and the counter-culture embraced the politicisation of personality to the point that personal feelings were now accorded unprecedented political significance. Roszak's call for a culture that celebrated 'the non-intellective capacity of the personality' implicitly drew attention to the need for validating emotionalism and a therapeutic version of personhood. Roszak went on to demonstrate the coexistence of an anti-scientific imagination with a crude psychologistic approach in his *The Gendered Atom: Reflections on the Sexual Psychology of Science* (1999). The target of his text was the male personality and the unhappy influence of its psychology on science. By this time, male personality traits were well on the way to being represented as inferior to female ones, mainly on the ground that men were not as emotionally expressive as women.

Commentators struggled to comprehend the origins and meaning of the cultural upheaval that they were witnessing. It was evident that many features of the taken-for-granted consensus that touched on the conduct of everyday life had become a focus for conflict. Matters that had been hitherto relatively untouched by political disputes – values, lifestyles, personal life – were suddenly engulfed by them. One of the first to note this shift was the scholar Gabriel Kolko, who in 1968 remarked that 'cultural realignment' rather than class led to conflicts which were 'pre-political'. He asserted that what 'ultimately explains the realignment in America's public culture are *allegiances to different formulations and sources of moral authority*'.[669]

Taken aback by the ferocity of the criticism hurled at the customs and values prevailing in western society, its defenders struggled to grasp and name the

---

668 Roszak (1970) pp.50–51.

669 G. Kolko (1968) *The Politics of War: The World and United States Foreign Policy 1943–1945*, New York: Vintage Books, p.118.

threat they were facing. In the end, the term 'adversary culture' came into use. Daniel Bell wrote of the 'power of this hostile "adversary culture"', which literally 'shattered' bourgeois culture to the point that almost no one is prepared to defend it.[670] He noted that, without any significant cultural support, capitalism lacked a 'moral justification of authority'.

The term 'adversary culture' was coined in 1965 by Lionel Trilling, who detected its influence in modernist literature. Trilling claimed that the work of its authors was oriented towards estranging their readers from their traditional culture and inculcating them with values that contradicted it. He stated that:

> Any historian of the modern age will take virtually for granted the adversary intention, the actual subversive intention, that characterizes modern writing – he will perceive its clear purpose of detaching the reader from the habits of thought and feeling that the larger culture imposes, of giving him a ground and a vantage point from which to judge and condemn, and perhaps revise, the culture that has produced him.[671]

Trilling's focus on modernist writers and on the cultural aesthetic critique of capitalism is understandable given his orientation towards literary criticism. His insightful appreciation of the attraction of a new cultural sensibility in literature provided others with an awareness of its role in other currents of public life.

Trilling's remarks about how modern writing had a 'clear purpose of detaching the reader from the habits of thought and feeling' of the 'larger culture' accurately identified the anti-traditionalist ethos of moral engineering, and particularly its practice in the sphere of education. The psychic distancing of readers from their culture served as the literary expression of a similar pattern at work in other sectors of society. In a similar vein the idealisation of an anti-conformist personality by psychology encouraged the value of distancing from the larger culture.

Trilling made an important distinction between the adversary spirit of modernism with what he perceived as an academically sanctioned adversary culture of the 1960s. He was dismayed by the adversary culture that permeated the higher education of his time and particularly by its willingness to engage in the 'socialization of the anti-social, or the acculturation of the anti-cultural'.[672] In his account of adversary culture, Trilling tried to make sense of a conflict that would soon erupt into a veritable culture war. His formulation 'socialization of the anti-social' allowed Trilling to come close to situating the phenomenon of

670 D. Bell (1976) *The Cultural Contradictions of Capitalism*, London: Heinemann, p.40.
671 L. Trilling (1965) *Beyond Culture*, New York: Viking Press, pp.xii–xiii.
672 Trilling (1965) p.26.

adversary culture within its origin in the re-engineering of socialisation. Others who embraced the concept of adversary culture overlooked the significance of the 'socialisation of the anti-social' and tended to portray it as a legacy of the romantic, anti-rationalistic and anti-bourgeois outlook of the 18th and 19th centuries.[673] Typically, they appeared oblivious to the adversarial cultural sensibility circulated through the powerful currents of social engineering that influenced political life from the late 19th century onwards.

The conceptualisation of an adversarial mentality was far too abstract to provide more than a limited insight into its cultural and political temper. Some attempted to attribute this development to what they described as a New Class. Trilling wrote that 'there has grown up a populous group whose members take for granted the idea of the adversary culture'. But he did not attempt to expound on the nature of this group or what its membership entailed.[674]

At the time opponents of adversary culture tended to perceive it as a reflection of the political ideology pursued by radical counter-cultural political activists. Yet, sensibilities that were designated as adversarial existed independently of any specific affiliations. Paul Hollander explained, 'specific ideology matters less and less, as groups of people have become socialized over a longer period of time into the adversarial position which has become increasingly reflexive, intuitive, nonintellectual – as all profoundly held cultural, or subcultural, beliefs are'.[675] Hollander was right to note that adversarial beliefs and attitudes were not external to the dominant culture; they were the products of its regime of socialisation. Conservative thinkers failed to appreciate this point and throughout the 1970s they were under the spell of a narrative that was conspiratorial in tone and insisted that what they faced was a wilful subversion by a group of highly committed nihilistic intellectuals. Consequently, they failed to understand the depth of the cultural threat that confronted them and to this day they have proved singularly unsuccessful in dealing with it. It was easier to imagine that what was at work was the outcome of conscious sabotage by resentful campus radicals than to acknowledge the internal crisis of culture confronting them.

673 P. Hollander (1988) 'Alienation and the adversary culture', *Society*, 25(4), 40–48, at 45.
674 Cited in Hollander (1988) p.45.
675 Hollander (1988) p.45.

The generational culture gap

By the 1960s, trends that had gradually gained momentum over the century coalesced and acquired a commanding influence. Their outcome was later characterised as the Cultural Turn by academics and social scientists.[676] A consciousness of cultural conflict and change permeated society, which had a profound effect on the conduct of public life. At the time a polarised conception of cultural values tended to be attributed to the so-called 'generation gap' and the conflict it provoked. The term 'generation gap' gained usage in the 1960s. It was not simply another term for generational conflict, for it also signalled something more profound – an unbridgeable cultural chasm between the generations. Bob Dylan's powerful generational hymn echoed this sentiment:

> Come mothers and fathers
> Throughout the land
> And don't criticize
> What you can't understand
> Your sons and your daughters
> Are beyond your command
> Your old road is rapidly agin'
> Please get out of the new one
> If you can't lend your hand
> For the times they are a-changin'

The emergence of a generation gap highlighted young people's alienation and animosity not just to their elders, but also to their values. As the therapist William Glasser put it; 'rather than the well-advertised generation gap, this is a cultural gap'! He wrote that in 'many families there are two cultures' and that 'we find most families with older children to be divided culturally'. Pointing to this development's unique character, Glasser stated that this 'cultural gap' was unprecedented in history.[677]

Like many social commentators at the time, Eisenstadt believed that this 'unprecedented' inter-generational discontinuity was underpinned by the rise of alienation from consumer society and a reaction to modernity.[678] What he, along with numerous commentators, failed to appreciate was that the youth re-

---

676 See K. Nash (2001) 'The "cultural turn" in social theory: towards a theory of cultural politics', *Sociology*, 35(1), 77–92.

677 W. Glasser (1972) *The Identity Society*, New York: Harper & Row Publishers, p.12.

678 S.N. Eisenstadt (1971) 'Generational conflict and intellectual antinomianism', *Annals of the American Academy of Political and Social Science*, 395, 68–79, at 69.

bellion was fuelled by many of the impulses that led to the idealisation of adolescence in the first place. Previously, the young were celebrated for their ability and willingness to adapt to change and to the consequences of a loss of cultural continuity. Yet, the disruption of cultural continuity was not without its problems, for it left the young without a map to guide them on their journey to adulthood.

The transition to adulthood requires a map where moral boundaries are clearly delineated. Through helping children to understand the meaning of these boundaries, they become prepared to make the transition from one stage of their life to another. Ideally, in this way children are able to form an identity of their selves that harmonises their needs with those of society. As Martin and Barresi note in their study of the history of personal identity:

> Ego identity requires knowing who you are and how you fit into society. It requires forming for yourself an identity of self that satisfies both your own internal needs and those of society. The task is easier if the society already has a clear role that you are expected to fill and respects you for filling it, and you have good role models. ... Under such conditions, there is little reason for an adolescent to experience a 'crisis' in making the transition from childhood to adulthood.[679]

In the absence of clear signposts, the boundary between childhood and adulthood becomes blurred, and everyone – adolescents and adults alike – becomes confused about their roles.

The disruption of cultural continuity raised important questions about what social roles the young should aspire to and what values should be transmitted to them in the process of socialisation. The adult world often failed to provide answers to these questions. Instead of offering solutions, the new regime of socialisation made a virtue of discontinuity and change, and encouraged the young to learn to adjust to it. They were expected to cultivate their selves and acquire the psychological skills required to adapt to a changing world. This sentiment was actively disseminated in education, particularly in colleges and universities. This new orientation suggested that, unlike in the past, socialisation should not transmit pre-existing values; nor should it dictate what social roles should be adopted by the young. Social theorists in particular legitimised this stance by calling into question forms of socialisation that sought to convey a sense of cultural continuity. Influenced by the therapeutic ethos, they preferred that young people learned to express themselves and realise their authentic selves.

679 Martin and Barresi (2006) p.275.

At the time, and in the decades to follow, many academic commentators embraced discontinuity as both a natural and desirable state of affairs and portrayed a stable form of socialisation as perverse. One sociologist asserted that socialisation need not be predictable because 'increasingly fluid symbolic surplus of cultural meanings, models, codes, and interpretations' mean that 'cultural models' can 'no longer serve as a reliable basis for predictability and consistency in behavior, even if internalized during childhood socialization'.[680] Such sentiments were framed in an even more exaggerated and dramatic form by postmodernists, who claimed that in a constantly changing, fluid environment the very notion of transmitting 'fixed' and 'stable' values was dysfunctional. Whereas the loss of stable identity was previously perceived as a source of serious concern, in more recent times the difficulty of adopting a stable identity has frequently been portrayed as a potentially creative development.

It was in the context of an omnipresent sensibility of cultural discontinuity that identity emerged as a name for the problems that were set in motion by the re-engineering of socialisation. Bauman explained this development well, when he stated that 'at no time did identity "become a problem"; it was a "problem" from its birth *was born as a problem*'.[681] In other words, identity became a graspable phenomenon and problem when, because of the discontinuity of culture, it had to be found and cultivated. Bauman's insight echoed an earlier influential sociological study, *The Homeless Mind* (1974), which concluded that the 'open ended' quality of 'modern identity engenders psychological strains and makes the individual peculiarly vulnerable to the shifting definitions of others'. Consequently, 'modern man is afflicted with a permanent identity crisis, a condition conducive to considerable nervousness'.[682]

Although the formulation of the crisis of identity preceded the cultural turn, it was very much a symptom of the awareness of discontinuity that made it permanent. The explosion of interest in the crisis of identity in the 1960s stemmed from this consciousness of discontinuity. Berger and his collaborators explained the relationship between the inherently unstable character of identity and its relationship to socialisation in the following terms:

> The norms and values on which the individual has been brought up are no longer reaffirmed in the presently relevant social relationships. They are no longer backed by the authority of the old primary groups. Thus they become less and less 'real' to the individual –

---

680 Marx (1980) p.189.

681 Z. Bauman (1996) 'From pilgrim to tourist – or a short history of identity', *Questions of Cultural Identity*, 1, 18–36, at 18–19.

682 Berger, Berger and Kellner (1974) p.73.

> as does his past identity itself. This causes an interesting reversal of the original socialization process. The norms that were originally internalized are now externalized once more, that is, they are located outside the self as belonging to the past or to others from whom one has become alienated. There appears a cleavage between past and present identity, with the former now being reinterpreted in terms of the latter.[683]

Their reference to the cleavage between past and present identity signified that the latter had become unmoored from the past. Its direction of travel was uncertain. The emergence of the polarisation between past and present identity was the point of departure for the gradual hardening of the cleavage between them. By the turn of the 21st century almost all the wedge issues that divided the public – guns, same-sex marriage, abortion, school prayer, euthanasia, Brexit – were symbols of this cleavage of identities.

Initially, the cleavage appeared to correspond to generational differences. But soon these identities attached themselves to different constituencies and cultural and political orientations. The cultural conflicts that erupted in the decades to follow are the politicised expressions of the rift between these two identities.

From its very inception as a newly constructed medium for understanding the self, identity was an inherently contradictory concept. For many, identity expressed an aspiration for a stable self, for a sense of permanence and certainty about where one belonged. At the same time, others who were concerned with their identity were conscious of its impermanence. Identity was framed as something to be found, constructed and, from the 1970s onwards, was even said to be invented. Some interpreted it as a statement about themselves while others regarded it as an attribute to the group to which they belonged.

Until the 1980s the literature on the subject of identity tended to express concern about its unstable features. Since this time, many have celebrated its fluid and unstable character.[684] Commentaries often warn against being fixated with the possession of stable identity and convey the sentiment that the identities they idealise are ones that are detached from the past; fluid and open ended.[685]

Proponents of deconstruction tended to show a preference for viewing identity as unstable and as not a 'pregiven entity bound by the fixed attributes of a

---

683 T. Luckmann and P. Berger (1964) 'Social mobility and personal identity', *European Journal of Sociology/Archives Européennes de Sociologie/Europäisches Archiv für Soziologie*, 5(2), 331–344.

684 Marx (1980) p.189.

685 Hall (1998) p.1.

group but as constituted in some type of processes'.[686] In so doing they sought to disassociate the self from possessing any inherent qualities and fixed characteristics. Often this approach was justified in the name of an 'anti-essentialist critique' of cultural identity. By detaching the self from any inherent qualities based on individual and collective experience, the anti-essentialist critique led to an arbitrary conception of identity. While the notion of identity-as-process appealed to groups of deconstructionist commentators, in real life people have tended to look for a more stable, coherent narrative for situating themselves and their place in the world.

The cultural turn coincided with the exhaustion of the main political ideologies of the 20th century – liberalism, conservatism, socialism, communism. The dominant narratives that were used to interpret political and socio-economic developments lost much of their legitimacy. Problems that were previously interpreted as principally social were increasingly presented as cultural and psychological. Academics in the social sciences and the humanities both invented and also fell under the spell of cultural narratives. *The one ideology that escaped demotion in this cultural turn was the one without a name.* The cultural turn was also a psychological turn and problems that were hitherto perceived as social were increasingly posited as psychological. One of the most important outcomes of this process was that identity became the vehicle through which a variety of problems and causes – individual and group – came to be grasped and eventually politicised. This occurred first in the Anglo-American sphere and later spread throughout the western world. Explanations oriented towards the emotions were increasingly applied to interpret social issues. 'Problems that were once considered political, economic, or educational are today found to be psychological', noted Moskowitz in her study of therapeutic culture in the US.[687]

Politicisation of identity

In 1960, when Bell published his famous essay *The End of Ideology*, he used the word 'exhaustion' to refer to the demise of the ideologies that haunted the interwar world. Bell's argument about the exhaustion of ideology did not simply pertain to the decline of communism and fascism but to the loss of relevance of many of the political concepts that inspired proponents of liberal democracy.

686 See Dunn (1998) p.30.

687 E.S. Moskowitz (2001) *In Therapy We Trust: America's Obsession with Self-Fulfillment*, Baltimore: JHU Press, p.2.

He wrote that older 'counter-beliefs' have 'lost their intellectual force as well'. The counter-beliefs that he alluded to were those of liberalism and conservatism.[688]

At the time, many commentators found it difficult to accept the end-of-ideology thesis. They argued that the rise of student radicalism and the upheavals of the late 1960s showed that ideology was very much alive. Yet, the radical rhetoric of the 1960s did not quite add up to an ideology. Moreover, in the decades to follow political parties with conventional ideological pretensions gradually unravelled and became marginalised.

In the discussion on the end-of-ideology thesis one important phenomenon was overlooked, which was the role of psychology in discrediting the status of ideology. As we noted earlier, political psychology was frequently used in the 1930s to depict fascism as a symptom of emotional deficits. Lasswell attributed the success of Hitler to his ability to 'alleviate the personal insecurity of many Germans'.[689] In the 1950s his version of political psychology became widely acclaimed and was used to explain the political behaviour of the public. Psychology was regularly applied as the instrument for diagnosing political behaviour. Indeed, it was often claimed that politics served as the medium through which individual psychological problems were expressed. Political ideologies, such as communism, were now depicted as 'subterfuges for something else'.[690] Ideology was explained away as a response to the emotional needs of people. This reduction of political ideologies to psychological issues contributed to discrediting them as both irrational and as providing a false solution to people's emotional needs. At the same time, the ideological assumptions that the adversary culture had assimilated from psychology became, if anything, more influential than in previous times.

The influence of psychology over the 1960s movements ensured that its radical rhetoric and utopian pretensions swiftly gave way to a focus on lifestyle, emotions and identity. At the time, one of the most prescient accounts of this development was offered by the sociologist Ralph Turner. Writing in 1969, he stated that 'the power of both the liberal humanitarian and the socialist conceptions of injustice has been largely exhausted' and displaced by a novel perception of injustice, which was framed through a therapeutic language.[691]

688 D. Bell (2000) *The End of Ideology: On the Exhaustion of Political Ideas in the Fifties*, Cambridge, Mass: Harvard University Press, p.402.
689 See discussion in Robin (2001) p.65.
690 Robin (2001) p.95.
691 Turner (1969) p.392.

A decade before the term 'identity politics' was coined, Turner succeeded in drawing attention to the significance of the turn of politics to the person and to the politicisation of identity. He observed that 'for the first time in history' it was now common for movements to express indignation 'over the fact that people lack personal worth' and that 'they lack an inner peace of mind which forms a sense of personal dignity or a clear sense of identity'.[692] Turner argued that this shift was paralleled by a new meaning given to the Marxist problem of alienation. Unlike the Marxist account, which emphasised people's alienation from the products of their work, its new meaning referred to a psychological state of alienation from the self. 'Man's alienation is now divorcement of the individual from himself or the failure of the individual to find his real self, which he must employ as a base for organizing his life', he noted.[693]

In effect, the dramatic development that occurred for the 'first time in history' was the assertion by the new social movements of the right to the validation of personal self-worth by society. Turner added that 'alienation in its more psychological meaning and the quest for identity become the main complaints'. He pointed out that the framing of the problem of lack of self-worth as a public injustice rather than a private misfortune was a 'novel idea – not yet generally accepted'.[694] But then, this was 1969, still at a very early stage in the development of identity politics. In the decades to follow, claim makers would insist that self-respect and self-worth are a human right and that government policy should direct its energy towards raising the self-esteem of individuals and communities.[695]

At the time Turner appeared to give the impression that the 1960s quest for identity and its demand for the validation of its self-worth could be a temporary phenomenon. As subsequent events would show, the early symptoms of identity politics in the late 1960s and early 1970s marked the modest beginning of what would turn out to be a powerful force in public life in the western world. The ground for the development of the politicisation of identity with its demand for the right to self-worth and to esteem was prepared by the decades-long practice of socialisation through validation. Socialisation through validation helped pave the way for the normalisation of the belief that there is a right for the self to be affirmed. These sentiments, which were initially widely practised in primary education, migrated upstream to adulthood. By the 1960s many grown-ups had concluded that they, too, deserved to be affirmed.

---

692 Turner (1969) p.392.

693 Turner (1969) p.396.

694 Turner (1969) p.404.

695 C. Bay (1982) 'Self-respect as a human right: thoughts on the dialectics of wants and needs in the struggle for human community', *Human Rights Quarterly*, 4(1), 53–75; and Furedi (2004) ch. 8.

Calls for the validation of self-worth and self-esteem were a short step to the politicisation of personality. If personality could be diagnosed in terms of political traits, then politics can become very personal. The late 1960s saw the politicisation of personal and everyday life. The flip-side of the end of ideology was an unprecedented emphasis on the search for personal solutions to the problems of existence. Changing yourself or realising yourself, expressing yourself or emancipating yourself became rallying calls for young people drawn towards the self-absorbed spirit of the time. For many, the project of changing yourself served as an end in itself. This was a time when former leaders of the 1960s cultural movement – Jerry Rubin, Abbie Hoffman – declared that it was 'more important to get your head together than to move the multitudes'.[696] The vociferous inward turn by the counter-culture served as the precursor to the politicisation of identity.

The politicisation of the emotional needs of the self was one of the most distinct contributions of the 1960s. This embrace of emotional and personal issues allowed activists to address a variety of 'prepolitical, "existential" concerns: issues pertaining to psychology, sexuality, family life, urbanism, and basic human intimacy', claims Wolin.[697] Carol Hanisch's 1969 essay 'The personal is political' highlighted this sensibility.[698] The rhetoric of the 'personal is political' and the attachment of the term 'political' to the emotional needs of the self were not simply confined to an individual quest for esteem and recognition. This sentiment was quickly assimilated into group identity. Identities based on wider affiliations, such as that of race, gender, ethnicity and community, came to be represented through the language of feelings. Once personal motivations and problems came to be regarded as the stuff of political activism, people's feelings and emotions could be seen as resources on which activists could draw. In its 1970 manifesto, the feminist San Francisco Redstockings Collective argued 'Our politics begin with our feelings'.[699] Supporters of a personalised and feelings-oriented movement frequently denounced what they perceived as the rigid separation of the emotional and the rational. The prevailing influence of lifestyle and therapeutic sensibilities played an important role in the crystallisation of the slogan the 'personal is political'.

Identity politics, with its emphasis on the affirmation of self, is generally perceived as the politics of the individual. However, once it is politicised identity

---

696 Cited in Lasch (1979) p.14.

697 R. Wolin (2010) *The Wind from the East: French Intellectuals, the Cultural Revolution and the Legacy of the 1960s*, Princeton: Princeton University Press, p.10.

698 See www.carolhanisch.org/CHwritings/PIP.html (accessed 4 May 2018).

699 www.redstockings.org/index.php/rs-manifesto (accessed 16 May 2021).

acquires the property of a thing in itself. Previously we discussed the fossilisation of personality traits and the way personality is grasped as something that can be typologised as a fixed entity. Contrary to the views of anti-essentialist deconstructionists, identity, too, has a tendency to become reified. The anti-essentialist rhetoric of difference, which influences academic discourse on identity, is contradicted by a reality where identity is increasingly endowed with a fixed pre-given content. Nevertheless, because many academic theorists are both analyst and protagonist of identity politics, they tend to overlook its tendency towards reification.[700]

While identity can be rendered fluid and open ended, the very act of politicising it forecloses such possibilities. The literary theorist Walter Benn Michaels hit the nail on the head when he asserted that there are 'no anti-essentialist accounts of identity' because 'the essentialism inheres not in the description of the identity but in the attempt to derive the practices from the identity – we do this because we are this'.[701] When it comes to public life, identity is its own script, and its narrative and practice are pre-given and non-negotiable. Back in 1992, when Benn made this point, the predetermined relationship between identity and its practice had only recently become visible. In the contemporary era, many identities proclaim their unmistakable fixed quality. In some instances identity is portrayed as an inheritance, something acquired at birth. That is why the journalist Joseph Harker could suggest that 'DNA technology' allows 'black people to trace their origins' which 'could be the route' to a new identity.[702] The growing interest in DNA testing indicates that many people are looking to find out 'who they really are'.[703]

In recent times, sexual identity – which was often depicted by 1960s radicals as a matter of choice – is often endowed with naturalistic qualities. The claim that being gay is not a choice naturalises this form of sexuality. The recently invented identity of whiteness conveys the implication of racism as the original sin of light-skinned folk. It is an identity that automatically implies privilege. Identity politics reduces the views of an individual to the common traits of a group. In some instances, this essentialist imagination credits identities with pre-given attitudes, emotions and even epistemologies. We have feminist epistemology,

---

700 See R. Brubaker and F. Cooper (2000) Beyond "identity"', *Theory & Society*, 29(1), 1–47, at 5.
701 W.B. Michaels (1992) 'Race into culture: a critical genealogy of cultural identity', *Critical Inquiry*, 18(4), 655–685, at 684.
702 See www.theguardian.com/world/2003/feb/14/race.science?INTCMP=SRCH.
703 See www.nytimes.com/2021/02/16/opinion/23andme-ancestry-race.html#click=https://t.co/8gbXdZ9Xjb (accessed 6 March 2021).

black epistemology, black feminist epistemology and queer epistemology, among others.[704]

The trend towards the fossilisation of identity has accelerated during the past decade as the policing of identity boundaries has acquired increased prominence. Instead of promoting difference, advocates of identity politics are busy protecting their group from the crime of cultural appropriation. The idea of appropriation has its foundation in the conviction that culture is the sacred property of its moral guardians. Through enforcing the cultural boundaries separating identities, the earlier claims about fluidity and choice are revealed as empty phrases.

Adversary becomes elite culture

Today, when identity has become so intertwined with cultural conflict, it is useful to remind ourselves that this development is of relatively recent historical vintage. It is important to situate this turn in its specific historical context because of a widespread tendency to perceive it as simply the latest version of age-old conflicts. As we noted earlier, it is common to project identity and the crisis surrounding it to previous historical epochs where it was not perceived as a problem. In a similar manner, identity and the need for its validation are often eternalised as a perpetual condition of life, as is the claim that 'human societies cannot get away from identity or identity politics'.[705]

Situating the politicisation of identity within the historical context of an awareness of cultural discontinuity is the precondition for understanding the depth of the transformation that has occurred. The cumulative impact of the decades-long conflict over socialisation and the customs and values guiding everyday life acquired an unprecedented intensity in the 1960s. Professional supporters of moral engineering became more confident and articulated their view in a more confrontational tone. To take one important example: that of parenting and family life. Until the 1960s professional intervention in socialisation was often justified on the ground that it aimed to strengthen the family to deal with the strains imposed on it by a changing world. In Britain positive family intervention sought to reinforce an institution that appeared fragile and in danger of extinc-

704 See www.tandfonline.com/doi/abs/10.1080/01419870.2015.1058496 (accessed 18 March 2021) and https://journals.sagepub.com/doi/abs/10.1068/d150223?journalCode=epda (accessed 19 March 2021).

705 F. Fukuyama (2018) 'The new tribalism and the crisis of democracy', *Foreign Affairs*, Sept.–Oct., 90–114, at 97.

tion. By the late 1960s and 1970s attitudes towards the family had fundamentally altered. The family was now viewed with hostility as 'a dangerous source of individual repression and mental pathology'.[706]

The backlash against the family was not confined to small groups of marginal activists. Establishment institutions were receptive to a negative representation of family life. The BBC's 1967 prestigious Reith Lecture indicated that the line dividing British elite and adversary culture had become blurred. In one broadcast, the Reith Lecturer, the Cambridge anthropologist Edmund Leach, rounded on 'soppy propaganda about the virtue of a united family life'. He insisted that the family needed to be changed since it could not cope with the emotional stress that it faced. 'Far from being the basis of the good society, the family, with its narrow privacy and tawdry secrets, is the source of all our discontents', warned Leach.[707] In 1967 a Reith Lecturer could not only denounce the British family but also propose that children 'need to grow up in larger, more relaxed domestic groups centred on the community rather than on mother's kitchen – something like an Israeli kibbutz perhaps or a Chinese commune'. The culture war against conventional family life and traditional forms of socialisation acquired institutional respectability.

In the US, too, criticism of the family was widespread among its cultural establishment. The sociologist Brigitte Berger noted that by the 'middle of the 1970s the stage had thus been set for the paradoxical situation in which the cultural elite was eager to deinstitutionalize the family in its conventional form and celebrate the rich variety of lifestyle options available, while ordinary people remained to be guided by more conventional ideals'.[708] Berger characterised this development as one of the outcomes of the 'war against the family'. The conflict that engulfed the family was paralleled by a series of similar disputes over cultural and identity-related issues.

In 1969, Turner underlined the novelty of the demand for self-worth to be politicised. He recognised that this 'novel idea' was not yet generally accepted and was less than certain about its future trajectory. Six years later he still was not sure about the depth of influence of this phenomenon. In 1975, Turner posed the question 'Is there a quest for identity?' He raised important questions about how extensive was the consciousness of this quest? He noted that though 'respected observers' were in no doubt about its pervasive influence, there was

706 Chettiar (2013) p.30.

707 Edmund Leach, 'Ourselves and others', Lecture 3, Reith Lectures, transmission 26 November 1967.

708 B. Berger (2002) *The Family in the Modern Age: More than a Lifestyle Choice*, New Brunswick: Transaction Publishers, p.23.

little empirical evidence to back up their observations. He asked, 'do the literati correctly perceive the inner struggle of ordinary people or do they project their own preoccupations and conventional plots onto their characters?' Similarly, he questioned whether the patients of psychiatrists 'express what is the hearts of silent majorities', and in any case do they 'express their naïve insights' or are the 'subtle encouragements' of the 'therapist responsible for the vocabulary they use'?[709]

Turner's own empirical research tentatively indicated that the 'overwhelming majority of university students acknowledge a personal quest for identity' in contrast to an 'equally overwhelming majority of the general adult population who deny such a quest'.[710] Though his conclusions were tentative, they indicated that, at least in higher education, the politicisation of validation had gained significant support. Its uneven influence among the population spoke to the cleavage between past and present identities. Trilling had already considered this trend in his discussion of the 'changed character of the university', which he claimed came about through the 'efforts of the adversary culture itself'. He suggested that a veritable class had formed around adversary culture, one that 'seeks to aggrandize and perpetuate itself'.[711] Like Turner, Trilling was not clear about whether or not it would acquire hegemony, since at the time of his commentary it had not yet succeeded in dominating the middle class.

By the late 1970s the influential status of adversary culture, particularly in the university, was indisputable. This development was ably analysed in Gouldner's study, *The Future of Intellectuals and the Rise of the New Class* (1979). Gouldner argued that a new class of intellectual and knowledge workers was successfully pursuing the culture war in society and especially inside the university. Gouldner explicitly connected this development to the re-engineering of socialisation which had damaged society's capacity to transmit its cultural legacy to the younger generations.

The most significant dimension of Gouldner's analysis was his insights regarding the relation between disrupted socialisation and the intensification of cultural conflict. He claimed that schools and chiefly universities assumed a central role in the socialisation of young people. They claimed the right to educate young people in line with their enlightened opinions, and even in schools teachers felt that they had no '*obligation*, to reproduce parental values in their chil-

709 R.H. Turner (1975) 'Is there a quest for identity?', *Sociological Quarterly*, 16(2), 148–161, at 149.

710 Turner (1975) p.153.

711 Trilling (1965) pp.xv-xvi.

dren'. The expansion of higher education further reinforced the insulation of parental cultural influence from their children. Gouldner wrote that

> The new structurally differentiated educational system is increasingly insulated from the family system, becoming an important source of values among students divergent from those of their families. The socialization of the young by their families is now mediated by a *semi*-autonomous group of teachers.[712]

As a result of this development, 'public educational systems' become a 'major *cosmopolitanizing* influence on their students, with a corresponding distancing from *localistic* interests and values'. Gouldner asserted that 'parental, particularly paternal, authority is increasingly vulnerable and is thus less able to insist that children respect societal or political authority outside the home'.[713] Parents now found it difficult to impose and reproduce their 'social values and political ideologies in their children'.[714]

Observers of the institutionalisation of adversary culture in higher education often underestimated the significance of Gouldner's argument. Campus radicalism was diagnosed as the work of noisy extremist students and faculty members. The powerful drivers leading to the institutionalisation of adversary culture tended to be overlooked, and time and again premature obituaries declared the death of campus radicalism and of identity politics.

Commentaries frequently portrayed identity politics in the past tense and prophesised its imminent demise. The authors of the first book to refer to identity politics (in 1973) claimed that 'identity politics swallowed itself'.[715]

Writing in 1995, Ross Posnock, a Professor of Literature, wrote that 'after twenty-five years of identity politics' a 'renascent cosmopolitanism is currently gaining ground on the left; indeed, belief that the prestige of identity politics is fading in the academy is fast becoming the received wisdom'.[716] 'After identity, politics: the return of universalism' is the title of an essay in *New Literary History*, in 2000.[717] Eight years later, Nicholson, in her history of identity, observed that 'identity politics seems now to be largely dead, or at minimum, no longer able to

---

712 A.W. Gouldner (1979) *The Future of Intellectuals and the Rise of the New Class*, London: Macmillan Press, p.3.

713 Gouldner (1979) p.14.

714 Gouldner (1979) p.2.

715 R.P. Wolff and T. Gitlin (1973) *1984 Revisited: Prospects for American Politics*, New York: Knopf, p.17.

716 R. Posnock (1995) 'Before and after identity politics', *Raritan*, 15(1), 95–115, at 99.

717 E. Lott (2000) 'After identity, politics: the return of universalism', *New Literary History*, 31(4), 665–680.

command the kind of public attention that it did from the late 1960s through the late 1980s'.[718] In the wake of the Brexit Referendum and the election of Donald Trump, the British journalist Janet Daley declared that 'Identity politics is dead'.[719]

The failure to grasp the ever-growing influence of identity politics was in part due to the inability of traditional political categories to make sense of this phenomenon. It was, and continues to be identified as a species of radical left-wing politics. Yet, at the time of its inception, observers understood that the success of identity politics was at the expense of the left and helped to accelerate its decline. The growing influence of the politicisation of identity always had its greatest impact on the sphere of culture rather than on political institutions. One reason why the conflict over values did not appear to excite the imagination of the political analyst was because the cultural revolt struck deepest in the pre-political sphere. At a time of East–West conflict, wars in South-East Asia, labour disputes in Europe and intense rivalries between soon to be extinct left- and right-wing parties, the disputes over values in the pre-political sphere were regarded as secondary to the big issues of the time. Although many commentators were concerned about the gradual spread of counter-cultural values in the pre-political sphere – particularly in relation to family life, parenting, sexuality, gender – they appeared to be unaware of its significance. Possessors of the values linked to the 'old identity' proved singularly ineffective in responding to the challenge to their outlook.

Critics of the cultural values transmitted through identity politics deceived themselves into believing that they had matters under control during the Reagan–Thatcher years. Yet, it was precisely during this era, when right-wing governments appeared to be in control, that adversary culture gained ascendancy. The right may have won the economic war but it suffered a serious setback on the terrain of culture. It was in the 1980s and early 1990s that proponents of adversary culture became the dominant force in higher education, schools, institutions of culture, the media and sections of the public sector.

The failure to comprehend that attitudes that were hitherto classified as adversarial had gained cultural ascendancy explains the prominence of the naive assumption that 'it was only a passing fad or phase'. This naivety re-surfaced in the aftermath of the destruction of the World Trade Center in September 2001. For a brief moment, it appeared that, in the face of terrorism, the tradition-

718 See L. Nicholson (2008) *Identity Before Identity Politics*, Cambridge: Cambridge University Press, p.4.

719 https://www.telegraph.co.uk/news/2016/11/26/identity-politics-dead-lefts-entire-electoral-strategy/%20 (accessed 5 October 2019).

al values of duty, patriotism and national unity would make a comeback in the United States. Hopeful commentators predicted that adversarial attitudes would evaporate in face of a dangerous common enemy. Yet, within a few months of this catastrophe, the usual divisions re-emerged. Counselling against the illusions that adversary culture was fatally undermined by 9/11, Hollander pointed to its spread 'through the media' and even through 'American commercial culture'.[720]

Commentaries pointing to the decline of adversary culture were looking for it in the wrong place; the sphere of formal politics. Yet, the flourishing of adversarial attitudes was most evident in areas that were peripheral to it, touching on a 'sense of identity, cultural norms, matters of taste'.[721] By the turn of the 21st century the ideals of adversary culture had been thoroughly absorbed by western society's cultural elites.

The politicisation of validation

Another reason why a comprehension of identity politics eluded so many observers was because they often overlooked its connection to the growing authority of the therapeutic ethos. Initially, therapeutic culture was not perceived as political by either its protagonists or its opponents. The manner in which young people were socialised led them to perceive the problems they faced as psychological rather than as social and political.

The 60s generation assumed that the right to validation was an integral element of social justice. What followed was a ceaseless demand for the recognition of self-worth and identity. Once identity acquires the form of right rather than as a state to be achieved through self-cultivation, action or work, it acquires a passive form. As Lasch pointed out, the therapeutic turn towards the demand for recognition has little to do with justice but reflects a new relationship between self and society. 'Today men seek the kind of approval that applauds not their actions but their attributes', observes Lasch.[722] Approval thus becomes an act of affirmation of self rather than an evaluation of individual achievement. Its corollary is that the refusal to affirm can constitute an act of psychological harm.

720 P. Hollander (2002) 'The resilience of the adversary culture', *National Interest*, No. 68, 101–112, at 103.

721 Hollander (2002) p.103.

722 Lasch (1979) p.116.

Ironically, the institutionalisation of the right to recognition leads to emptying it of any moral content. Human struggles for recognition are mediated through specific historical and cultural forms. Such activity contains the potential for making history, enhancing self-consciousness, making moral choices, entering into dialogues and accomplishing the construction of identities organic to one's circumstances. Arendt stresses this point when she notes that, like freedom, identity must be attained through action. Through action and speech, 'men show who they are, reveal actively their unique personal identities and thus make their appearance in the human world'.[723] Struggling for, is fundamentally different from gaining recognition on demand. The former involves an active engagement of construction while the latter implies being acted upon by those conferring recognition. Such a right can never satisfy the craving to be recognised – it merely incites the individual for more assurances of respect.

Official recognition overlooks individual differences and needs, and fails to distinguish between achievement and failure and wisdom and ignorance. A real recognition of the individual requires that choices are made between knowledge and opinion and contributions that are worth esteeming and those that are not. Both the granting and the demand for universal esteem serve to transform recognition to an empty ritual. Such formulaic reassurance cannot meet the existential quest for recognition. It can merely divert energy from constructive social engagement towards the quest for more institutional guarantees.

The very demand for the right to be esteemed posits a uniquely feeble version of the self. It places the individual in a permanent position of a supplicant, whose identity relies on a form of bureaucratic affirmation. The self is not so much affirmed or realised through the activities and relationships of the individual but through the legal form. In effect, autonomy, an essential component of human dignity, is exchanged for the quick fix of an institutionally affirmed identity.

In his discussion of identity formation, Erikson hinted at the ineffectiveness of socialisation through validation. He underlined the importance of activity and experience for gaining 'realistic self-esteem' and stated;

> Children cannot be fooled by empty phrase and condescending encouragement. They may have to accept artificial bolstering of their self-esteem in lieu of something better, but their ego identity gains real strength only from wholehearted and consistent recognition of real accomplishment – ie. of achievement that has meaning in culture.[724]

723 Arendt (1998) p.173.
724 Erikson (1963) pp.235–236.

Erikson's warning about artificial bolstering went against the grain of the culture that gained ascendancy throughout the cultural and educational institutions of western society. At the time that Erikson raised concern about the dysfunctional consequence of the artificial bolstering of self-esteem, the regime of validation was still in its early stage of institutional development. In the decades to follow a veritable movement emerged around the cause of raising self-esteem and numerous governments developed policies designed to support this cause.[725]

Towards the end of her life, in one of her last lectures, the psychiatrist Anna Freud recognised that something was not quite right with the pedagogy of validation that she promoted from the 1920s onwards. She stated that 'we have tried too hard to turn all work into play, neglecting the fact' that work, unlike play, is 'governed by the reality principle, which means that it also is pursued in the face of difficulties until an intended aim is reached'.[726] Work and, as Arendt argued, action are the precondition for developing a meaningful identity. Unfortunately, this outlook went against the cultural zeitgeist of the 1960s and 1970s, and since that time every generation of young children have been subjected to an ever-expanding regime of validation.

Validated personhood and the devaluation of moral agency

Since the 1960s, the demand for the validation of self-worth has expanded and policies promoting the affirmation of identity have become institutionalised. In practice the demand for recognition constitutes an invitation to paternalistic intervention in people's lives. This demand has been wholeheartedly embraced by moral engineers for whom the management of recognition and validation has provided important opportunities for cultivating their authority. The phenomenal growth of what Ronald Dworkin has called the caring industry is instructive in this respect. According to Dworkin, 'although the general population of the United States has only doubled since the mid-20th century, this industry has already increased 100-fold'![727]

The most striking manifestation of the institutionalisation of validation has been its continuous expansion into new domains of human experience. Policies designed to secure the right to self-esteem have been complemented by declara-

725 See Furedi (2004) ch. 7.

726 A. Freud (1976) 'Dynamic psychology and education', in Freud, A., *Writings of Anna Freud*, vol. 8, London: Hogarth Press, p.311.

727 www.nationalaffairs.com/publications/detail/the-politicization-of-unhappiness (accessed 16 May 2021).

tions that claim that sexual health is also a right, as are well-being and happiness. The cumulative effect of these initiatives is to create the impression that if people do not enjoy these rights, they are likely to feel unhappy, unwell, weak or vulnerable.

Through the imperative to medicalise human experience a feeble sense of moral agency has been engineered. Since the conceptualisation of a 'sick society' in the 1920s a growing number of human disorders – crime, terrorism, unrest – have been diagnosed as forms of illness. In this way health has been transformed into a normative concept that serves as the functional equivalent of morality.

Health has been redefined as not so much a physical condition as a political right. From its birth in 1948, the WHO has assumed that it possesses an extremely broad remit, not only to deal with medical and scientific matters but also with issues to do with people's lifestyle and personal behaviour. From the perspective of this organisation, health is much more than the absence of disease. According to the definition adopted in 1948, health is a 'state of complete physical, mental and social wellbeing and not merely the absence of disease or infirmity'.[728] Such a broad definition of health goes way beyond the problems that doctors and medical science can fix.

Given its interest in a complete state of well-being, it is not surprising that in 1974 the WHO expanded the meaning of health by inventing the term 'sexual health'. The WHO called for 'the integration of the somatic, emotional, intellectual, and social aspects of sexual being, in ways that are positively enriching'. In the decades to follow, its focus became the provision of a 'pleasurable and safe sexual experience'.[729] The WHO's ever-broadening definition of health underpinned an obsession with the politics of lifestyle regulation and the management of people's personal behaviour. The engineering of pleasurable sex – satirised by Aldous Huxley in his *Brave New World* – was adopted as one of the WHO's missions. In 2002, the WHO adopted a broader definition of sexual health which added concepts of mental health and sexual rights to the mix.

Policy makers are also busy promoting policies designed to help people feel good about themselves. Such policies are frequently justified on the ground that unless people's identity is affirmed they are likely to have mental health problems. As in previous times, the main target of these initiatives is the school. It was in this vein that in April 2007 England's former School Minister Alan Johnson instructed teachers to routinely praise their pupils. According to guidelines,

728 www.who.int/governance/eb/who_constitution_en.pdf (accessed 16 May 2021).
729 www.who.int/governance/eb/who_constitution_en.pdf (accessed 16 May 2021).

teachers ought to reward children five times as often as they punish them for disrupting lessons.[730] The exhortation to institutionalise the praising of children is not an isolated attempt to flatter the egos of young people. Increasingly the therapeutic objective of making children feel good about themselves is seen as the primary objective of schooling.[731]

Happiness education has become integrated into the curriculum of many schools. Numerous feelings-related fads are deployed to make children happy. A report on the Second Annual European Happiness & Its Causes Conference in October 2008 included a session where the presenter talked about a 'feelings meter', peer massages and meditation in the classroom and other 'innovations' designed to improve student well-being. Others advocated 'holistic spirituality' while the 'leading experts' in the 'psychology of happiness' lectured on how to make schools more happy.[732]

Perversely, the more professional validators attempt to make children feel good about themselves, the more young people become distracted from engaging in experiences that have the potential for giving them the sense of achievement they require to cultivate their sense of self-worth. Since these programmes encourage a mood of emotionalism in the school it inevitably follows that young people become more and more self-absorbed.

Throughout the western world the complex emotional tensions that are integral to the process of growing up are now depicted as stressful events with which children and young people cannot be expected to cope. Yet, it is through dealing with such emotional upheavals that young people learn to manage risks and gain an understanding of their strengths and weaknesses and come to understand who they are. The pedagogy of validation short-circuits this policy and encourages many children to feel fragile and vulnerable. As I have noted elsewhere, since the turn of the 21st century childhood has been turned into a permanent state of mental illness.[733] Judging by media reports, the mental health crisis afflicting young people seems to increase year on year. The phenomenon of

---

730 See 'Schools discipline and pupil behaviour guidelines: guidance for schools' on Teachernet (www.teachernet.gov.uk/wholeschool/behaviour/schooldisciplinepupilbehaviourpolicies/ (accessed 25 October 2019)); and Richard Garner, 'Teachers told to praise the unruly as strike looms over discipline', *Independent*, 11 April 2007.

731 See K. Ecclestone and D. Hayes (2019) *The Dangerous Rise of Therapeutic Education*, London: Routledge.

732 Teacher Support Network, Press Release, 14 October 2008, http://teachersupport.info/news/press-releases/2008-Happiness-Conference.php (accessed 18 June 2019).

733 www.spiked-online.com/2017/12/13/turning-childhood-into-a-mental-illness/ (accessed 15 April 2020).

the so-called 'snowflake generation' and the fragility demonstrated by university students has become a widely discussed issue.

That validation had the perverse consequence of diminishing the capacity of children to deal with the problem of existence is demonstrated by a never-ending quest for new education fads to manage the situation. Some schools have looked to mindfulness and meditation to tackle this problem. Others advocate teaching resilience or providing young people with character and grit in order to help children deal with adversity.[734] Unfortunately, the use of psychological techniques – whether of validation or of promoting resilience – overlooks the fact that they have a tendency to disempower children and render them passive. A validated version of personhood reinforces the problem that it is designed to solve since identity needs to be achieved through individual effort. By medicalising the problems of existence, children are likely to regard themselves as potential patients rather than as agents who possess the capacity for exercising agency.

The medicalisation of personhood diminishes its moral agency. It displaces the normative foundation of personhood with virtues that derive from a therapeutic sensibility. Outrage at the refusal of society to recognise one's self-worth is often couched in the language of victimisation, as is its demand for an entitlement to be validated and protected from hurt. From this standpoint the refusal to affirm the demands of an identity group is perceived as not only an outrage but also a likely cause of a medical harm. Since institutional affirmation is rarely able to satisfy the demand for recognition, the crisis of identity and its different political expressions have become a permanent feature of contemporary life.

734 See L.K. Thaler and R. Koval (2015) *Grit to Great: How Perseverance, Passion, and Pluck Take You from Ordinary to Extraordinary*, New York: Crown Business.

Conclusion: Awareness as Its Own Cause

The patterns set in motion a century ago – the imperative of leaving the past behind, the constant fetishisation of change, the tendency to represent previous forms of socialisation as obsolete – continue to reinforce the perception of culture as discontinuous. This condition of cultural discontinuity is constantly reproduced by the perception of rapid change. The constant references to rapid change over the past 150 years indicate that this perception has acquired a life of its own and, as Bell pointed out, 'overshadows the dimensions of actual change'.[735] The consciousness that corresponds to this sensibility assumes that the new necessarily represents an improvement over the old. This attitude is not only attached to technologies and their products but also to values. What follows is 'ceaseless searching for a new sensibility'.[736]

The discontinuity of culture coexists with the loss of the sense of the past. The loss of this sensibility has had an unsettling effect on culture itself and has deprived it of moral depth. A consciousness of culture as unsettled and discontinuous renders it volatile. Inner tensions within culture are refracted through what Trilling characterised as the 'acculturation of the anti-cultural'.[737] Acculturation refers to the transfer and adoption of values and hints at the transient and fragile status of prevailing norms.

In 1961, when he penned these words, Trilling's remarks were directed at the uncritical cultural criticism that prevailed among his university students. Today, the acculturation of the anti-cultural exercises a powerful role over the imagination of western society. Culture is frequently framed in instrumental and pragmatic terms and rarely perceived as a system of norms that endow human life with meaning. Culture has become a shallow construct to be disposed of or changed. Calls for 'changing culture' are casually and regularly echoed in management circles and by policy makers. 'The fastest way to change a culture', advises a commentator in *Forbes*.[738] With the exception of references to aboriginal exoticised people, culture tends be a target of change rather than preservation.

One of the by-products of the cultural turn was a redefinition of culture itself. It has become downgraded, rendered shallow and deprived of normative

---

735 D. Bell (1972) 'The cultural contradictions of capitalism', *Journal of Aesthetic Education*, 6(1–2), 11–38, at 12.

736 Bell (1972) p.12.

737 Trilling (1965) p.23.

738 www.forbes.com/sites/davidrock/2019/05/24/fastest-way-to-change-culture/?sh=4cda0763d50c (accessed 15 March 2021).

https://doi.org/10.1515/9783110708899-011

content. Phrases like a 'culture of bullying', 'negative organisation culture', 'toxic work culture' or a 'canteen culture' both trivialise and render culture meaningless. Typically, this usage of the term 'culture' serves as an invitation to changing it to, for example, a 'culture of learning' or an 'inclusive workplace culture'. The acculturation of the anti-cultural and the spirit of the counter-culture are integral features of the contemporary zeitgeist. Cultural norms and attitudes that emerged as a reaction to those of the past soon suffer the same fate and are cast aside by the latest version of adversary culture. Bell observed;

> Today, each new generation, starting off at the benchmarks attained by the adversary culture of its cultural parents, declares in sweeping fashion that the status quo represents backward conservatism or repression, so that, in a widening gyre, new and fresh assaults on the social structure are mounted.[739]

An illustration of this trend is the reaction of different waves of feminism to one another, in particular the tension between the second and fourth waves of feminism.[740]

Even though what was once described as adversary culture has acquired a hegemonic status, it continues to search for adversaries. It finds it easier to question, condemn and disparage than to offer a positive account of itself. Identities mirror this trend, continually creating a demand for new ones and attempting to assert themselves, often at the expense of other identities.

The main achievement of the acculturation of the anti-cultural was to detach values from normativity. In this way culture serves as an object of competitive claims making. Cultural norms are continually tested by competing claims based on the needs of identity, self-fulfilment and the supposed evidence of science. In this way, culture itself becomes a permanent site of conflict; a never-ending process of attempting to secure moral authority through pathologising supposedly outdated cultural practices. Individuals are condemned for their outdated behaviour or language. As I write, I hear of a local councillor in Bolton apologising for using 'outdated language' to describe disabled people.[741] His cultural crime was to use the term 'invalid carriages' in a newsletter.

---

739 Bell (1976) p.41.

740 See www.vox.com/2018/3/20/16955588/feminism-waves-explained-first-second-third-fourth; and S.G. Cook (2011) 'Feminists differ in second and third waves', *Women in Higher Education*, 20(8), 7.

741 www.theboltonnews.co.uk/news/18808310.councillor-apologises-using-outdated-language-describe-disabled-people/ (accessed 20 March 2021).

Becoming an ideology

The greatest impact of the cultural turn was on the norms and customs that prevailed in the pre-political sphere. The decades-long targeting of socialisation, parental authority and taken-for-granted customs has had a significant impact on people's personal lives. The weakening of adult authority and the new regime of socialisation led to the explosion of identity consciousness and crisis, which in turn found expression in the politicisation of the person. What lent this development a momentous quality was that it coincided with the growing awareness that the classical ideologies had become exhausted and that mainstream political movements struggled to motivate the public.

The precondition for the explosion of identity consciousness and the disputes surrounding it was the 'end of ideology' and the politicisation of the self.

The end of ideology also provided an opportunity for a science- and expertise-informed form of technocratic governance to gain extraordinary influence.

Back in 1969 Habermas observed that, in the post-war period, technology and science worked as a quasi-ideology: he wrote of the 'scientization of political power' and argued that politicians had become increasingly dependent on professionals.[742]

Since the late 1960s the scientisation of political power has continued to expand, leading to the consolidation of technocratic governance. Technocratic governance draws on the legitimacy of science and the authority of expertise. It seeks to justify itself on the basis of expertise and process rather than political vision. It self-consciously eschews politics and attempts to de-politicise controversial issues by outsourcing their management and decision making to expert institutions, courts and international bodies such as the International Monetary Fund. Except in unusual circumstances, such as during the coronavirus pandemic, when politicians explicitly gave way to scientists, technocratic governance rarely exists in a pure form. And with good reason: on its own, technocratic governance cannot motivate or inspire people. This is why a technocracy relies for its credibility on policies and ideals that are external to itself.

Technocratic governance, with its reliance on the authority of science and expertise, lacks the moral depth required to motivate citizens. From time to time it attempts to harness the motivating power of other causes, such as that of environmentalism. But the most important supplement to its form of governance is provided by the therapeutic ethos. The use of psychology and mass therapy for legitimating authority was forcefully promoted by Parsons. He sought

742 Habermas [1967] (1987) p.63.

to harness the potential of the therapeutic relationship for validating authority in a wider social setting.[743]

For Parsons, professionalism, with its moral connotation of a calling and its promotion of the public good, provided technocratic expertise with a moral dimension. Reconciling scientific rationality with the moral was at the heart of his project of promoting therapeutic authority of the professional. After noting that 'it is essential to establish a position of impersonal authority', Parsons stated that in the case of medicine this 'involves primarily two elements, technical competence and moral integrity'.[744] It is significant that his model was the therapist, not the scientist or the administrator. Therapy, with its promise to connect with the public's emotion, validate it and gain its trust, appeared to Parsons to be the most promising medium for gaining authoritative influence over individual behaviour. This synthesis of professional expertise with therapeutic guidance turned out to be the most effective form of moral engineering.

Technocratic governance has mobilised the techniques of validation developed by institutions of socialisation for supporting policies oriented towards identity management. The reorientation of the state towards the management of individual well-being is one of the most important developments in recent times. Technocratic governance draws on the contemporary version of personhood as one that is defined by its fragility and vulnerability. Its policies are justified on the ground that the fragility of personhood demands the 'support' of officialdom and the state.

In effect, technocratic governance has embraced a synthesis of the therapeutic ethos and identity politics to help manage and engineer public opinion. It offers an institutional response to the quest for identity. Policies directed at offering recognition and validation of identities aim to provide officialdom with authority and responsibility for managing the psychological and identity-related concerns of citizens. This orientation towards policy making in the sphere of the personal is underwritten by the internalisation of a synthesis of therapeutic ethos and identity politics by the key institutions of western society.

The coexistence of technocratic governance and the cultural politics of identity is most dramatically expressed through the legal and quasi-legal recognition of identity groups. The promotion of identity-related interests has led to its pursuit through groups which are affirmed and recognised by the state. Consequently, when rules are enacted and discussed in areas like education, social policy

743 F. Furedi (2013) *Authority: A Sociological History*, Cambridge: Cambridge University Press, pp.367–375.

744 Parsons [1942] (1964) 'Propaganda and social control', in Parsons, T. *Essays in Sociological Theory*, Glencoe: The Free Press, p.160.

and health their implication for different identity groups invariably comes to the fore. As technocratic governance has become more and more involved in supporting group aspirations, it has become more active in the informal and pre-political domain of life. In the UK, it has developed the legal concept of protected characteristics, which makes it illegal to discriminate against someone whose characteristic is protected.[745] In this way human relations have become increasingly formalised and subjected to a technocratic disciplinary regime.

In light of the developments discussed in the previous chapters, the reorientation of the institutions of the state towards the repair of psychical injury and related therapeutic functions represents an attempt to contain the effect of the unravelling of moral authority. The politics of recognition attempts to offer a provisional solution to the disassociation of identity from normativity. It does so by offering recognition and validation in exchange for the adoption of new forms of psychologically informed, evidence-based behaviour.

In the current era, moral engineering is principally promoted through the *politics of behaviour*.[746] The politics of behaviour is based on the assumption that people's emotional lives, lifestyles, private conduct and relationships are legitimate objects of policy making, which can and must be reformed through the benevolent application of social engineering. That personal issues such as loneliness, happiness, well-being, sexual satisfaction, self-esteem and parental values have become the target of government policy illustrates the extent to which officialdom has become intertwined with the management of private affairs. For example, in early 2018 the British Conservative Government decided to devote its attention to dealing with what it characterised as an epidemic of loneliness by appointing the world's first Minister of Loneliness. The official 'loneliness strategy' promised to link up lonely and isolated people with support groups and welfare organisations.[747] The document outlining this strategy stated that the government would be 'incorporating loneliness into ongoing policy decisions with a view to a loneliness "policy test" being included in departments' plans', and approvingly cited a comment made by one of its advisors:

---

745 www.equalityhumanrights.com/en/equality-act/protected-characteristics (accessed 12 February 2021).

746 For a discussion of the politics of behaviour see Leggett (2014) 'The politics of behaviour change: nudge, neoliberalism and the state', *Policy & Politics*, 42(1), 3–19.

747 See www.gov.uk/government/news/pm-launches-governments-first-loneliness-strategy (accessed 21 February 2021).

> This is a serious strategy that's not only going to help people feel more connected in their everyday lives but is also inspiring other Governments and communities around the world to see loneliness for what it is: a heart-breaking emotion and a major public health issue.[748]

The young Werther's terrible emptiness and loneliness is today a potential target of state intervention. As Goethe so eloquently reminded readers, loneliness is heartbreaking. But since when has people's existential pain become the business of government? And if a Werther's emotional life becomes reframed as a public health issue, are any important matters left for private decision making?

Paternalistic techniques of behaviour management are promoted by officialdom as solutions to people's emotional needs. So-called 'happiness experts' insist that public policy should shift its emphasis from economics and wealth creation towards a strategy that enhances the happiness of the population. Like officialdom's objective of tackling loneliness, policies that attempt to increase the state of individual happiness are mental health interventions targeting citizens' internal lives. Promoters of the politics of happiness claim that 'governments could have more success in improving people's lives if they prioritised improving mental health over traditional top goals such as boosting economic growth'.[749] This point was echoed by former British Prime Minister David Cameron, when he stated that 'we should be thinking not what is good for putting money in people's pockets but what is good for putting joy in people's hearts'.[750] For Cameron, happiness was nothing less than a central goal of government.[751]

Policies directed at governing people's emotions are not simply about making people feel good about themselves. The policy of instrumentalising happiness implicitly conveys a narrative about how people should behave, encouraging them to adopt attitudes that conform to specific public norms and ideals. Such policies de-personalise feelings and reframe them as emotionally correct public attitudes. Consequently, the instrumentalisation of happiness leads to fashioning this emotion as a political resource. At a 2016 conference organised

748 Cited in www.gov.uk/government/news/pm-launches-governments-first-loneliness-strategy (accessed 19 September 2020).

749 Tamsin Rutter (2016) 'New research boosts crusade to embed happiness in public policy', Global Government Forum, 15 December, www.globalgovernmentforum.com/new-research-boosts-crusade-to-embed-happiness-in-public-policy/ (accessed 4 March 2021).

750 Cited in Mark Easton (2006) 'The politics of happiness', *BBC Home*, 22 May, http://news.bbc.co.uk/2/hi/programmes/happiness_formula/4809828.stm.

751 Frank Furedi (2006) 'Politicians, economists, teachers: why are they so desperate to make us happy/', *The Daily Telegraph*, 7 May, www.telegraph.co.uk/comment/personal-view/3624819/Politicians-economists-teachers-why-are-they-so-desperate-to-make-us-happy.html (accessed 23 January 2019).

by the London School of Economics, the OECD and the Paris School of Economics, Gus O'Donnell, the former UK Head of civil service, argued that embedding happiness in public policy would reduce the electoral appeal of populism. O'Donnell stated that both the victory for Brexit in Britain's EU referendum and Donald Trump's success in the US Presidential elections could be 'explained by an analysis of people's wellbeing': the implication being that if people had felt happier they would have voted to stay in the EU and elected Hillary Clinton as President.[752]

Within the parameter of technocratic governance, social engineering has acquired unprecedented significance. It was explicitly pursued by David Cameron during his tenure as Prime Minister of the UK. Cameron helped set up the Behavioural Insight Team in 2010, which was charged with the task of developing policies that could shape people's thoughts, choices and actions. This team, known as the 'Nudge Unit', operated on the assumption that attempting to convince the electorate of government policies is pointless; subliminal psychological techniques and manipulation were considered more effective than democratic debate and argument. When Britain's former Deputy Prime Minister Nick Clegg casually remarked that the Nudge Unit 'could change the way citizens think', he spoke a language usually associated with a totalitarian propaganda agency.[753]

Nudge-like classical forms of social engineering are justified on the assumption that the expert knows best. In *Law and Leviathan* two prominent American supporters of Nudge and of expert authority insist that administrative technocrats must be trusted since they personify the binding law of morality. Their re-engineered form of instrumental morality is realised through rule making.[754] From their standpoint, morality is reduced to obedience to the law.

The displacement of moral norms by psychological and other types of administratively produced values has been integral to the project of moral engineering for over a century. In its current form, it appears to be prepared to go beyond the traditional forms of moral engineering. It is not simply directed towards the objective of changing the way people to think but also to shape their moral values. Virtue engineering through technologies of moral enhancement constitutes the new frontier of moral engineering. Neuroenhancement to

---

752 Tamsin Rutter (2016) 'New research boosts crusade to embed happiness in public policy', Global Government Forum, 15 December, www.globalgovernmentforum.com/new-research-boosts-crusade-to-embed-happiness-in-public-policy/ (accessed 4 March 2021).

753 www.theguardian.com/society/2010/sep/09/cameron-nudge-unit-economic-behaviour (accessed 23 September 2016).

754 See C.R. Sunstein and A. Vermeule (2020) *Law and Leviathan: Redeeming the Administrative State*, Cambridge, Mass: Belknap Press.

engineer morality is supported by so-called transhumanist lobby groups, like the World Transhumanist Association. Their leaders advocate 'technoscientific means to achieve happiness, a total control of emotions, and an improvement of human character'.[755] Moral neuroenhancement, unlike previous forms of moral engineering, 'operates by altering brain states or processes directly', through the application of drugs or the use of brain modulation techniques.[756]

Although occasionally there are outcries against the influence and power of experts, technocratic and therapeutic governance itself is rarely a focus of political dispute. During the coronavirus pandemic the different sides of the argument over the efficacy of lockdown and quarantine measures sought to legitimate their argument by justifying it on the ground of their mental health impact. All sides of the debate appeared to have internalised the fundamentals of the therapeutic ethos but drew different political conclusions from it.

The politics of behaviour resonates with the cultural confusions of our times. Socialisation has become even less devoted to the transmission of virtues than it was last century. The guidance offered to young people by institutions of socialisation are typically shallow and leave it up to them to make their way in the world. Lack of clarity about moral norms and on the conduct of human relationships has led to an explosion of rule making throughout society. The micro-management of relationships and conduct is most expansive in institutions of education and the public sector, but in recent years its usage has rapidly accelerated in the private sector.

The politics of behaviour and its proclivity for inventing new rules and procedures represents an attempt to provide an alternative to the moral guidance that is organic to community life. The invention of new rules and the impulse to moralise is most evident in relation to problems to do with cultural identity, emotions and lifestyles. In recent decades the politics of behaviour has shifted attention from poverty, exploitation and social equality to the moralisation of people's lifestyles, sexuality, gender roles and identity.

The politics of behaviour does not simply demand good behaviour but the abandonment of what was previously held to be unexceptional and normal features of life. Behaviour managers renounce them as outdated and unhealthy customs and practices. As in the past with the re-engineering of socialisation, the politics of behaviour is as much about rendering unacceptable the norms of the past as it is about embracing new enlightened ones.

---

755 Cited in F. Jotterand (2011) 'Will post-humans still need the virtues?', *AJOB Neuroscience*, 2(4), 3–9, at 4.

756 T. Douglas (2015) 'The morality of moral neuroenhancement', in Clausen, J. and Levy, N. (eds) *Handbook of Neuroethics*, Netherlands: Springer.

Awareness as its own cause

Psychology provides the medium through which the symbiotic relationship between moral engineering and the cultural politics of identity is forged. Though noisy advocates of identity causes inhabit a different world from no-nonsense technocrats, differences in their outlook are reconciled through their embrace of the politics of behaviour. The goal of managing attitudes and identities, promoting new forms of behaviour and cultures and validating them resonates with both sides of this unlikely alliance. Its demand that people 'raise their awareness' serves as the functional equivalent of a traditional political slogan.

The impulse fuelling the demand for awareness in the 21st century is not unlike the one that motivated the early generations of professional socialisers. In part it was the conviction that socialisation was far too complex a process to be left in the hands of the 'unaware' members of adult society that justified their project. In some instances – as in the case of Stanley Hall – raising awareness assumed the character of a quasi-religious mission.

At first sight Hall's assertion in 1921 that the university was the 'chief shrine', the 'new church of science' and 'powerhouse' of the spirit of social engineering comes across as fanciful and widely utopian.[757] As it turned out, the university lacked the moral authority to serve as the functional equivalent of a church of science. However, its institutional and cultural power has steadily expanded so that today it has become a formidable entity. It serves as the main source of cultural capital, both directly through its influence on pedagogy at all levels of education and also indirectly in shaping the outlook of all the main professions and the institutions they inhabit. Through its impact on millions of educated members of society it exercises a commanding influence on the media and popular culture. It has contributed to the fostering of a climate that is hospitable to the discrediting of 'outdated' ideas and embracing new ones. The emergence of identity politics, new social and cultural movements, and new speech codes all bear the imprint of campus culture.

Almost six decades after Hall's call for a new church of science, the universities succeeded in assuming a pivotal role in the socialisation of young people. Gouldner highlighted the role played by what he called a 'new class of intellectual and knowledge workers' in distancing the younger generations from the value system of their elders.[758] Contrary to Hall's expectations, the university did not quite become a new church. Though it lacked a coherent dogma, it

757 Hall (1921) p.116.
758 Gouldner (1979) p.●.

was sufficiently powerful to undermine long-standing norms and values and identities, and motivate generations of young people to interpret the world through therapeutic and counter-cultural terms.

Conservative critics of the university overlooked the connection between the decades-long tradition of socialisation by validation and its practice in higher education. They focused their concern on student militants, tenured radicals and political subversives. Some objected to the rise of groupthink and the exclusion of conservatives from academic positions. What these criticisms fail to grasp is that the defining feature of campus politics is not a commitment to a radical ideology or to a subversive cause but the conviction that its understanding of the world is far superior to that of normal citizens', that it knows better than they do what is in their best interest, and that it has the right and duty to shape and reshape people's minds.

A key cultural role of the university is to transmit the sensibility and value orientation of moral engineering. It has adopted a form of socialisation that aims to distance its subjects from the values of their parents and encourage them to adopt new, more enlightened ones. As in the past, it attempts to motivate the younger generation by denouncing the old and celebrating the new. What it offers is not an ideology as such, but something that approximates a *l'esprit de corps*. To idealist young people in search of meaning, it provides a common spirit of distinction and difference; a set of symbols and signals that serves to legitimate their identity.

Previously we noted that as identity permeates the world the appetite for differentiation becomes difficult to satisfy. Encouraging young people to adopt the perception that their values and behaviour are more enlightened than the rest feeds the craving for distinctiveness. It was this craving that motivated fans of Werther to adopt their tragic hero's dress and mannerisms. They regarded themselves as possessing superior sensibilities to the conformist ways of others. Today, this sensibility is expressed through calls for 'raising awareness'. The term 'raising awarenewss' implicitly draws attention to the superiority of people over those who are not aware. This distinction corresponds to the cleavage between past and present identity, discussed in the previous chapter. The state of being aware serves as a mark of cultural distinction connoting an identity of superiority towards those who are presumably unaware and still in the dark.

Justman wrote that awareness is a 'good impossible to question and a power impossible to oppose'.[759] Initiatives designed to raise awareness provide participants with virtues and moral qualities that distinguish them from those who do

759 Justman (2015) p.159.

not see the light. The very gesture of 'raising awareness' thus involves the drawing of symbolic distinctions between those who possess this quality and those who do not. According to the *OED*, in recent decades the meaning of being aware has shifted from being on guard to becoming well informed. In its 2008 revision of the term, the *OED* added that being aware meant 'generally concerned and well informed' and being sensitive and 'savvy'.

The imputation of intelligence, sensitivity, broadmindedness, sophistication and enlightenment ensure that campaigns oriented towards awareness raising provide an important cultural resource for their participants. Those who draw on these resources have every incentive to inflate the behavioural and cultural distinction between themselves and the rest of society. That is why awareness raisers are preoccupied with constructing lifestyles that contrast so sharply with those of their perceived inferiors.

Despite its innocuous and feel-good appearance, the word 'awareness' is a politically loaded one. To be aware is to be informed but it also signifies being watchful, vigilant, being on one's guard. In its most neutral form, raising awareness can mean enhancing people's consciousness of a problem. But in practice the call on someone to raise their awareness is a demand to adopt the awareness raiser's outlook and values. Raising awareness targets outdated norms and values, customs and forms of behaviour, and claims to unmask prejudice and hurtful and dangerous assumptions. The possession of awareness is a marker of a superior status, while its absence represents moral inferiority. That is why the refusal to abide by the exhortation to 'be aware' invites the act of moral condemnation.

Raising awareness can be about anything that touches on people's behaviour and lifestyle. In the UK and the US there are literally hundreds of different Health Awareness Days every year.[760] It is a trope that is rooted in psychology and the therapeutic ethos. Unlike its 1960s predecessor of 'raising consciousness', it does not simply refer to what we do to ourselves but to others. Campaigns devoted to raising awareness are often focused on altering lifestyles and health-related behaviours. It can refer to changing the behaviour and practices of parents to demanding that a particular group's hitherto unacknowledged issues should be recognised. It serves as an all-encompassing device for re-educating its target audience on a variety of disparate subjects. Unlike traditional methods of socialisation, its target audience is not confined to children and

760 See www.healthline.com/health/directory-awareness-months (accessed 4 March 2012) and www.theatlantic.com/health/archive/2015/04/what-good-is-raising-awareness/391002/ (accessed 7 April 2020).

young people. Raising awareness need not be about a particular cause. It is represented as a value in its own right. As one higher education institute website declared, 'both the Student's Union and University will be looking to continue raising awareness'.[761] The act of raising awareness is perceived as good in and of itself. Why? Because it signals an openness to change attitude and behaviour. In some instances it refers to the willingness to change oneself; in others it implies a commitment to help others to change the way they behave and think.[762]

Promoters of awareness frequently exhibit an enthusiasm not unlike that shown by zealous missionaries. Awareness entitles one to frame a problem in a manner that is not susceptible to discussion and debate. A narrative that attaches itself to being aware of a problem is not just a version of the truth, but truth itself. Frequently such truths claim to draw on the authority of science and assert that it is beyond dispute. The implicit intolerance towards dissident views shown by impatient awareness raisers is communicated in the recently invented put-down of choice, 'Educate Yourself'. Educate Yourself does not mean go to a library and read some books. What it means is re-educate yourself and accept our values and outlook on the world. In many institutions in both the public and private sectors, educating yourself is not an option and people are instructed to attend awareness-raising courses, seminars, and workshops on a variety of subjects such as unconscious bias, gender sensitivity and consent.

Calls for raising awareness and to re-educate yourself represent a demand to re-socialise the person. In practice it represents the expansion of socialisation from the sphere of young people to that of adulthood. Since it calls for a change in behaviour, it is not surprising that its practice resembles those of social engineers. Technocratic-minded social engineers argue that since it is not enough to campaign to raise awareness their professional skills are essential for changing people's behaviour. They contend;

> Because abundant research shows that people who are simply given more information are unlikely to change their beliefs or behavior, it's time for activists and organizations seeking to drive change in the public interest to move beyond just raising awareness. It wastes a lot of time and money for important causes that can't afford to sacrifice either. Instead, social change activists need to use behavioral science to craft campaigns that use messaging and concrete calls to action that get people to change how they feel, think, or act, and as a result create long-lasting change.[763]

---

761 Cited in F. Furedi (2017) *What's Happened to the University? A Sociological Exploration of its Infantilisation*, London: Routledge, p.138.

762 www.happeemindz.com/self-awareness-a-mechanism-to-chang (accessed 23 March 2021).

763 https://ssir.org/articles/entry/stop_raising_awareness_already (accessed 23 March 2021).

It is not evident whether or not behavioural science actually achieves its objective of 'long-lasting change'. However, what is certain is that at the very least its project of re-socialisation unsettles prevailing cultural norms and practices.

Moral engineering is deeply implicated in the project of awareness raising. Technocrats are constantly asking the question 'which nudging techniques can we use to further increase awareness?'[764] They believe that through psychological manipulation they can create public awareness that ensures that 'very large numbers of people form powerful groupings, like a "swarm", to produce massive social outcomes'.[765] The extensive use of nudging and behavioural economics during the coronavirus pandemic illustrates how the engineering of people's 'decision making' rapidly displaced open politically informed guidance and leadership.

The ethos and practice of raising awareness is based on the unstated and often unacknowledged assumption that behavioural change is important for both the individual and for society. It is often devoted to gaining support for attitudes that as yet lack significant support in society. Awareness raising is not a response to a public demand for new ways of conducting life. On the contrary, its aim is to create a demand for social and cultural practices that a relatively small coterie of self-ascribed awareness raisers believe is good for its putative beneficiaries. Although its promoters perceive themselves as part of a movement to raise awareness it is far more accurate to characterise it as a top-down affair. It is also an activity that assists possessors of aware views to forge a sense of cohesion and group consciousness.

The cultivation of a *l'espirit de corps* through the attribution of a state of awareness endows its possessors with a group identity. Shared awareness allows those affiliated to the caste of awareness raisers to recognise one another.

Through the possession of aware attitudes people set themselves apart, reinforce their status and draw a moral contrast between their styles of life and those of others. Weber referred to this process of forging a distinctive pattern of living as the 'stylisation of life'. The stylisation of life provides a group with status while highlighting the moral distinction between itself and others. As Pierre Bourdieu noted in his influential sociological essay, *Distinction:* 'aversion to different life-styles is perhaps one of the strongest barriers between classes'.

764 http://diposit.ub.edu/dspace/bitstream/2445/152912/1/TFG_GEI_ROIG_ANNA_JUN19.pdf (accessed 21 March 2021).

765 www.businessballs.com/improving-workplace-performance/nudge-theory/ (accessed 19 March 2021).

Struggles over the 'art of living' serve to draw lines between behaviour and attitudes considered legitimate and those deserving of moral condemnation.[766]

In recent times these struggles have led to an unprecedented degree of cultural polarisation. This trend is actively promoted by The Aware, which continually creates and inflates behavioural and cultural distinctions between itself and the rest of society. What is important about its lifestyle is not so much the values that it invokes, but that it is different in every detail from those obese, junk food-eating, gas-guzzling, gun-obsessed, emotionally illiterate fundamentalist Joe Sixpacks. The previous psychological contrast drawn between the traits associated with an authoritarian personality and those blessed with enlightened ones services identities consistent with awareness.

The cultural politics of the 21st century is inherently disposed towards struggles over the art of living. This trend is most strikingly expressed through conflicts over competing assertions of identity consciousness. Not infrequently, raising awareness leads to a conflict of cultural values. Such conflicts are immanent to the cultural politics of identity. As we pointed out earlier, identity's claim for recognition can never be satisfied. The demand for identity is its own cause, and drawing attention to it often leads to new claims for recognition. The acculturation of the anti-cultural deprives the cultivation of selfhood of authoritative guidance. Lack of clarity about the moral values through which an identity is sustained creates a demand for external validation, which makes it susceptible to politicisation. Without the sustenance of moral clarity society will continue its self-inflicted crisis of identity. In these circumstances, the normative lag between the values of the 'aware' and those of common sense is likely to perpetuate itself into the future.

As we discussed in previous chapters, the demand for identity and its subsequent politicisation are neither the direct outcome of rapid socio-economic change nor of some inherent feature of the human condition. The crisis of identity emerged as an unintended consequence of moral engineering and in particular through its culture war against prevailing forms of socialisation. So long as society is prepared to live with its loss of the sense of the past and continues to neglect the positive legacy of the human experience, it will remain prisoner to a perpetual conflict of values. It is not possible to retrace our steps and retrieve what we left behind. But it is possible to take ourself more seriously, and challenge the childish demand to be validated. For that to occur we need to teach ourselves that the identity that really matters is the one that is the outcome of our achievement through work and action. This can all begin by socialising

766 Bourdieu (2010) p.49.

and educating the young for independence rather than training them to become recipients of validation.

Bibliography

Abrams, P. (1972) 'The sense of the past and the origins of sociology', *Past & Present*, No. 55, 19–32.

Adorno, T.W. (1950) 'Democratic leadership and mass manipulation', in Gouldner, A. (ed.) *Studies in Leadership: Leadership and Democratic Action*, New York: Harper & Brothers.

Adorno, T.W., Frenkel-Brunswik, E., Levinson, D.J. and Sanford, R.N. (1969) *The Authoritarian Personality*. New York: W.W. Norton & Company.

Allport, G.W. (1945) 'Human nature and the peace', *Psychological Bulletin*, 42(6), 376–378.

Andrews, F.E. (1932) 'Human engineering', *North American Review*, 233(6), 511–518.

Arendt, H. (1998) *The Human Condition*, Chicago: University of Chicago Press.

Arendt, H. (2003) *Responsibility and Judgment*, New York: Schoken Books.

Arendt, H. [1954] (2006) 'The crisis in education' in Arendt, H., *Between Past and Future*, New York: Penguin.

Aries, P. (1962) *Centuries of Childhood*, New York: Vintage.

Ayling, J. (1930) *The Retreat From Parenthood*, London: Kegan Paul, Trench, Trubner & Co.

Ball, T. (1987) 'Authority and conceptual change', in Pennock, J.R. and Chapman, J.W. (eds) *Authority Revisited*, New York: New York University Press.

Bamta, M. (1996) 'Review: *Machine-Age Ideology, Social Engineering and American Liberalism, 1911–1939* by John M. Jordan', *American Quarterly*, 48(1), 121–127.

Banicki, K. (2017) 'The character–personality distinction: an historical, conceptual, and functional investigation', *Theory & Psychology*, 27(1), 50–68.

Bantock, G.H. (1952) *Freedom and Authority in Education: A Criticism of Modern Cultural and Educational Assumptions*, London: Faber & Faber Ltd.

Barry, F.R. (1923) *Christianity and Psychology*, London: Student Christian Movement.

Bauman, Z. (1991) *Modernity and Ambivalence*, Cambridge: Polity.

Bauman, Z. (1996) 'From pilgrim to tourist – or a short history of identity', *Questions of Cultural Identity*, 1, 18–36.

Bauman, Z. (2004) *Identity: Conversations with Benedetto Vecchi*, Cambridge: Polity Press.

Baumeister, R.F. (1986) *Identity: Cultural Change and the Struggle for Self*, Oxford: Oxford University Press.

Bay, C. (1982) 'Self-respect as a human right: thoughts on the dialectics of wants and needs in the struggle for human community', *Human Rights Quarterly*, 4(1), 53–75.

Beauchamp, T.L. (1999) 'The failure of theories of personhood', in *Personhood and Health Care*, International Library of Ethics, Law, and the New Medicine, vol. 7, Dordrecht: Springer.

Beck, U. (1992) *Risk Society: Towards a New Modernity*, London: Sage.

Bell, D. (1972) 'The cultural contradictions of capitalism', *Journal of Aesthetic Education*, 6(1–2), 11–38.

Bell, D. (1976) *The Cultural Contradictions of Capitalism*, London: Heinemann.

Bell, D. (2000) *The End of Ideology: On the Exhaustion of Political Ideas in the Fifties*, Cambridge, Mass: Harvard University Press.

Bell, R. (2011) 'In Werther's thrall: suicide and the power of sentimental reading in early national America', *Early American Literature*, 46(1), 93–120.

Benedict, R. (1934) 'Anthropology and the abnormal', *Journal of General Psychology*, 10(1), 59–82.

https://doi.org/10.1515/9783110708899-012

Benedict, R. [1934] (1989) *Patterns of Culture*, Boston: Houghton Mifflin.

Benedict, R. (2017) *An Anthropologist at Work*, London: Routledge.

Berger, B. (2002) *The Family in the Modern Age: More than a Lifestyle Choice*, New Brunswick: Transaction Publishers.

Berger, P. (1965) 'Towards a sociological understanding of psychoanalysis', *Social Research* 32(1), 26–41.

Berger, P. (1966) 'Identity as a problem in the sociology of knowledge', *European Journal of Sociology/Archives Européennes de Sociologie/Europäisches Archiv für Soziologie*, 7(1), 105–115.

Berger, P., Berger, B. and Kellner, H. (1974) *The Homeless Mind*, Harmondsworth: Penguin.

Bergman, M. (2015) 'Minimal meliorism: finding a balance between conservative and progressive pragmatism', *Action, Belief and Inquiry*, 2, 2–28.

Bernays, E.L. (1947) 'The engineering of consent', *Annals of the American Academy of Political and Social Science*, 250(1), 113–120.

Bernstein, B. (1977) *Class, Codes and Control*, vol. 3, London: Routledge & Kegan Paul.

Binder, R.M. (1903) *Feeling as the Principle of Individuation and Socialization*, New York: Columbia University Press.

Blatterer, H. (2007) *Coming of Age in Times of Uncertainty*, New York: Berghahn Books.

Blatterer, H. (2010) 'The changing semantics of youth and adulthood', *Cultural Sociology*, 4(1), 63–79.

Boas, G. (1938) 'The century of the child', *American Scholar*, 7(3), 268–276.

Bourdieu, P. (2010) *Distinction: A Social Critique of the Judgment of Taste*, London: Routledge.

Bourdieu, P. and Passeron, J.C. (1990) *Reproduction in Education, Society and Culture*, London: Sage.

Bourne, R.S. (1913) *Youth And Life*, New York: Houghton Mifflin.

Bracken, P. (2002) *Trauma: Culture, Meaning and Philosophy*, London: Whurr Publishers.

Bridges, J.W. (1928) 'The Positive Hygiene movement', *Public Health Journal*, 19(1), 1–8.

Brinkmann, S. (2010) *Psychology as a Moral Science: Perspectives on Normativity*, Berlin: Springer Science & Business Media.

Bristow, J. (2015) *Baby Boomers and Generational Conflict*, New York: Palgrave Macmillan.

Brubaker, R. and Cooper, F. (2000) 'Beyond "identity"', *Theory & Society*, 29(1), 1–47.

Bruch, H. (1952) *Don't Be Afraid of Your Child*, New York: Farrar, Straus and Young.

Bryson, D. (1998) 'Lawrence K. Frank, knowledge, and the production of the "social"', *Poetics Today*, 1, 401–421.

Bryson, D. (2009) 'Personality and culture, the Social Science Research Council, and liberal social engineering: the Advisory Committee on Personality and Culture, 1930–1934', *Journal of the History of the Behavioral Sciences*, 45(4), 355–386.

Bryson, D. (2015) 'Mark A. May: scientific administrator, human engineer', *History of the Human Sciences*, 28(3), 80–114

Burnham, J.C. (1960) 'Psychiatry, psychology and the progressive movement', *American Quarterly*, 12(4), 457–465.

Burt, S. (2007) *The Forms of Youth: Twentieth-Century Poetry and Adolescence*, New York: Columbia University Press.

Callahan, R.E. (1962) *Education and the Cult of Efficiency*, Chicago: University of Chicago Press.

Carlson, B. (2005) 'Social engineering, 1899–1999: an odyssey through The New York Times', *American Studies in Scandinavia*, 37(1), 69–94.

Chettiar, T. (2013) *The Psychiatric Family: Citizenship, Private Life, and Emotional Health in Welfare-State Britain, 1945–1979*, Ann Arbor: Northwestern University Press.

Chisholm, G. (1946) *The William Alanson White Memorial Lectures*, Baltimore:
W.A. White Psychiatric Foundation.

Chisholm, G. (1947) 'Can man survive?', *A Review of General Semantics*, 4(2), 106–111.

Churchill, W. (1930) *My Early Life*, London: Thornton Butterworth Limited.

Cohen, S. (1983) 'The mental hygiene movement, the development of personality and the school: the medicalization of American education', *History of Education Quarterly*, 23(2), 123–149.

Cohen, S. (1990) 'Review: the triumph of the therapeutic', *History of Education Quarterly*, 30(3), 371–379.

Cohen-Cole, J. (2014) *The Open Mind: Cold War Politics and the Sciences of Human Nature*, Chicago: University of Chicago Press.

Cole, S. (1938) 'Education for change', *Journal of Higher Education*, 9(1), 7–17.

Cook, S.G. (2011) 'Feminists differ in second and third waves', *Women in Higher Education*, 20(8), 7.

Cushman, P. (1995) *Constructing the Self, Constructing America: A Cultural History of Psychotherapy*, New York: Da Cappo Press.

Danziger, K. (1976) *Socialization*, Harmondsworth: Penguin.

Danziger, K. (1997) *Naming the Mind*, London: Sage Publications.

Davis, K. (1940a) 'The child and the social structure', *Journal of Educational Sociology*, 14(4), 217–229.

Davis, K. (1940b) 'The sociology of parent–youth conflict', *American Sociological Review*, 5(4), 523–535.

Demos, J. and Demos, V. (1969) 'Adolescence in historical perspective', *Journal of Marriage and Family*, 31(4), 632–638.

Denney, R. (1963) 'American youth today: the problem of generations', in Erikson, E. (ed.) *Youth: Change and Challenge*, New York: Basic Books.

Derksen, M. (2017) *Histories of Human Engineering: Tact and Technology*, Cambridge: Cambridge University Press.

Dewey, J. (1902) 'The school as a social center', *Elementary School Teacher*, 3(2), 72–86.

Dewey, J. (1920) *Reconstruction in Philosophy*, New York: H. Holt.

Dewey, J. (1937) 'Education and social change', *Bulletin of the American Association of University Professors*, 23(6), 472–474.

Dewey, J. (1954) *The Public and Its Problems*, Denver: Alan Swallow.

Diner, S.J. (1998) *A Very Different Age: Americans of the Progressive Era*, New York: Hill and Wang.

Djilas, M. (1957) *New Class*, London: Thames and Hudson.

Dollard, J. (1939) 'Culture, society, impulse, and socialization', *American Journal of Sociology*, 45(1), 5–63.

Dollard, J., Miller, N.E., Doob, L.W., Mowrer, O.H. and Sears, R.R. (1939) *Frustration and Aggression*, New Haven: Yale University Press.

Douglas, T. (2015) 'The morality of moral neuroenhancement', in Clausen, J. and Levy, N. (eds) *Handbook of Neuroethics*, Netherlands: Springer

Douglass, H.R. (1949) 'Education of all youth for life adjustment', *Annals of the American Academy of Political and Social Science*, 265, 108–114.

Dowbiggin, I. (2011) *The Quest For Mental Health: A Tale of Science, Medicine, Scandal, Sorrow, and Mass Society*, Cambridge: Cambridge University Press.

Dunn, R.G. (1998) *Identity Crises: A Social Critique of Postmodernity*, Minneapolis: University of Minnesota Press.

Eby, C.V. (1994) 'Thorstein Veblen and the rhetoric of authority', *American Quarterly*, 46(2), 139–173.

Ecclestone, K. and Hayes, D. (2019) *The Dangerous Rise of Therapeutic Education*, London: Routledge.

Editorial (1963) 'Diagnosis of a sick society', *British Medical Journal*, 1(5324), 97.

Eisenstadt, S.N. (1963) 'Archetypal patterns of youth', in Erikson, E.H. (ed.) *Youth: Change and Challenge*, New York: Basic Books.

Eisenstadt, S.N. (1971) 'Generational conflict and intellectual antinomianism', *Annals of the American Academy of Political and Social Science*, 395, 68–79.

Eisenstadt, S.N. (1998) 'The construction of collective identities: some analytical and comparative indications', *European Journal of Social Theory*, 1(2), 229–254.

Eisenstadt, S.N. and Aizensḥtadṭ, S.N. (1995) *Power, Trust, and Meaning: Essays in Sociological Theory and Analysis*, Chicago: University of Chicago Press.

Eksteins, M. (1989) *Rites of Spring: The Great War and the Birth of the Modern Age*, Boston: Houghton Mifflin.

Elliott, A. (2013) *Reinvention*, London: Routledge.

Entwistle, H. (1979) *Child-Centred Education*, London: Methuen & Co. Ltd.

Epstein, R. (2010) *Saving Our Children and Families from the Torment of Adolescence*, Fresno: Quill Driver Books.

Erikson, E.H. (ed.) (1963) *Youth: Change and Challenge*, New York: Basic Books.

Erikson, E.H. (1964) 'Identity and uprootedness in our time', in Erikson, E.H. *Insight and Responsibility: Lectures on the Ethical Implications of Psychoanalytic Insight*, London: Faber & Faber.

Erikson, E.H. (1968) *Identity: Youth and Crisis*, New York: W.W. Norton & Company.

Erikson, E.H. (1970) 'Reflections on the dissent of contemporary youth', *International Journal of Psychoanalysis*, 51, 154–176.

Erikson, E.H. (1974) *Dimensions of a New Identity: The 1973 Jefferson Lectures in the Humanities*, New York: W.W. Norton & Company.

Erikson, E.H. [1950] (1993) *Childhood and Society*, New York: W.W. Norton & Company.

Erikson, E.H. [1950] (1995) *Childhood and Society*, London: Vintage.

Farley, J. (2009) *Brock Chisholm, the World Health Organization, and the Cold War*, Vancouver: UBC Press.

Fass, S.P. (2016) *The End of American Childhood: A History of Parenting from Life on the Frontier to the Manged Child*, Princeton: Princeton University Press.

Ffytchee, M. and Pick, D. (eds) (2016) *Psychoanalysis in the Age of Totalitarianism*, London: Routledge.

Fox, V.C. (1977) 'Is adolescence a phenomenon of modern times?' *Journal of Psychohistory*, 5(2), 271–290.

Frank, L. (1940) 'The family as cultural agent', *Living*, 2(1), 16–19.

Frank, L.K. (1941) 'What can psychiatry contribute to the alleviation of national and international difficulties? A symposium: social order and psychiatry', *American Journal of Orthopsychiatry*, 11(4), 620–627.

Frank, L.K. (1953) 'The promotion of mental health', *Annals of the American Academy of Political and Social Science*, 286, 167–174.

Frawley, A. (2020) 'Self-esteem, happiness and the therapeutic fad cycle', in Nehring, D., Madsen, O.J., Cabanas, E., Mills, C. and Kerrigan, D. (eds) *The Routledge International Handbook of Global Therapeutic Cultures*, Abingdon and New York: Routledge.

Freud, A. (1976) 'Dynamic psychology and education', in Freud, A., *Writings of Anna Freud*, vol. 8, London: Hogarth Press.

Fromm, E. (1955) *The Sane Society*, Greenwich: Fawcett Publications.

Fromm, E. [1941] (1969) *Escape From Freedom*, New York: Holt.

Fukuyama, F. (2018) 'The new tribalism and the crisis of democracy', *Foreign Affairs*, Sept.–Oct., 90–114.

Fukuyama, F. (2019) *Identity: Contemporary Identity Politics and the Struggle for Recognition*, London: Profile Books.

Furedi, F. (2004) *Therapy Culture: Cultivating Vulnerability in an Anxious Age*, London: Routledge.

Furedi, F. (2007) 'From the narrative of the Blitz to the rhetoric of vulnerability', *Cultural Sociology*, 1(2), 235–254.

Furedi, F. (2008) *Paranoid Parenting*, London: Continuum Press.

Furedi, F. (2013) *Authority: A Sociological History*, Cambridge: Cambridge University Press.

Furedi, F. (2014) *First World War – Still No End In Sight*, London: Bloomsbury.

Furedi, F. (2015) *The Power of Reading: From Socrates to Twitter*, London: Bloomsbury.

Furedi, F. (2017) *What's Happened to the University? A Sociological Exploration of its Infantilisation*, London: Routledge.

Furedi, F. (2020) *Why Borders Matter and Why Humanity Must Relearn the Art of Drawing Borders*, London: Routledge.

Fussell, P. (1975) *The Great War and Modern Memory*, Oxford: Oxford University Press.

Giddens, A. (1991) *Modernity and Self-Identity: Self and Society in the Late Modern Age*, Cambridge: Polity.

Giddings, F.H. (1897) *The Theory of Socialization: A Syllabus of Sociological Principles for the Use of College and University Classes*, New York: Macmillan & Co.

Giddings, F.H. (1924) 'Social work and societal engineering', *Journal of Social Forces*, 3(1), 7–15.

Giorgi, L. (2017) 'Travelling concepts and crossing paths: a conceptual history of identity', *European Journal of Social Science Research*, 30(1), 47–60.

Glasser, W. (1972) *The Identity Society*, New York: Harper & Row Publishers.

Gleason, P. (1983) 'Identifying identity: a semantic history', *Journal of American History*, 69(4), 910–931.

Goffman, E. (1963) *Stigma: Notes on the Management of Spoiled Identity*, Englewood Cliffs: Prentice-Hall.

Golden, J. (2018) *Babies Made Us Modern: How Infants Brought America into the Twentieth Century*, Cambridge: Cambridge University Press.

Gottfried, P. (2002) *Multiculturalism and the Politics of Guilt: Toward a Secular Theocracy*, Columbia: University of Missouri Press.

Gouldner, A.W. (1979) *The Future of Intellectuals and the Rise of the New Class*, London: Macmillan Press.
Graebner, W. (1980) 'The unstable world of Benjamin Spock: social engineering in a democratic culture, 1917–1950', *Journal of American History*, 67(3), 612–639.
Graebner, W. (1986) 'The small group and democratic social engineering, 1900–1950', *Journal of Social Issues*, 42(1), 137–154.
Graubard, S.R. (1978) 'Preface' to Erikson, E. (ed.) *Adulthood*, New York: W.W. Norton.
Guild, P.J. and Guild, A.A. (1936) *Handbook on Social Work Engineering*, Richmond: Whittet & Shepperson.
Habermas, J. [1967] (1987) *Toward a Rational Society*, London: Polity Press.
Hall, S. [1904] (1916a) *Adolescence: Its Psychology and Its Relation to Physiology, Anthropology, Sociology, Sex, Crime, Religion, and Education*, vol. 1, New York: D. Appleton & Company.
Hall, S. [1904] (1916b) *Adolescence: Its Psychology and Its Relation to Physiology, Anthropology, Sociology, Sex, Crime, Religion, and Education*, vol. 2, New York: D. Appleton & Company.
Hall, S. (1921) 'The message of the Zeitgeist' *Scientific Monthly*, 13(2), 106–116.
Hall, S. (1971) 'Adolescence and the growth of social ideals', in Rapson, R. (ed.) *The Cult of Youth in Middle-Class America*, Lexington: D.C. Heath and Co.
Hall, S. (1998) 'Introduction: who needs "identity"?', in Hall, S. and du Gay, P. (eds) *Questions of Cultural Identity*, London: Sage.
Halmos, P. (1965) *The Faith of the Counsellors*, London: Constable.
Handler, R. (1990) 'Boasian anthropology and the critique of American culture', *American Quarterly*, 42(2), 252–273.
Haskell, T.L. [1977] (2000) *The Emergence of Professional Social Science: The American Social Science Association and the Nineteenth-Century Crisis of Authority*, Baltimore: Johns Hopkins University Press.
Hayek, F.A. (1952) *The Counter-revolution of Science: Studies on the Abuse of Reason*, Glencoe: Free Press.
Hayward, R. (2009) 'Enduring emotions: James L. Halliday and the invention of the psychosocial', *Isis*, 100(4), 827–838.
Hayward, R. (2012) 'The invention of the psychosocial: an introduction', *History of the Human Sciences*, 25(5), 3–12.
Heale, M.J. (2005) 'The sixties as history: a review of the political historiography', *Reviews in American History*, 33(2), 133–152.
Helm, P. (1979) 'Locke's theory of personal identity', *Philosophy*, 54(208), 173–185.
Hendrick, H. (2016) *Narcissistic Parenting in an Insecure World: A History of Parenting Culture 1920s to Present*, Bristol: Policy Press.
Herman, E. (1995) *The Romance of American Psychology: Political Culture in the Age of Experts*, Berkeley: University of California Press.
Herman, S.R. (1995) 'Alva Myrdal's campaign for the Swedish comprehensive school', *Scandinavian Studies*, 67(3), 330–359.
Hewitt, J.P. (1998) *The Myth of Self-Esteem: Finding Happiness and Solving Problems in America*, New York: St. Martin's Press.
Hilgartner, S. (2000) *Science on Stage: Expert Advice as Public Drama*, Stanford: Stanford University Press.

Hobsbawm, E. (1972) 'The social function of the past: some questions', *Past & Present*, 55, 3–17.

Hobsbawm, E. (2020) *The Age of Extremes: 1914–1991*, Hachette UK.

Hoff Sommers, C. and Satel, S. (2005) *One Nation Under Therapy*, New York: St. Martin's Press.

Hoffman, M.L. (1958) 'Conformity, conviction, and mental health', *Merrill-Palmer Quarterly*, 4(3), 145–150.

Hollander, P. (1988) 'Alienation and the adversary culture', *Society*, 25(4), 40–48.

Hollander, P. (2002) 'The resilience of the adversary culture', *National Interest*, No. 68, 101–112.

Huddy, L. (2001) 'From social to political identity: a critical examination of social identity theory', *Political Psychology*, 22(1), 127–156.

Hughes, J.L. (1900) *Dickens As An Educator*, New York: D. Appleton & Co.

Hunter, D.J. and Nedelisky, P. (2018) *Science and the Good: The Tragic Quest for the Foundations of Morality*, New Haven: Yale University Press.

Ibarra, P. and Kitsuse, J. (2003) 'Claims-making discourse and vernacular resources', in Holstein, J. and Miller, G. (eds) *Challenges and Choices: Constructionist Perspectives on Social Problems*, New York: Aldine de Gruyter.

Illich, I. (1975) 'The medicalization of life', *Journal of Medical Ethics*, 1(2), 73–77.

Illouz, E. (2008) *Saving the Modern Soul: Therapy, Emotions, and the Culture of Self-Help*, Los Angeles: University of California Press.

Izenberg, G. (2016) *Identity: The Necessity of a Modern Idea*, Philadelphia: University of Pennsylvania Press.

James, W. [1890] (1950) *The Principle of Psychology*, Mineola: Dover Publications.

Jaques, E. (1965) 'Death and the mid-life crisis', *International Journal of Psychoanalysis*, 46(4), 502–514.

Jewett, A. (2012) *Science, Democracy and the American University: From the Civil War to the Cold War*, Cambridge: Cambridge University Press.

Jewett, A. (2020) *Science under Fire: Challenges to Scientific Authority in Modern America*, Cambridge, Mass.: Harvard University Press.

Jordan, J.M. (1994) *Machine Age Ideology: Social Engineering and American Liberalism, 1911–1939*, Chapel Hill: University of North Carolina Press.

Jordan, W.D. (1976) 'Searching for adulthood in America', *Daedalus*, 105(4), 1–11.

Jotterand, F. (2011) 'Will post-humans still need the virtues?', *AJOB Neuroscience*, 2(4), 3–9.

Justman, S. (1998) *The Psychological Mystique*, Evanston: Northwestern University Press.

Justman, S. (2010) 'Bibliotherapy: literature as exploration reconsidered', *Academic Questions*, 23(1).
125–135.

Justman, S. (2015) *The Nocebo Effect: Overdiagnosis and Its Costs*, New York: Palgrave.

Kaplan, S. (1956) 'Social engineers as saviors: effects of World War I on some American liberals', *Journal of the History of Ideas*, 17(3), 347–369.

Kardiner, A. (1946) 'Western personality and social crisis: a psychiatrist looks at human aggression', *Commentary* 2, 436–442.

Keck, C. (1908) 'The socialization of the child', *Journal of Education*, 67(4), 91–92.

Keniston, K. (1963) 'Social change and youth in America', in Erikson, E.H. (ed.) *Youth: Change and Challenge*, New York: Basic Books.

Keniston, K. (1970) 'Youth: a "new" stage of life', *American Scholar*, 39(4), 631–654.

Kerlinger, F.N. (1960) 'The implications of the permissiveness doctrine in American education', *Educational Theory*, 10(2), 120–127.

Kessen, W. (1979) 'The American child and other cultural inventions', *American Psychologist*, 34(10), 815–820.

Kett, J.F. (2003) 'Reflections on the history of adolescence in America', *History of the Family*, 8(3), 355–373.

Key, E. (1909) *The Century of the Child*, New York: G.P. Putnam's Sons.

Kloppenberg, J.T. (1986) *Uncertain Victory: Social Democracy and Progressivism in European and American Thought, 1870–1920*, New York: Oxford University Press.

Kluckhohn, C. and Murray, H.A. (1953) 'Outline of a conception of personality', in Kluckhohn, C. and Murray, H.A. (eds) *Personality: In Nature, Society, and Culture*, London: Jonathan Cape.

Kolko, G. (1968) *The Politics of War: The World and United States Foreign Policy 1943–1945*, New York: Vintage Books.

Koops, W. (2019) 'Does adolescence exist?', *Japanese Journal of Adolescent Psychology*, 30(2), 89–98.

Koops, W. and Zuckerman, M. (2003) 'Introduction: a historical developmental approach to adolescence', *History of the Family*, 8(3), 345–354.

Korsgaard, C.M. (2009) *Self-Constitution: Agency and Integrity*, Oxford: Oxford University Press.

Kotinsky, R. (1933) *Adult Education and the Social Scene*, New York: D. Appleton-Century Company.

Kuhlmann, H. (2005) 'Walden Two: a behaviorist utopia', in *Living Walden Two: B. F. Skinner's Behaviorist Utopia and Experimental Communities*, Urbana-Champaign: University of Illinois Press.

Kultgen, J. (1988) *Ethics and Professionalism*, Philadelphia: University of Pennsylvania Press.

LaBarre, W. (1948) 'The age period of cultural fixation', an address presented at the 39th Annual Meeting of the National Committee for Mental Hygiene, Inc., 4 November 1948, New York City.

LaBarre, W. (1949) 'The age period of cultural fixation', *Mental Hygiene*, 33, 209–221.

Lakoff, G. (2014) *Don't Think of an Elephant! Know Your Values and Frame the Debate*, White River Junction: Chelsea Green Publishing.

Langness, L.L. (1975) 'Margaret Mead and the study of socialization', *Ethos*, 3(2), 97–112.

Lasch, C. (1977) *Haven in a Heartless World: The Family Besieged*, New York: Basic Books.

Lasch, C. (1979) *The Culture of Narcissism: American Life in an Age of Diminishing Expectations*, New York: Warner Books.

Lasch, C. (2013) *The True and Only Heaven: Progress and Its Critics*, New York: Norton.

Lasswell, H.D. (1930) *Psychopathology and Politics*, Chicago: University of Chicago Press.

Leggett, W. (2014) 'The politics of behaviour change: nudge, neoliberalism and the state', *Policy & Politics*, 42(1), 3–19.

Lemert, C. (2011) 'A history of identity: the riddle at the heart of the mystery of life', in Elliott, A. (ed.) *Routledge Handbook of Identity Studies*, London: Routledge.

Levy, D.M. (1968) 'Beginnings of the child guidance movement', *American Journal of Orthopsychiatry*, 38(5), 799–804.

Lewis, S. (1920) *Mainstreet*, New York: Harcourt.

Lewis, S. [1922] (1996) *Babbitt*, Harmondsworth: Penguin.

Lott, E. (2000) 'After identity, politics: the return of universalism', *New Literary History*, 31(4), 665–680.

Lucassen, L. (2010) 'A brave new world: the left, social engineering, and eugenics in twentieth-century Europe', *International Review of Social History*, 55(2), 265–296.

Luckmann, T. (1967) *The Invisible Religion: The Problem of Religion in Modern Society*, London: Macmillan.

Luckmann, T. and Berger, P. (1964) 'Social mobility and personal identity', *European Journal of Sociology/Archives Européennes de Sociologie/Europäisches Archiv für Soziologie*, 5(2), 331–344.

Lynd, F.M. (1958) *On Shame and the Search for Identity*, London: Routledge & Kegan Paul.

Lynd, J. (1932) 'The modern American family', *Annals of the American Academy of Political and Social Science, 160, 197–204.*

MacDonald, J.R. (2017) *Reel Guidance: Midcentury Classroom Films and Adolescent Adjustment*, Thesis submitted to the faculty of the Virginia Polytechnic Institute and State University in partial fulfilment of the requirements for the degree of Master of Arts In History.

Mandler, P. (2013) *Return from the Natives: How Margaret Mead Won the Second World War and Lost the Cold War*, New Haven: Yale University Press.

Mandler, P. (2019) 'The language of social science in everyday life', *History of the Human Sciences*, 32(1), 62–82.

Marsden, W.E. (1997) 'Contradictions in progressive primary school ideologies and curricula in England: some historical perspectives', *Historical Studies in Education*, 9(2), 224–236.

Martin, R. and Barresi, J. (2006) *The Rise and Fall of Soul and Self*, New York: Columbia University Press.

Marx, J.H. (1980) 'The ideological construction of post-modern identity models in contemporary cultural movements', in Robertson, R. and Holzner, B. (eds) *Identity and Authority: Explorations in the Theory of Society*, Oxford: Basil Blackwell.

McLean, K. and Syed, M. (eds) (2015) *The Oxford Handbook of Identity Development*, Oxford: Oxford Library of Psychology.

Mead, M. (1940) 'Social change and cultural surrogates', *Journal of Educational Sociology*, 14(2), 92–109.

Mead, M. (1942) *And Keep Your Powder Dry: An Anthropologist Looks at America*, New York: William Morrow and Company.

Mead M. [1970] (1972) *Culture and Commitment: A Study of the Generation Gap*, London: Panther Books.

Mead, M. (1973) 'Preface' to *Coming of Age in Samoa*, New York: Wm. Morrow & Co.

Mead, M. [1942] (2000) *And Keep Your Powder Dry: An Anthropologist Looks at America*, New York: Berghahn Books.

Merton, R. (1942) 'Science and technology in a democratic order', *Journal of Legal and Political Sociology*, 115–126.

Merton, R. (1948) 'The self-fulfilling prophecy,' *Antioch Review*, Summer, 193–210.

Mészáros, I. (1989) *The Power of Ideology*, New York: Harvester Wheatsheaf.

Meyerowitz, J. (2010) 'How common culture shapes the separate lives: sexuality, race, and mid-twentieth-century social constructionist thought', *Journal of American History*, 96(4), 1057–1084.

Michaels, W.B. (1992) 'Race into culture: a critical genealogy of cultural identity', *Critical Inquiry*, 18(4), 655–685.

Mills, J.A. (1998) *Control: A History of Behavioral Psychology*, New York: New York University Press.

Minois, G.C. (1999) *The History of Suicide: Voluntary Death in Western Culture*, Baltimore: Johns Hopkins University Press.

Mintz, S. (2015) *The Prime of Life: A History of Modern Adulthood*, Cambridge, Mass: Harvard University Press.

Moore, S. (2010) *Ribbon Culture: Charity, Compassion, and Public Awareness*, Houndmills: Palgrave.

Moran, M. (2015) *Identity and Capitalism*, London: Sage.

Morawski, J.G. (1982) 'Assessing psychology's moral heritage through our neglected utopias', *American Psychologist*, 37(10), 1082–1095.

Morawski, J.G. and St Martin, J. (2011) 'The evolving vocabulary of the social sciences: the case of "socialization"', *History of Psychology*, 14(1), 1–25.

Moscovici, S. (1961) *La Psychoanalyse – Son Image et Son Public*, Paris: Presses Universitaires de France.

Moskowitz, E.S. (2001) *In Therapy We Trust: America's Obsession with Self-Fulfillment*, Baltimore: JHU Press.

Muller, J.W. (2009) 'The triumph of what (if anything)? Rethinking political ideologies and political institutions in twentieth-century Europe', *Journal of Political Ideologies*, 14(2), 211–226.

Muller, J.W. (2013) *Contesting Democracy: Political Ideas in Twentieth Century Europe*, New Haven: Yale University Press.

Murphy, G., Murphy, L. and Newcomb, T. (1937) *Experimental Social Psychology: An Interpretation of Research Upon the Socialization of the Individual*, New York: Harper & Brothers.

Naegele, K. (1962) 'Youth and society: some observations', *Daedalus*, 91(1), 47–67.

Nash, K. (2001) 'The "cultural turn" in social theory: towards a theory of cultural politics', *Sociology*, 35(1), 77–92.

Nicholson, I.A. (1998) 'Gordon Allport, character, and the "culture of personality" 1897–1937', *History of Psychology*, 1(1), 52–68.

Nicholson, L. (2008) *Identity Before Identity Politics*, Cambridge: Cambridge University Press.

Nuttall, J. (2005) 'Labour revisionism and qualities of mind and character, 1931–79', *English Historical Review*, 120(487), 667–694.

Oberle, E. (2018) *Theodor Adorno and the Century of Negative Identity*, Stanford: Stanford University Press.

O'Riordan, K. (2012) 'The life of the gay gene: from hypothetical genetic marker to social reality', *Journal of Sex Research*, 49(4), 362–368.

Pangle, T. (1993) *The Ennobling of Democracy: The Challenge of the Postmodern Age*, Baltimore: JHU Press.

Parsons, T. (1942) 'Age and sex in the social structure of the United States', *American Sociological Review*, 7(5), 604–616.

Parsons, T. [1942] (1964) 'Propaganda and social control', in Parsons, T. *Essays in Sociological Theory*, Glencoe: The Free Press.

Parsons, T. and Bales, R.F. (1956) *Family: Socialization and Interaction Process*, London: Routledge & Kegan Paul.

Parsons, T., with White, W. [1961] (1970) 'The link between character and society', in Parsons, T., *Social Structure and Personality*, Chicago: Free Press.

Pérez-Ibáñez, I. (2018) 'Dewey's thought on education and social change', *Journal of Thought* 52(3–4), 19–31.

Petrina, S. (2006) 'The medicalization of education: a historiographic synthesis', *History of Education Quarterly*, 46(4), 503–531.

Plumb, J.H. (1969) *The Death of the Past*, London: Macmillan.

Popper, K. (1986) *The Poverty of Historicism*, London: Ark Paperbacks.

Posnock, R. (1995) 'Before and after identity politics', *Raritan*, 15(1), 95–115.

Rakos, R.F. (2013) 'John B. Watson's 1913 "Behaviorist Manifesto": setting the stage for behaviorism's social action legacy', *Revista Mexicana de Análisis de la Conducta*, 39(2), 99–118.

Ravitch, D. (2000) *Left Back: A Century of Failed School Reforms*, New York: Simon & Schuster.

Raz, J. (ed.) (1990) *Authority*, Oxford: Basil Blackwell.

Ribot, T.A. (1910) *The Diseases of Personality: Authorized Translation*, Chicago: Open Court Publishing Company.

Rich, P. (1989) 'Imperial decline and the resurgence of British national identity', in Kushner, T. and Lunn, K. (eds) *Traditions of Intolerance*, Manchester: Manchester University Press.

Richards, G. (2000a) 'Psychology and the churches in Britain 1919–39: symptoms of conversion', *History of the Human Sciences*, 13(2), 57–84.

Richards, G. (2000b) 'Britain on the couch: the popularization of psychoanalysis in Britain 1918–1940', *Science in Context*, 13(2), 183–230.

Richardson, T.R. (1989) *The Century of the Child: The Mental Hygiene Movement and Social Policy in the United States and Canada*, New York: State University of New York Press.

Rieff, P. (2006) *The Triumph of the Therapeutic: Uses of Faith After Freud*, Wilmington: ISI Books.

Robbins, A. and Wilner, A. (2001) *Quarterlife Crisis: The Unique Challenges of Life in Your Twenties*,

New York: Tarcher.

Robin, R. (2001) *The Making of the Cold War Enemy: Culture and Politics in the Military-Intellectual Complex*, Princeton: Princeton University Press.

Ross, D. (1991) *The Origins of American Social Science*, Cambridge: Cambridge University Press.

Ross, D. (1994) 'Modernist social science in the land of the new/old', in Ross, D. (ed.) *Modernist Impulses in the Human Sciences, 1870–1930*, Baltimore: Johns Hopkins University Press.

Ross, E.A. (1906) 'The nation's need of moral experts', *Current Literature (1888–1912)*, XLI.

Roszak, T. (1970) *The Making of a Counter Culture: Reflections on the Technocratic Society*, London: Faber & Faber.

Roszak, T. (1999) *The Gendered Atom: Reflections on the Sexual Psychology of Science*, Newburyport: Conari Press.

Russell, B. (1919) *The Scientific Outlook*, London: George Allen & Unwin Ltd.

Rutherford, A. (2017) 'BF Skinner and technology's nation: technocracy, social engineering, and the good life in 20th-century America', *History of Psychology*, 20(3), 290–312.

Samelson, F. (1986) 'Authoritarianism from Berlin to Berkeley: on social psychology and history', *Journal of Social Issues*, 42(1), 191–208.

Sapir, E. (1924) 'Culture, genuine and spurious', *American Journal of Sociology*, 29(4), 401–429.

Schön, D. (1973) *Technology and Change: The New Heraclitus*, Oxford: Pergamon Press.

Schorer, M. (1961), 'Main Street', *American Heritage*, 12(6).

Schwartz, S.J., Côté, J.E. and Arnett, J.J. (2005) 'Identity and agency in emerging adulthood: two developmental routes in the individualization process', *Youth & Society*, 37(2), 201–229.

Selleck, R.J.W. (1972) *English Primary Education and the Progressives: 1914–1939*, London: Routledge & Kegan Paul.

Simmel, G. (1909) 'The problem of sociology', *American Journal of Sociology*, 15(3), 289–320.

Skolnick, A. (1975) 'The limits of childhood: conceptions of child development and social context', *Law and Contemporary Problems*, 39(3), 38–77.

Soffer, R.N. (1969) 'New elitism: social psychology in prewar England', *Journal of British Studies*, 8(2), 111–140.

Stewart, J. (2011) '"The dangerous age of childhood": child guidance and the "normal" child in Great Britain, 1920–1950', *Paedagogica Historica*, 47(6), 785–803.

Stoczkowski, W. (2009) 'UNESCO's doctrine of human diversity: a secular soteriology?', *Anthropology Today*, 25(3), 7–11.

Strong, S. (1944) 'A review of a book on the educational theories of George H. Mead's approach to behaviourism by A.S. Clayton', *American Journal of Sociology*, 50, 7–11.

Sunstein, C.R. (2014) *Why Nudge? The Politics of Libertarian Paternalism*, New Haven: Yale University Press.

Sunstein, C.R. and Vermeule, A. (2020) *Law and Leviathan: Redeeming the Administrative State*, Cambridge, Mass: Belknap Press.

Sussman, M.B. (1955) *Sourcebook in Marriage and the Family*, New York: Houghton Mifflin.

Szasz, T. (1989) *Law, Liberty and Psychiatry*, Syracuse: Syracuse University Press.

Taft, J. (1921) 'Mental hygiene problems of normal adolescence', *Annals of the American Academy of Political and Social Science*, 98(1), 61–67.

Thaler, L.K. and Koval, R. (2015) *Grit to Great: How Perseverance, Passion, and Pluck Take You from Ordinary to Extraordinary*, New York: Crown Business.

Thomson, I.T. (1997) 'From conflict to embedment: the individual–society relationship, 1920–1991', *Sociological Forum*, 12(4), 631–658.

Thomson, M. (2006) *Psychological Subjects: Identity Culture, and Health in Twentieth-Century Britain*, Oxford: Oxford University Press.

Trilling, L. (1957) 'The sense of the past', in Trilling, L., *The Liberal Imagination: Essays on Literature and Society*, New York: Doubleday Anchor Books.

Trilling, L. (1965) *Beyond Culture*, New York: Viking Press.

Tucker, A. (1777) *The Light of Nature Pursued*, 1st edition, 1768–1777, vol. 3, pt 1, London: W. Oliver.

Turner, R. (1969) 'The theme of contemporary social movements', *British Journal of Sociology*, 20(4), 390–405.

Turner, R.H. (1975) 'Is there a quest for identity?', *Sociological Quarterly*, 16(2), 148–161.

Vansieleghem, N. (2010) 'The residual parent to come: on the need for parental expertise and advice', *Educational Theory*, 60(3), 341–355.
Vicedo, M. (2012) 'Cold War emotions: mother love and the war over human nature', in Solovey, M. and Cravens, H. (eds) *Cold War Social Science*, New York: Palgrave Macmillan.
Wall, W.L. (2009) *Inventing the 'American Way': The Politics of Consensus from the New Deal to the Civil Rights Movement*, Oxford: Oxford University Press.
Wallach, G. (1997) *Obedient Sons: The Discourse of Youth and Generations in American Culture, 1630–1860*, Amherst: University of Massachusetts Press.
Walsh, D. (1997), *The Growth of the Liberal Soul*, Columbia: University of Missouri Press.
Watson, G. (1931) ['No title'], *Journal of Education*, 114(2).
Watson, G., Rivlin, H.N., Jersild, A.T., Shoben, Jr, E.J. and McKillop, A.S. (1956) 'Twenty-five years of educational research', *Review of Educational Research*, 26(3), 241–267.
Watson, J.B. (1924) *Behaviorism*, New York: People's Institute.
Weber, M. [1919] (1958) 'Science as a vocation', in Gerth, H. and Mills, C.W. (eds) *From Max Weber: Essays in Sociology*, New York: Oxford University Press.
Weigert, A.J., Teitge, J.S. and Teitge, D.W. (1986) *Society and Identity: Towards a Sociological Psychology*, Cambridge: Cambridge University Press.
Weinstein, D. (2004) 'Culture at work: family therapy and the culture concept in post-World War II America', *Journal of the History of the Behavioral Sciences*, 40(1), 23–46.
Weinstein, D. (2013) *The Pathological Family: Postwar America and the Rise of Family Therapy*, Ithaca: Cornell University Press.
Wells, H.G. [1911] (2005) *The New Machiavelli*, London: Penguin Books.
White, W. (1844) *Christ's Covenant the Best Defence of Christ's Crown, etc: Our National Covenant, Scriptural, Catholic, and of Permanent Obligations*, Edinburgh: Kennedy.
White, W.A. (1921) 'Childhood: the golden period for mental hygiene', *Annals of the American Academy of Political and Social Science*, 98, 54–60.
Whitehead, A.N. [1933] (1961) *Adventures of Ideas*, New York: Free Press.
Whyte, W. (1956) *The Organization Man*, New York: Simon and Schuster.
Williams, F.E. (1934) *Russia, Youth and the Present-Day World*, New York: Farrar and Rinehart.
Wolff, R.P. and Gitlin, T. (1973) *1984 Revisited: Prospects for American Politics*, New York: Knopf.
Wolin, R. (2010) *The Wind from the East: French Intellectuals, the Cultural Revolution and the Legacy of the 1960s*, Princeton: Princeton University Press.
Wolpert, J.F. (1950) 'Towards a sociology of authority', in Gouldner, A. (ed.) *Studies in Leadership: Leadership and Democratic Action*, New York: Harper & Brothers.
Wuthnow, R. (1989) *Meaning and Moral Order: Explorations in Cultural Analysis*, Berkeley: University of California Press.
Yerkes, R. (1941), 'Psychology and Defense', *Proceedings of the American Philosophical Society*, 84, 527–542.
Zilversmit, A. (1993) *Changing Schools: Progressive Education Theory and Practice, 1930–1960*, Chicago: Chicago University Press.
Zorbaugh, H.W. and Payne, L.V. (1935) 'Adolescence: psychosis or social adjustment?', *Journal of Educational Sociology*, 8(6), 371–377.

Index

https://doi.org/10.1515/9783110708899-013